The

White

Bedouin

The White Bedouin

by George Potter

Council Press
Springville, Utah

The views expressed within this work are the sole responsibility of the author and do not necessarily reflect the position of Cedar Fort, Inc., or any other entity.

This is a work of fiction. The characters, names, incidents, places, and dialogue are products of the author's imagination, and are not to be construed as real.

ISBN 13: 978-1-59955-074-9

Published by Council Press, an imprint of Cedar Fort, Inc., 2373 W. 700 S., Springville, UT, 84663
Distributed by Cedar Fort, Inc., www.cedarfort.com

LIBRARY OF CONGRESS CATALOGING-IN-PUBLICATION DATA

Potter, George, 1949–
   The White Bedouin / George Potter.
      p. cm.
   ISBN 978-1-59955-074-9 (acid-free paper)
   1. Petroleum industry and trade—Fiction. 2. Saudi Arabia—Fiction. 3. Mormons—Fiction. 4.
Interpersonal relations—Religious aspects—Fiction.
   5. Religious fiction. I. Title.

   PS3616.O852W48 2007
   813'.6—dc22
         2007026410

Cover design by Nicole Williams
Cover design © 2007 by Lyle Mortimer
Edited and typeset by Lyndsee Simpson Cordes

Printed in the United States of America

10 9 8 7 6 5 4 3 2 1

Printed on acid-free paper

Dedicated to Randolph W. M. Linehan, Hugh W. Nibley, and my father, Kenner T. Potter—the three most brilliant and independent thinkers I have known.

Acknowledgments

I am obliged to recognize Robert Sterforth, Ila Jenson, and Brian Tate for their patience in editing this work. Their friendship and talents are greatly appreciated. I am indebted to Brad Monson and Wendy Ulrich for reading the book and sharing their insights with me. Special thanks must be expressed to my wonderful Arab friends who have freely shared with me their culture, poetry, and religious beliefs for fifteen years. To my friends of all faiths, I quote Emily Brontë: "Whatever our souls are made of, his and mine are the same."

Contents

Maps

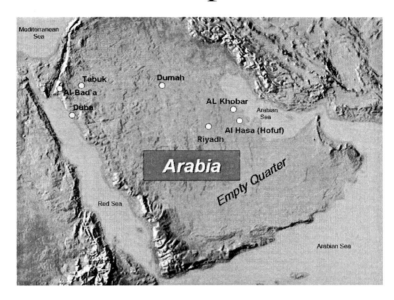

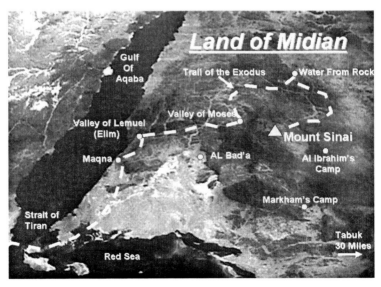

One who has never met an Arab in the desert can have no conception of his terrible appearance. The worst pictures of the Italian bandits or Greek mountain robbers I ever saw are tame in comparison. . . . The celebrated Gasperini, who ten years ago kept in terror the whole country between Rome and Naples . . . [and] told me he could not remember how many murders he had committed, . . . looked civil and harmless compared to a Bedouin of the desert. The swarthy complexion of the latter, his long beard, his piercing coal-black eyes, and a rusty matchlock in his hand, make the best figure for a painter I ever saw.

John Lloyd Stephens, *Incidents of Travel in Egypt,* 1837

Chapter 1

Welcome to Saudi Arabia

The most cherished locus of the lost tribes, and the one that
met with almost universal approval in the Jewish world, was
the area around the Red Sea: the land of Cush redolent of the
tales of Eldad the Danite to the west, and the Arabian Desert to
the east. The great twelfth-century Jewish traveler Benjaimin
of Tudelah located . . . half the tribe of Manasseh squarely in
Arabia.

Tudor Parfitt, *The Lost Tribes of Israel*

Jake Sorensen
Summer 1989
Dhrahan, Saudi Arabia
Day One of Ten-week Internship

"So this is Arabia," I mused. The vista from my tiny window was unpromising to say the least. For the past two hours the plane had flown over nothing but desert wasteland. The endless sand pit below made southern Utah look like the Garden of Eden. I saw no rivers or lakes, nor even a distant object that resembled a tree. I was having trouble registering it in my mind. How could the Arabs have stretched out a living here for the last five thousand years? And how could this barren nothingness be the spiritual wellspring for the billion people who call themselves Muslims, the submitters to God?

"Narjo rabt hizam almigaad min ajel alhaboot fey Matar Al-Dhahran Al Dawley."

"Excuse me," I said to the middle-aged Arab businessman sitting next to me on the Saudia Airlines 747. "What did that announcement mean?"

The well groomed Arab gave me a friendly smile. "You know the routine," he replied. "Please fasten your seat belt in preparation for our descent into the Dhrahan International Airport."

"Thank you."

No sooner had I buckled my seat belt than a stewardess repeated the announcement in English. The Saudi seated next to me continued in perfect American English, "We should be touching down in about ten minutes."

He was flying economy class, but the Arab wore an expensive looking Italian-cut suit. In contrast, I was dressed in jeans, tennis shoes, a sweatshirt, and a dark blue sports cap that plastered a big Y over my forehead. Although the Arab seemed polite, it felt like he was giving me that "you poor naïve American" look. It's the look Europeans give American tourists as they pass around the old joke that if you speak three languages, you're trilingual. If you speak two languages, you're bilingual. If you speak one language, you're American. The version of that joke I overheard during my Paris France Mission ended with "You're a dumb American."

Perhaps the look of superiority the Arab gave me was not intentional, but just in case, I thought I would shatter any misconceptions by using all the Italian words I knew that are not found on a menu. "Dieci minuti. Grazie."

"Have you traveled much in Italy?" the man asked. "I have a summer villa at Ischia Porto."

"Never traveled in Italy, but I lived in France for two years."

"I figured you were a Mormon," the man quickly replied. "Drinking only orange juice all the way from New York to the Middle East. Most Americans your age would have been soaking up all the free airline booze they could before landing in alcohol-free Saudi Arabia."

"How did you know Mormons serve two-year missions?" I asked.

Setting down the copy of the *Wall Street Journal* he had been reading, he continued. "Just checking my hedge funds. My name is Bandar Al-Ameri." He reached out to shake my hand. "I own a Jet ski shop in Al-Khobar. I studied for my MBA at UC Berkeley. I had several Mormon friends there. Good people. From what I remember, most of them served Christian missions in some poor third world country. At Berkeley they were preparing for international careers where they could use their language skills. The last I heard, they all got married and now live in Utah or Idaho."

I laughed. "I'm Jake Sorensen. I'm a journalism major at Brigham Young University."

"First time in Saudi Arabia?" he asked.

"Yes, I'll be spending ten weeks here as a summer intern for Pan Arabian American Oil Company."

"I didn't realize that PAMMCO hired Americans as interns."

"I guess I'll be the first. It was through my father's friend Mac Pastore that I landed a short internship writing articles for PAMMCO's *Moon Crest* magazine."

"So it was not straights A's that got you a summer job? If you know Mr. Pastore, you have considerable *wasta*! I have heard of Mac Pastore. He will be the last non-Saudi vice president at PAMMCO. Once he retires, there probably won't be another American vice president at PAMMCO."

"What is wasta?" I asked.

"You'll see. By the time you leave Saudi Arabia, you will know that all things in this desert flow from either oil or wasta. Loosely speaking, the word means 'influence.' The more wasta you have, the more money you will have. I come from a small tribe; we have little wasta. That's why I have to work hard and ride in economy class. Those families riding in first class, they have first-class wasta. They come from the right tribes, marry within their wasta group, and know all the right people." Shifting gears abruptly, he asked, "What are your plans after leaving the university?"

"My ultimate career goal is to join the editorial staff of the Washington DC muckraker Jack Anderson."

"That's a strange word," the Saudi mused. "Sounds like some kind of rodent. What is a muckraker?"

"In a way, they're professional rats. They rat on influential people. A muckraker is a journalist who searches out and exposes misconduct by public officials."

"Sounds like a poor career choice for someone living in the Middle East. Besides," he said with a laugh, "maybe you need exposing. You got yourself an internship at PAMMCO by using the influence of your father's friend. I don't mean to offend. I am just trying to see if I am correctly understanding the word *muckraker.*"

We both laughed. I was beginning to see that Saudis have a good sense of humor. "The muckraker I admire most is Jack Anderson," I continued. "He uses a bulldog's approach in getting to the facts. For example, as a foreign correspondent for the *Deseret News,* Anderson's first byline accompanied the story of his World War II rendezvous with nationalist Chinese guerrilla fighters. Perhaps during my summer in Arabia I'll discover a story important enough to get published in a mainstream newspaper. That would be a first for me."

We continued our conversation until I felt the familiar disconcerting but relieving jolt. Our plane had just landed in Saudi Arabia.

Mr. Al-Ameri reached in his pocket, pulled out a business card, and handed it to me. "Welcome to Saudi Arabia," he said. "It has been nice meeting you. My family owns the Al-Ameri Jet Ski Shop at Half Moon Bay. Come out some weekend and be my guest. Just tell the manager at the rental shop Bandar sent you. There will be no charge. As you will see, the Saudis appreciate their American friends, especially the Mormons."

Chapter 2

Demons and Ghosts

For we wrestle not against flesh and blood, but against principalities, against powers, against the rulers of the darkness of this world, against spiritual wickedness in high places.

Ephesians 6:12

Jake Sorensen
Summer 1989
Oil Boom Town of Al-Khobar
Week One of Ten-week Internship, 1989

I had barely recovered from jet lag when Mac Pastore invited me to the Commissary Inn. The all-American fare restaurant was discretely hidden away in a corner of the King Fahad Royal Airbase. Operated by the U.S. Department of Defense Mission to Saudi Arabia, the dining club, Mr. Pastore noted, allowed a limited number of civilians to join the private restaurant. Apparently the inn was highly valued as a culinary refuge for Americans. Instead of the Saudi Arabian cuisine of goat grabs, spicy curries, and chicken cooked every which way, the menu here included burgers, fries, and other typical American cuisine. As Mac put it, the Commissary Inn was the only place in Arabia where asking for mashed potatoes didn't result in blank stares from clueless waiters.

Mac explained that after Americans had lived in Saudi Arabia for several years, the Commissary Inn became a lifeline to their homeland. He humorously called those who patronized the restaurant Expat Jacks and Janes. He said the inn was their mother ship in the strict Islamic universe of Saudi Arabia. Stretching my neck in both directions, I could see that the Expat Jacks and their European guests seemed to be enjoying the contraband pork, the prohibited alcohol, and the outlawed background music. Though I had been in the porkless kingdom less than one week, I was tempted by the forbidden fruits. I ordered a BLT sandwich.

After the waiter took our orders, a dapper, well-dressed man entered the dining room. He looked around, saw Mac, and came over to our table. This didn't surprise me. I had come to realize that Mac knew absolutely everyone, no matter where we went. Mac introduced him to me as Willy O'Malley, a geologist with PAMMCO. He was short, about five feet six inches or so, and slim. His weather-beaten face had the texture and color of tanned leather. His hair was pure white and stood out starkly against the dark chiseled features of his narrow face. He had a bit of an Irish lilt in his voice as he greeted us heartily. Mac invited him to join us for dinner, and he accepted.

As the waiter returned to take Willy's order, I noticed another man across the room rise from his seat and head for our table. "Willy!" he cried, greeting our new dinner guest like a long-lost brother. They welcomed each other with much back-slapping, "Haven't seen you in a dog's age!" and that sort of thing. Willy introduced the man as Hank Parkerson, another geologist who used to work for PAMMCO but now did consultant work for one of their manpower suppliers. Hank's face was every bit as dark as Willy's but had more wrinkles than any face I had ever seen. Their appearances were rather similar, except for height. Hank was a much taller version of Willy, standing maybe six feet two inches or so. Both Willy and Hank exuded a kind of nervous energy beneath their calm surfaces. I could easily picture the two of them tipping pints together and arguing vehemently over some fine point in the history of Ireland or the Korean War.

"So, you're still prostituting yourself and calling it consulting work I see," said Willy to his old companion.

"You're not going to pretend hanging around PAMMCO and living off your Arab buddies' goodwill is making an honest living, are you?" replied Hank.

On they went for a while about Hank's consultant status versus Willy's remaining on the PAMMCO payroll. I got the feeling that this was an old argument, like a warm-up for the less-rehearsed insults that they would soon be hurling at each other. Their exchanges were full of the good-natured ribbing that only old friends can exchange. They were like actors reciting their lines in a play they both knew well.

When our dinners arrived, we fell upon them ravenously. The silence of men in good company, savoring good food, descended. What passed for conversation over the next half hour or so was confined to grunts and mmms. Pushing back from the table with the intoxication that comes from a satisfying meal, the others ordered coffee. Willy pulled out a fat black cigar and went about the process of lighting it. I was about to object to being engulfed in a cloud of smoke but decided to bite my tongue. I was young and newly arrived, and these men appeared to have lived hard, lonely lives with few comforts.

Hank produced a pipe and a pouch of tobacco and began his ritual of filling, tamping, and lighting his post-meal smoke. I was beginning to understand that people could smoke anywhere in Saudi Arabia, even in a crowded restaurant with "No Smoking" signs posted on the wall just above them. This wasn't Provo, Utah, and few people on this side of the world knew or cared about the effects of second-hand smoke or the ingrained idiosyncrasies of a Mormon.

Trapped between two billows of smoke, I decided to silently bear it and see what I could glean from these two men. The Arabian desert had chiseled them into rough human oddities, and they intrigued me. There was some listless chatter, but I noticed that Hank had fallen silent. He almost seemed contemplative. Willie and Mac struck up a conversation about the old days. Mac had been in Saudi Arabia for an impressive twenty-five years, but I was sure that Willy and Hank had been here a good deal longer. Willy humored Mac, however, and they were soon swapping "Do you remember when?" stories. I had a suspicion Hank was wrestling with some inner demon, and I was determined to take a stab at bringing it out. I acted on a reporter's hunch.

"I take it your employment with PAMMCO didn't end pleasantly," I ventured. Hank was fussing with his pipe. I thought perhaps he hadn't heard me. After what seemed like a long time, he turned to face me and pointedly said, "You don't have any idea, young man, what goes on out there in the deep desert, do you? I can see by your soft skin that you have never seen the likes of a real desert, one that can kill you in a few hours. PAMMCO let me go because I refused to go back into the Empty Quarter, the most dangerous place on earth."

Taken aback by his sharpness, I answered, "No, I'm from San Diego. I have not yet seen Arabia's great Empty Quarter, but I had hoped someone would take me there this summer."

"The Empty Quarter ain't Palm Springs, laddie, and it doesn't have Burger Kings or Coke machines either. It's a sea of sand dunes that stretches over an expanse the size of Arizona. The Arabs call it the Rub' Al-Khali or the Rub, which means the Empty Quarter. Do you have any idea why they call it that?"

"No," I admitted.

"It's because no one has ever been able to permanently survive there. The Eskimos can hack it on the ice caps, but no one can make it year around in the Empty Quarter. The Rub knows a hundred different ways to kill a man. The nomadic Bedouin travel around its edges, but even they don't try to cross the heart of it," Hank explained with a sour expression.

Like a naive collegiate, I continued trying to reason with a man who had a lifetime of experiences that I had only read about in books. "I understand it's an unpleasant place, but many things in life can seem harsh and barren yet are still beautiful in their own way."

My lack of respect for the dangers of the Empty Quarter must have struck a sensitive nerve with rock-hard Hank. Saying not a word, he just stared at me.

Finally, he blew smoke in my direction and said, "I guarantee it, church boy; the Empty Quarter ain't empty. Dark and toxic evil survives there."

Willy and Mac stopped conversing and were now listening. I'd had just about enough of Hank's insults, and our eyes were locked in a standoff. I had the good breeding of my Mormon mother, but having knocked on the doors of the sarcastic Parisians and the gates of the broad-shouldered Catholic French villagers, I wasn't about to allow some old Irish roughneck to intimidate me. While I didn't want to do something foolish in front of my father's friend, this Hank character had knocked down too many beers. I reached for a pitcher of ice water. "Try blowing your smoke in my face again, and I'll put out the fire."

Hank slowly reached for a table knife. Willy finally broke the spell. "Hank, I think it's time we leave these fine gentlemen and walk off all that food before we end up looking like everyone else in this room." With that, he pushed his chair back from the table and began to rise.

Hank stopped him. "No, Willy. It's time the story was told. I'd feel better to finally get it off my chest." Willy eased back in his chair, folded his arms across his chest, and settled in for the long haul. "Help me out, Willy," said Hank. "I don't quite know where to begin."

But Willy was having none of it. "No, Hank, it's your story. I didn't see what you say you saw out there. I was knocked out cold, and you're the one who still has the nightmares, not me."

Hank nodded slowly and began. "Sorry for the poor use of words, kid. It's just that you remind me of myself at your age, back when I didn't have these nightmares. Willy and I came into this part of the world when we were brisk young lads. It was 1950. We were fresh out of engineering school, degrees in hand and eager to show the world what we could do. We were so full of energy and ideas; they just spilled out of us like rainwater from a downspout. Oil wasn't a new idea. The world had been pumping oil for two decades or more, but in 1950, finding where to drill was still the tricky part. Setting up those old rigs was hard work and an expensive proposition. Saudi Arabia is a big land. You can't just go poking holes all over the place. That's where we came in.

"It was our job to say 'Drill here,' and then hope our observations and calculations were right. We were right often enough because they kept finding oil right where we said it would be. We had our share of successes, you might say. In the early days, PAMMCO used American and European geologists because they knew they would work. We tried to use some of the local talent, but they proved to be very iffy."

"Iffy?" Willy came to life, jolting up out of his semi-comatose state. "You will find hardworking locals here or there, but for the most part, they won't get their hands dirty. The first oilmen to arrive here, back in the late thirties, told us that before they struck oil, the Arabs were some of the hardest-working people they'd ever met. Today, it's like the working man's world has completely passed them by. With each passing generation, the oil money makes them that much more spoiled. Before the big oil money flowed in, there were no roads, schools, hospitals, telephones, or electricity. There were none of the things that we in the western world take for granted. Today we offer Saudis jobs as highly paid laborers, mechanics, and rig workers, and they turn their noses up at them.

"You see, there are two kinds of Saudis," Willy continued, "the townspeople and the Bedus. When it comes to manual work, the townies aren't worth a goat grab's leftovers. They'll do anything to avoid working up a sweat. They wouldn't survive a day in the deep desert. But the desert Arabs—the Bedu or the Bedouin—are tough. They're hard workers, but aren't impressed by a paycheck. It's just not their way. They have survived in the desert for thousands of years, and they're not about to change just because we're here sucking out their oil. I remember one time when we hit a gusher. We danced around shouting 'Eureka!' as oil rained down around us. When word came to the local sheikh that we were celebrating, he came out to see what all the ruckus was about. The Bedouin patriarch rode up on a camel with his entire clan. Unimpressed with our growing pool of black gold, the disappointed sheikh got back on his camel and rode off. He had no use for oil. We learned later that he thought we had been drilling for water and was annoyed that we had found more of that black stuff."

When Willy ran out of descriptions of the Bedouin, Hank took up the narrative.

"Willy and I were paired together from the start. There were about fifty geologists who worked for PAMMCO at that time. We were headquartered in Dhahran, the site of the old CALTOC camp. The first big strike was made in 1938 at Jebel Dhahran. PAMMCO eventually decided to set up its permanent headquarters here. Each two-man team was assigned a sector in the eastern province of Saudi Arabia in which to search for oil. Calling it a province doesn't seem quite right. That would imply the existence of a government, a police force, telephones, and other trappings of civilization. Back then the nearest town was Al-Khobar, which had grown from a small fishing village into a boom town with a population of around fifteen thousand. The town was flooded with migrants who came from all over Arabia and the rest of the world looking for jobs with PAMMCO.

"In the fifties we lived in WWII army-style Quonset huts. We drove WWII surplus jeeps and trucks with specially outfitted balloon tires for use in the desert sand. Willy and I poked around the eastern sector for almost five years, having the drillers punch holes here and there. Every year we went farther and farther out, spending first weeks, then months out in the desert. We found enough oil to keep our jobs and even developed some respect among the PAMMCO brass. I guess that's why our names came up to help out when word came down that the suits wanted to survey for oil in the Empty Quarter. We knew this was going to be our most difficult assignment. We had five years of desert experience behind us, but this assignment would be in the Rub Al-Khali, the Empty Quarter, the biggest, hottest, most desolate place in the world. It would be a challenge, but we felt we were up to it. We had experience, we were confident, and we were tough—or so we thought.

"We loaded our gear into a Dodge Power Wagon and headed out across the desert along a graded road that led toward the PAMMCO base camp. The camp was located south of the tiny village of Yabrin. It was on the very edge of the great sand desert. Because of where we were going, we were loaded down pretty good. There was no chance to replenish supplies or repair equipment without returning to the base camp. You took out what you needed, and when you ran out, you came back for more. We navigated by compass and sextant over the dunes. There were no roads down there and no maps—that was part of the job, to start mapping the wilderness. Funny, with all the wealth in this place, there are still no roads or accurate maps of the entire area.

"It was pretty slow going. The Power Wagons were pretty good in the sand, but they were geared down for traction, not speed. The big tires helped in the soft sand, but they made for tedious traveling. Four days out of Dhahran, we reached the PAMMCO base camp. The other eight men on our team were already there: four geologists and four 'desert rats.' The Sudanese got their nickname because they were so good in the deep desert.

"We were there seven or eight months, going out to different quadrants and surveying the terrain. We didn't know what the execs back at headquarters thought we'd find without drilling for core samples. There wasn't much to observe since all the geological outcrops were buried beneath mountains of sand. For whatever reason we were there, we didn't think much of the desk jockeys back in Dhahran. Seemed to us they spent more time in their offices than we did in our tents, and we stayed in our tents a lot during the hot noontime hours. I'll admit that the heat down there was tougher to take than I thought it would be. At times it felt like the sun was just six feet above my head and followed me everywhere I went. No shade anywhere. Not a living thing visible to the eye, just sand and the ever-present, merciless, oppressive heat. I remember one day it reached 147 degrees, and I thought the cursed sun would never go down.

"From time to time we were visited by Bedouin, riding their camels and moving from one desolate place to another on the fringes of the Empty Quarter. They searched endlessly for fodder for their camels. They were a strange lot. A different sort of human from any I'd ever met before, primitive, as if from a different time period. They never said much. They would just stay the requisite seventy-two hours, eat our food, drink our water, and move on."

"Come again?" I asked. "Seventy-two requisite visiting hours?"

"The Bedouin bond of salt, young man. It's the unwritten law of the desert. If a stranger comes to your camp, you must invite him into your tent, feed him, and care for his animals. It's the nomad's covenant of mutual survival. One day you assist a man you have never met and will probably never see again. The next day it might be you who is in need of care. It's worked for the Bedouin for thousands of years, and without their bond of salt, travel would be impossible in Arabia. The isolated desert tribes can't understand that the outside world is not so kind and generous. If they see a PAMMCO camp, it's their right to enter it and set themselves as the honored guests. Sometimes the same group of Bedouin would visit our camp, sometimes another. We got to know them a little. We learned which group was which. There were twenty or thirty people in each party of Bedus. Not knowing Arabic, we talked to them through the Sudanese rats who had learned English at PAMMCO's Training Center. We figured out that all Bedouin considered themselves to be part of the same tribal family, the Murrahs. The Bedouin were then divided into clans or families. Each family had a leader, but there was only one sheikh. The sheikh was the head honcho of the combined clans of the Murrahs in the Empty Quarter. They considered the entire Rub' al Khali their tribal lands. Lucky them. Save Antarctica, they owned the most desolate spot on the face of the earth.

"We tried to do our work early in the morning and late in the afternoon, when it was not so hot, but the Bedouin seemed to take no notice of the heat. It was nothing to see a group of men squatting in a circle in the height of the noonday sun, no shade in sight, just chattering away as if they were watching the World Cup on the telly. It can be 140 degrees out in the sun, and the sand can reach 180 degrees! The sand gets so hot it blisters your hands if you touch it. Even so, you never saw the Bedouin sweat. Their skin looked as hard and dry as tanned leather. Their hair and eyes were coal-black. I don't think I have ever seen people with such pure black eyes . . ."

Willy trailed off, and Hank picked up the story.

"Late one morning, Hank and I were coming back from surveying, when we spotted a speck against a sand dune in the distance. It was moving, but barely. We didn't know what to make of it. We were low on fuel and water, but we headed for it anyway. As we approached, we could see that it was a man, walking alone in the desert. He collapsed just as we came upon him. He was not far from dying, but since he had been on his feet a few minutes before, we had hope. We laid him down in the shade of the Power Wagon and wet his face and gave him water to drink. His robe was stained in dry blood, and he had a deep cut on his head. He began babbling something in Arabic we didn't understand. We took him back to camp where he slept on and off for three days. We nursed him with water and some broth one of the desert rats had concocted. When his condition improved enough to talk, we got one of the rats to find out what had happened to him. He told us his name was Ziad. Members of his clan were on their way to Mecca to worship when Yemeni raiders ambushed them. They killed all the pilgrims but him and one other man. The other survivor had died in the desert. As it turned out, Ziad had been in the scorching sand without water for two days.

"As usual, our radio was on the fritz, so we had no way to contact base camp. The nearest little mud village was three days' journey, and the base camp south of Yabrin was a hard four-day drive to the north. We knew we needed to get medical help for Ziad, but he insisted on showing us the scene of the massacre, so we refueled and headed out.

"When we arrived at the site, we wished we'd never come. We could smell the scene well before we reached it. It was the most horrendous sight I had ever seen before or since. Perhaps sixty bodies were spread out in the sand. The dead pilgrims were strewn over three or four acres. In a panic, they must have fled in all directions, just to be cut down, robbed, molested, and butchered. Men lay shot dead, half covered by the sand, their arms and legs akimbo. Mothers and daughters lay prone, raped and their throats cut. Children's little bodies lay broken in the sand. Their frozen eyes stared up at us as if asking why we hadn't arrived in time. The sand was saturated with blood. You can't imagine the smell of rotting flesh in the hot desert. We threw up until there was nothing left, and then we lapsed into dry heaves.

"No one said a word. The only sound was the buzzing of millions of flies and the pages of the pilgrim's Qur'ans flapping in the wind. I picked up a little girl's doll and wondered what kind of souls could order such an act. I reckoned whoever murdered these poor people must hate Muslims. He must have been sending them a message that he ruled the wilderness, and that he ruled it by means of sheer terror. We wanted to bury the victims, but Ziad wouldn't hear of it. He said his tribal sheikh would have to see the scene before it was removed. Then his tribesmen would bury what was left of the victims' bodies facing Mecca."

Mac and I sat there in stunned silence. Out of the blackness of that June night came an eyewitness account of real-life horror. It took a few minutes for me to realize my mouth was gaping open, and only with an act of conscious will did I shut it. The look on Mac's face mirrored the shock we both felt. Suddenly this was no longer a story about the good old days of oil exploration in Saudi Arabia. It was a dark reality in the country where I was spending the summer. We waited patiently for Willy to go on, but he couldn't. After a long silence, Hank picked up the thread of thought.

"Willy and I drove Ziad to the nearest Bedouin camp and got some folks to care for him. Two days later we were back at our camp only to discover that the Sudanese desert rats had all taken off. Ziad's account must have terrified them. Seems they slipped into one of the Power Wagons while the others slept and headed for who knows where. PAMMCO eventually found the truck and four beheaded Sudanese.

"That left just the six of us with three trucks and no way to contact anyone. The only weapon we had was Willy's .45. In all the years we had lived in Arabia, we had never heard of anything like this before. It had never occurred to us to pack firearms. But then, we had never been this deep into the Rub' al Khali before either. I mean, the desert was dangerous enough with the heat, lethal vipers, scorpions, camel spiders, quicksand, and countless other deadly risks. Now we had bloodthirsty raiders to contend with too.

"The six of us held a meeting. It was decided that two men would head back to the base camp, where they could contact Dhahran and get a chopper to the rest of us as fast as possible. We reasoned that two men in a light truck, without our heavy gear and with just enough food, water, and gasoline to make it to base camp, could travel a lot faster. There would be less risk of getting stuck in the sand than if we all broke camp and evacuated all our equipment and survey records. The plan was for the rest of us to stay and guard our camp and valuable survey records. It was our best shot for survival. Even so, it would take four or five days for the two men to get help, depending on how fast they could push their truck, and that depended on not getting stuck in the soft *sabkha*. If they became embedded in the quicksand, it would take at least another day to dig themselves out."

"What's a sabkha?" I interrupted, now more interested in the various details of how I could die in Arabia.

"A series of great lakes once covered the Empty Quarter. Before the lakes, the area was an ancient sea floor, and that's what they call a sabkha. If you drive across a long flat area where the dunes haven't collected, your truck is likely to break through the hardened surface and sink into the thick mud of a forgotten sea floor. Rarely will your truck completely sink into the moist abyss, but it might as well. If you can't dig your way out, you can go ahead and dig your own grave. No one can walk out of the Empty Quarter. Without a truck, your first steps are those of a walking dead man.

"As I was saying, we sent two geologists off, but like the Sudanese rats, that was the last anyone heard of them. After three weeks of air searches, PAMMCO stopped hunting for them. The remaining four were left to look to our defenses. But we were only four men and a couple of tents in the middle of thousands of square miles of nothing. What was there to defend and what could we defend it with? So we hunkered down and waited for the PAMMCO helicopter to arrive.

"On the third day we all started feeling it. Something evil was about to befall us, but we didn't know quite what. Whatever it was, it wouldn't be good. We didn't have to wait long. The next morning over the dunes came a group of Bedouin on camelback, armed to the teeth and looking like something out of Lawrence of Arabia. We were right scared by this time, but it turned out they were friendly toward us. They were the Murrah warriors sent by the sheikh to find out what had happened to Ziad and his group. For all the world, they looked like an Apache war party from the Old American West out to avenge their brothers. All that was missing was war paint and feathers. It was hard to communicate with them without the Sudanese rats. They thanked us for saving their clansman. We tried to tell them the little we knew about the raid, and then we took them to the massacre site. Their eyes grew darker as they approached the scene. They silently examined what was left and buried their dead. They held a meeting, prayed, and then headed out in pursuit of the raiders. It wasn't as if they could simply follow tracks across the sand, but the Murrah are famed above all other Bedouin tribes for their tracking abilities."

Willy butted in here, and Hank went back to fussing with his pipe.

"The next day passed quietly enough in our camp, but on the dawn of the fifth day, we heard the grunts of far-off camels. In a few minutes, a half dozen riders appeared over a dune to the south. They were moving at a fast clip in our direction. As they drew nearer, we realized that they were all that was left of the Murrah warriors. They were riding as if their lives depended on a flawless escape. Chills ran up our spines. We all knew what had happened. They had been overcome by the Yemenis and were now trying to stay one sand dune ahead. We grabbed a jerry can of drinking water and another of gasoline, jumped into our trucks, and roared out of there without a second thought for our expensive equipment and research notes.

"We had no idea what the Yemenis would do to foreign oilmen if they overtook us, but it couldn't be good. We felt we held the advantage in the safety of our trucks. However, that remaining element of security was short lived. In our dash for safety, our lead truck, carrying two American geologists, tried to take a straight-line dash across a patch of sabkha. They must have decided it was worth the risk to avoid a slow traverse over the large sand dunes on each side of the sabkha. Less than half way across the salt flats, their truck cracked the sabkha and fell fender-deep through the crust. They were hopelessly stuck in the thick mire. Following a hundred yards back, we slammed on the brakes as quickly as possible to avoid getting too close to the weakened crust. We yelled to the others to abandon their truck and join us. Just as we got their attention, we heard the sickening sound of cracking sabkha beneath our Power Wagon. With a jolt, our truck dropped into the muddy quicksand of a primordial seabed.

"It was useless trying to walk out, so we rested in the shade inside our trucks and prayed help would arrive before the Yemenis found us. What wishful thinking. In less than two hours, we spotted a dust cloud forming over the dunes to the south. In their panicked retreat, the surviving Murrah warriors had inadvertently led the raiders straight to our camp. Judging by the size of the dust cloud, some if not all of the Yemenis chose to follow the tracks of our trucks. We were up a creek without a paddle and about to face an army of bloodthirsty terrorists.

"Hank and I tried to devise some kind of strategy for how we should negotiate with the raiders. Then all of the sudden, we felt a hot wind blast us in the face, and there they were. The Yemeni raiders appeared over the ridge of a dune no more than two hundreds yards from our truck. Seeing their prey, they started yelling their Arabic war cry, pounding their rhythmic drums, and firing their rifles. An instant later, bullets started whizzing past us. We ducked in the cab of the truck, hoping for a temporary sanctuary. Bullets were piercing the truck, and I remember thinking this was no way for an Irishman to die. I grabbed the handgun and jumped out of the truck to do battle, but after firing a few wild shots, I was hit in the leg. I struggled for a few more steps and released another round or two before I was hit in the back of the head by what must have been a rifle butt. That's all I remember."

Hank slowly swallowed. Then he picked it up from there. "When the shooting started, I knew we didn't stand a chance. Willy was blazing away with that .45, but he was taken out before he even ran out of ammo. I concluded that we were goners, but I found myself instinctively getting out of the cab to help Willy. I thought I was a dead man when a bullet pierced my shoulder. I felt warm blood flowing down my chest. I fell to the ground as stiff as a stone. Of course I wasn't dead. I was frozen with fear. I smelled something far worse than even the rotting bodies of the Murrah pilgrims. The stench was beyond anything imaginable. My nervous system locked up on me, and I couldn't have moved a finger even if I had wanted to.

"Through the sound of gunfire, I could hear the terrified screams of the geologists in the other truck. I could smell the fumes of their truck burning. Then I heard an explosion. The yells for help stopped, but the smell of their burning flesh wafted my way. I will never forget the sounds of the Yemeni war cries, their drums, and their camels grunting. It was the sound of bedlam, and it only ended with the silence of death.

"I laid there in sheer terror, suspended in the rigor mortis of total neuron shock. Then someone, I mean something, delivered a sharp kick to my back. The revolting odor was overwhelming. I felt a film of vomit covering my face. My body moved, but I did not react to being kicked. My muscles were frozen in place. I didn't dare cry out, nor could I.

"You might think I was afraid of dying, but death wasn't what I feared at that moment. It was the evil of that thing! And the thought of what the evil creature would do to my soul. I can't describe the stench that reeked from the beast or the coldness that encompassed me. As the creature passed over me, I could see that it had the form of a man, but it was not human. The further away he moved, the weaker the grip his coldness had on my body. The thing was dressed in black robes and a black head wrap. In his left hand he held the head of the chief Murrah warrior and in the other hand, a sword. It turned to take one last look back at us. To my surprise, it had the face of a handsome man, except for a large, deformed right eye that had a slimy liquid dripping from it. The evil thing shouted instructions to the Yemenis, and they started mounting their camels. At that moment, I blacked out.

"What must have been days later, the light slowly reappeared. I could make out the dreary cinder block walls of a beige room. I must have been heavily medicated. It seemed as if I was floating in a dream without any sense of time. That first day of consciousness, Willy and I could see and hear the nurses but had no strength to communicate.

"After a day or two, I was able to ask the Filipina nurse where we were and how we got there. I'll never forget what she said.

" 'You're in the public health clinic of the village of Yabrin. The White Bedouin brought you here hunched over the back of camels. You owe him your lives and some money. He paid for your care before he left.'

" 'What the . . . ? What kind of Bedouin brought us here?' I asked again.

" 'He's the Caucasian Bedouin who the Arab tribesmen say travels with the nomads. They say he's the chief of a small clan of camel traders, but no one in this village really knows who he is or even if he has a proper name. He speaks both English and Arabic and has a long white beard. I've heard the old folks say he's the ghost of a lost crusader, dressing and talking like an Arab. But believe me, he's no ghost. I saw him myself. He's a tall man with an American accent.' When the nurse asked him his name, he only said, 'I am Al-Mormon.' "

I could hardly believe what I had just heard. Al-Mormon? I was only a week into my summer internship, but I knew what my investigative story would be for my short time in Arabia. I had to find out all I could about this white Bedouin. Where did he come from? Why did he call himself Al-Mormon? Was he a man or only an initiatory joke perpetrated by the two old oilmen on young newcomers?

"How did the White Bedouin find you way out there in the

desert?" I asked.

"The nurse could only tell us that this Al-Mormon character said 'Alhamdallah'—which means 'Thanks to Allah'—'I was led to them by his grace.' So I guess I also owe my life to God! The White Bedouin told the clinic staff something about being in his tent and having the impression that someone was lost in the desert and needed his help. Following the impression, he took some camels and went out searching for strangers in need."

What Hank had just told me touched a spiritual nerve deep inside my soul. I momentarily lost my train of thought in a whirlpool of emotions. If Al-Mormon was real, he was like a modern-day Abraham. This Al-Mormon sounded like a man with the spiritual sensitivity and heightened humanity of the great patriarch. With Willy and Hank dying in the desert, I imagined this American Bedouin sitting in his tent on an insufferably hot day. I remembered a lecture in my religion class at BYU in which Dr. Nibley told of a similarly hellish day when Abraham rested in the protection of his thick goat-skinned tent. Suddenly, the prophet sensed that a wanderer was lost on the desert plain of Mamre and was in dire need of help. The sun on such a day can crush the will of even the strongest man and take his life in a few short hours. Anyone lost on such a day is bound to suffer a most painful death.

Sensing that the stranger's life was in danger, Abraham sent his servant to look for him. The servant returned and told Abraham that his search was in vain, that he found no one on the desert plain. Still knowing that someone needed his help, Abraham walked into the blistering heat of the desert. He would risk his own life to help someone he had never met. Abraham searched and searched, but he finally returned to his tent exhausted. As he approached the tent, he saw three men. He immediately realized that it was the Lord and two disciples. He fell to his knees and worshiped the Lord, the one who would give his own life to save Abraham and the rest of mankind. The story meant so much to me, for it helped me understand the principle that by giving our lives in the service of others, we find our own meaning in life and obtain salvation through the Lord. Abraham's reward that day was the promise that his wife would bear him a son, Isaac.[1]

But who was this white Bedouin, and what was his motive for saving these two crusty oilmen? Rejoining the conversation, I asked Hank if he ever met the White Bedouin.

"Never," he answered. "The more we think about it, the more we have come to believe that the nurse was filling our heads with a tall desert tale. No white man could survive in that desert. If he does exist, he's a ghost."

"If he is a ghost, how do you explain how you ended up in the Yabrin clinic?" I persisted.

"I don't know. Whether he's a ghost or man, I don't care. What I do know is that as long as I live, I will never return to the Empty Quarter. I will never step another foot in the domain of that evil creature that tried to kill us. That's the reason PAMMCO finally canned me. I refused to go back. Honestly, I'd rather die than face the evil beast again."

"But you said yourself you saw the evil man, the one dressed in black from head to toe. He sounds like a tall tale to me."

Hank locked his piercing eyes on me again. "You stupid kid! You fool! He's real all right, just as real as I am sitting here next to you. Why do you think I refuse to go back into the Empty Quarter? He cost me the best job I ever had. My advice to you, sprout, is to stay out of that desert and don't tell anyone what you heard tonight. The gringos around here already think I'm crazy. When I reported to PAMMCO what happened, they sent me off to a psychologist. I was diagnosed with post-traumatic stress disorder, and my coworkers kept asking if I had seen the boogey man lately."

"And what do the Arabs say about the beast in black?" I asked.

"Oh, they know who he is all right. The Muslims call him Al-Dajja, the evil one. They claim he comes from the mountains of Syria, has armies of assassins throughout the Middle East, and rules freely the deep deserts and the open seas. They say he is the reason there will be no peace in this part of the world until the Day of Judgment. He's the one their Prophet Mohammed said would come in the last days and would have one swollen eye. He is Al-Dajja. He's the anti-Christ."

Notes

1. Story adapted from Hugh Nibley's account. See *Faith of an Observer: Conversations with Hugh Nibley,* DVD, directed by Brian R. Capener (Provo, UT: BYU and FARMS, 1985).

Chapter 3

A Cowboy Lands in Arabia

I did not go to the Arabian desert to collect plants, nor to make a map. . . . I went to find peace in the hardship of desert travel and the company of desert peoples.

Wilfred Thesiger, *Arabian Sands*, 1959

Stephen Markham

August 1936
The Sleepy Fishing Village of Al-Khobar

"Al-Khobar! Now disembarking!" came the difficult-to-decipher announcement from the ship's enthusiastic first mate. The cargo steamer *S.S. Lady Ann* was now securely moored to the single jetty that formed the harbor at Al-Khobar. The *Lady Ann* was the only metal ship resting in port among several dozen small wooden fishing boats and a tubby open-decked wooden craft that ferried passengers and their cargo from the Arabian mainland to the small island emirate of Bahrain.

From one of the *Lady Ann's* portholes, Stephen Markham got his long-anticipated first glance at his new home. However, all he could glimpse through the steamed-up porthole were the shabby mud huts that made up the tiny fishing village. After rubbing the glass, he could make out a single mud-brick tower that looked as if it would tumble over at any moment. The leaning minaret was the only structure that accentuated the skyline of the small community. It was a Sunni Islamic minaret, and it reminded the young American that he was about to enter the guarded Muslim Holy Land—the land of Mohammed, Mecca, veiled women, and a thousand more secrets hidden from the West. Until oil was discovered just fifteen miles to the east on the island of Bahrain, westerners were not welcome in Saudi Arabia. However, with the discovery of oil in Bahrain, the Saudi king contracted Americans to hunt for his loot of black gold. That was the reason Markham came to this backward desert kingdom—to find oil.

Preparing to leave the fan-cooled cabin, Stephen took a deep breath, opened the ship's sliding door, and stepped into the oppressively hot, muggy air of his first Persian Gulf August. For a moment, the heat and the pungent odor of fishing boats staggered the six-foot three-inch geologist. Having driven cattle in southern Utah, Markham knew he could handle heat. But the 120-degree temperature was only the first punch. It was followed a split second later by an even stronger blow—a thick film of steamy humidity that enveloped his body.

"Hot Tamales!" he murmured. He removed his cowboy hat and wiped his brow with a handkerchief. By the time he had brushed back his blond hair and rested his Stetson back on his head, he realized that his forehead was as wet as before.

Trying to mentally block out the humidity, Markham knew this was no time to become disoriented. The young American needed his wits to retrieve his two small trunks. The luggage had already been placed on deck along with the other freight that was to be off-loaded at Al-Khobar. As Stephen made his way toward the trunks, all he could make out was a busy swarm of white-robed men fighting over the baggage. It was pure mayhem. He was no longer in the civilized world of the English porters at Southampton who had carefully and politely put his personal items aboard the *Lady Ann*. He was all too aware that the ship had sailed from what he knew as civilization into a world that seemed lost in time. He was realizing with both eyes and both ears that he would soon be stepping into the impoverished, yet exotic, world of Arabia. Seeing Arab men dressed in threadbare robes and screaming at each other for a chance to pick up minuscule tips reminded him of the Great Depression back home. Even so, to this newcomer from Utah, the Arab porters looked like a band of greedy pirates scouring the plunder of their latest shipwreck.

One toothless old Arab couldn't help but get Stephen's attention. He stuck his face right in front of Stephen's. His breath could have knocked over an ox. The aged porter gave Stephen a big gummy smile and pointed to his heart. *"Habibi! Habibi!"* (Friend! Friend!), he shouted.

Why not? Stephen thought. *He looks as needy as any of these other poor hombres.*

Stephen nodded his head in approval. The old Arab took the cowboy's big hand and led him toward the trunks. Instinctively, Stephen jerked his hand free. The toothless porter panicked, perhaps thinking he had offended the foreigner and would lose his day's meal ticket. The old man gently smiled, lowered his eyes in respect for the foreigner, and again took Stephen's hand to continue leading him toward the cargo deck. Stephen could only wonder why this man was holding his hand. He was starting to question his wisdom in coming to Arabia. *What on earth have I gotten myself into for a salary of three hundred dollars a month plus expenses?* Stephen thought. *Have I just arrived in the land of the fairies? Good golley, the men wear dresses and toothless Butch can't stop holding my hand.*

By the time they reached the trunks, Stephen was ready for an emotional meltdown. *Has anyone heard of deodorant here?* he wondered. *This is unbearable. These people smell worse than a herd of cattle that's gotten into crazy weed.* Between the heat, the ripe aroma of fishing boats, and the sweat of bodies that hadn't soaked in bath water in months, the new arrival was about to faint. Nothing his Mormon mother taught him about good social graces could have prepared him for this. Suddenly, a perplexing feeling triggered an anomalous thought. *I am home.* Stephen could only shrug his shoulders. *What an odd notion! I am home.*

There was no reason to try communicating with the porter in English. Stephen simply pointed to his trunks, and the old porter quickly subcontracted the real lifting to four younger Arabs. With his luggage in able hands, they all headed across the gangplank and on down the jetty toward a wooden shack. The hut had some crude English writing painted on its side. In rough brush strokes, Stephen read: *CUSTOMS HOME. Oh well,* he thought. *If I don't find oil here, maybe I can get a job teaching English.*

The short walk down the jetty gave Stephen time to gather his thoughts. If these poor fellows were an example of middle-class Arabs, Stephen figured this new nation of Saudi Arabia must be the poorest place on earth. The infamous shabby towns of Calcutta or Shanghai couldn't be much worse.

Stephen's cowboy boots had strolled down the jetty less than four hundred feet before he reached the customs home. By then his cloths were completely drenched in perspiration. He was dripping sweat like a roasting goose. Before opening the door to the customs home, Stephen closed his eyes and said a silent prayer that the room would have one of those new machines that cooled air. Stepping inside, he opened his eyes. His prayer had not been answered, but before him sat what looked like a prophet straight out of his Old Testament primary lessons. The customs inspector was the spitting image of Father Abraham! He was dressed in a robe and a headscarf with an *agaal* (a woven head rope, resembling two fan belts, that Arabs use to hold their headscarves on). But the officer's most striking feature was his foot-long white beard that would have made Brother Brigham proud!

Without a desk, the officer conducted his business sitting cross-legged on a well-worn Persian carpet. What must have been his receipt book and documents log were on the floor next to him. The inspector said, *"Salaam aleikumm."* He motioned to the newly arrived American to be seated on the carpet.

Stephen removed his hat and sat down on the rug. "Same to you, sir."

The young American was pleasantly surprised that the Arab, though dressed in clothes Stephen thought were better suited for walking beside Moses, spoke intelligible English.

"It be your first time here. Welcome to Saudi Arabia," the customs inspector said in broken English.

"How do you know it's my first time?" Stephen asked.

"Because you insult me. Three time you insult me and you be here less than minute."

Apologetically, the Utahn requested the inspector's forgiveness and asked what he had done. "I'm sorry. I took off my hat and politely called you sir."

"Taking off your strange headdress is no being polite to Arab. No one takes off their headdress when they go inside. But don't worry, young man. They call me Abullah the Patient. I guess that is why they have me as the customs home man. But remember, I am more old than you. It is our way that you, the young man, say 'salaam aleikum' before their elders do. It means 'Peace be upon you.' Then you added even more insult by not replying to my greeting by saying 'Wa aleikum as-salaam' or 'And upon you be peace.' I suggest you learn our greeting good before you go into the desert and meet a Bedouin. If you show a Bedouin such disrespect, he might pierce your heart with his jumbia. For now, please stop pointing the bottom of your funny shoes at me."

"Why's that?" Markham questioned.

"Because that is insult number three. Not your father and mother teach you no to point the bottom of your feet at someone?"

"Oh, sorry," Stephen said as he quickly rearranged his long legs while trying to make heads or tails of his first lesson in Arab cultural traditions. *Clearly*, the Utahn thought, *I have gotten off on the wrong foot with this Saudi.*

"I check your trunks for *haram* things," the inspector announced as he rose and walked toward Stephen's trunks. Stephen followed, not sure what the inspector would be looking for.

"*Haram*," the inspector said, "is another word you will need learn. It mean 'prohibited,' and there are many things in Arabia that is haram. You have no gold on your finger. You not got wife or concubine? Let me warn you, young man, there are many things that are prohibited here, but the most haram thing for you is our women. Violate one of Allah's pure daughters and the sands of Arabia will soak up your blood."

Stephen was a returned Mormon missionary. He didn't know whether to laugh or take offense at the inspector's lecture on morals. "You don't need to worry, sir. I don't smoke, I don't drink alcohol, and I guarantee you, I will take absolutely no interest in your women. I am engaged to be married to a girl back in America. Going home and marrying her is the first thing I'll do after my two-year contract is up."

"*Inshalal*" (God willing), the officer said as he started searching through Markham's trunks. "No whisky? No wine?"

"No, sir. Like I said, I don't drink alcohol."

"What is this? If it is bacon, you'll spend a week in jail and get ten lashes."

"That's only elk jerky. I cured it from the meat of a wild animal that lives in America. I shot the elk and dried the meat. It is definitely not pork. More like a camel with horns. It's good. Try some if you want."

"We Muslims don't eat old flesh. This has blood in it; it's haram. It has terrible odor. You Americans eat this kind of food?" With a disgusted look on his face, the old Arab set the bag of jerky back in the trunk.

Then, as if he discovered a great treasure, his expression suddenly changed to a broad smile. "Now what is these?" the inspector said, removing Stephen's Bible and Book of Mormon from the trunk. "Your company no tell you that Bibles is forbidden in Arabia. This is the land of Holy Qur'an. We no need your Bible and this other book." Carefully reading the cover, he laughed. "Book of Mormon, ha, corrupting our holy people. The rest you can take, but books stay with me."

"Then you can tell these men to put my trunks back on the ship," the cowboy said defiantly. "I won't stay here without them, and you can explain to the California Arabian Texaco Oil Company and your king why I got back on the ship." Stephen's eye showed that he meant it.

"So you is religious infidel, is you? Is you a Christian missionary here to try and make us believe Jesus is partner with Allah?"

"No, sir, as my documents show, I am a geologist for the California Arabian Texaco Oil Company, and these books are for my eyes only."

"You work for CALTOC, do you? They should tell you about our laws. You say you only here for two years and then leave Arabia." Then he added with an increased touch of sourness in his voice, "That short time. You can be without your Bibles that long."

Stephen said a silent but earnest prayer that helped him to be a little less reactive and a lot wiser. He looked directly into the old Arab's eyes. "My friend, I am very sorry that I insulted you, and I ask your forgiveness. If I broke a law that I was not aware of, I apologize. But please understand, partner, I am a believer in God, your Allah, and I will be lost and alone without these two books. They keep me close to Allah, and my heart will be sad without them, just the way you would feel if you visited my country and the customs officer took away your Holy Qur'an."

The inspector was both surprised and touched by the young American. Hearing a westerner respect the one true God by invoking his Arabic name caught the customs officer off guard. He placed both his hands on Stephen's shoulders and looked up into the tall Mormon's eyes. In that moment, the two believers in God understood each other's most important priority in life. Then, without warning, the inspector embraced Stephen in a long, brotherly hug and whispered in his ear, "We are brothers. Allah is love."

In the very core of his soul, Stephen Markham knew that the old man spoke the truth—they were brothers. The warmth in his heart confirmed the truthfulness of something that he was yet to comprehend.

The inspector respectfully placed the Book of Mormon and Bible back in Stephen's trunk and officially pronounced, "You are clear. You go."

Stephen had been in Arabia less than fifteen minutes and was already whispering his third prayer, "Oh Lord, thank you for saving my scriptures."

Just outside the customs shack, Stephen spotted a burly American among the Arabs. He was holding up a piece of paper with the handwritten word *Markham*. The stocky oilman and his low-budget sign drew a smile from the cowboy, and another instant mental prayer—a plea of gratitude like so many foreigners say the first time they arrive in Arabia. *Thank you, Lord. I've made contact with someone from the real world. Amen.*

"Ya must be Stephen. Nice boots ya got dere. I'm Timmy Cullerson. As ya can hear from my talk, I am a Texan."

"Well, partner, you're a sight for sore eyes," Stephen replied.

"Glad ya here in one piece. The boss sent me to pick ya up. Here, let me give ya some local fallus to pay off 'em friends of yers. These here bills are riyals. The picture on the money is der King Abulaziz, so don't ya write anyding on it or accidentally tear it or they'll throw ya in the clink and whip ya. Jus give 'em a tenner apiece, and they'll be in camel heaven."

Stephen laughed to himself at how even the English idioms had to be modified for this Islamic land. The trunks were loaded into the back of the CALTOC Ford pickup in slow motion, a speed reflective of the scorching heat. Stephen paid the toothless porter and his sidekicks. The luggage safely onboard, the two gringos hopped into the cab and headed out of town on a dusty dirt road. *Finally*, Stephen thought, *the air is moving through the open windows, and I no longer feel like a stick of melting butter.*

"Got something fur ya." Cullerson reached in a small ice chest he had in the cab and pulled out an ice-cold bottle of Pepsi. "Bet ya'd like one of them right now. Der's a church key on the dash."

"A what?"

"Church key. Ya know, a beer bottle opener."

Stephen usually avoided caffeinated drinks, but this heat and humidity constituted a crisis. Without thinking twice, he took the bottle and the opener, popped off the cap, and took a drink. "Ahhh . . . Thanks, Mr. Cullerson."

"Name's Timmy."

Driving through the village of Al-Khobar was like turning back the pages of time. The single-story mud-brick houses had flat roofs where laundry hung to dry. Exterior staircases led to the rooftops, and along the rooflines, beams made of palm trunks projected out the front and back of the building. Since it was the hottest time of the day, the streets were deserted, except for the haunting view of several women covered entirely in black cloth. To Stephen, the women looked like aliens from a distant planet.

But most curious of all, and to Stephen's delight, there, in the middle of the main street, were at least a dozen camels. He had seen black and white photographs of camels in zoos, but these were the first he had ever witnessed in the flesh. What strange animals! They were bigger than he had supposed, and their feet were shackled with ropes to keep them from wandering away. To keep them content, their owners had piled desert bushes at their feet. The strange beasts slowly lowered their long necks to snatch mouthfuls of bush. Their heads rose again, chewing the fodder by wildly moving their lower jaw back and forth.

The only thing in the village that seemed to be going somewhere was a far-off donkey cart heading into the desert. "So this is Saudi Arabia," Markham concluded.

"Where ya from?" Cullerson asked as they bounced their way out of the fishing village and headed up a graded track toward the CALTOC camp some five miles inland.

"Born and raised in Richfield, Utah, but for the last year I've been working odd jobs in the oil fields of west Texas. I graduated eighteen months ago from the Colorado School of Mining and Engineering, but with the depression and all, it's tough to land an oil job, even in Odessa."

"Your kin still live in Utah?"

"No, my parents were killed in a car accident when I was fourteen. My only sister lives in Oakland, California. She's eleven years older than me. During high school I lived with my grandfather on his cattle ranch, but he's gone now too. I thought that tough old pioneer would never die, but even he passed away while I was in college. So what little family I have is spread around small towns in southern Utah."

"Cattleman. I knew der were something I liked about ya. Sorry about yer kin. Don't sound like ya got much waiting for ya in the States. Might as well settle in here and make some big-time dough working for CALTOC."

"Partner, you can take this to the bank. I'll be out of here in two years. I have someone special waiting for me back home. So you can tell CALTOC to have my return ticket ready. I will be here twenty-four months—just long enough to pay back a loan for my schooling, put a down payment on a second-hand car, and buy a wedding ring."

"Glad to hear yer engaged. There's not much wine or women around these parts. A lot of time, though, for thinkin'. I don't know your preference for chapel, but beings yer from Utah, you's probably one of 'em Mormons. If you feel so inclined, ya's sure welcome to join some of us church boys. We hold Bible classes in my room each Friday. That's the Sabbath day in Muslim countries. I'm an oilman by trade, but Daddy was a preacher, and he taught me the Good Book well enough to lead some lively Bible discussions."

"I thought the Bible was outlawed in Saudi Arabia," Stephen said, fresh from his encounter with the customs inspector.

"Law? What law? There's less law here than in a zoo. These Arabs use their Qur'an as their national constitution, the criminal code, and even for their traffic regulations. It's more confusing than watching my dog chase a raccoon. The law here all depends on who thinks he has the right to enforce his interpretation of the Qur'an. Yea, ya must have run into old Abdullah back there at the customs shack. He loves nothin' more than taking away folks' Bibles and lecturing 'em on the virtues of Islam. Thank goodness he only works there two days a week. The regular dude lets everybody through with deir Bibles, but watch out for that feller too. He's got quick fingers when it comes to stealing men's underwear. I reckon his wife gets a thrill out of havin' the only buck in the village in American briefs. Take note, Stephen, the next time ya come back from America, bring a few extra pair of drawers."

"That won't be a problem for me. I'm really not coming back. I'll work the two years of my contract, and then its back to God's country to marry Jan Roberts." But as Stephen was saying those words, they didn't seem to come out with as much confidence as he wanted them to. That eerie thought entered his mind again. *This strange place is home.*

"By the way," Stephen said, "that customs inspector, Abdullah, called me his brother and said, 'God is love.' "

"Now that there is a real odd thing. The heat must be gettin' to old Abdullah. He's a devout Muslim. What they call a *matawa* or volunteer religious sheriff. He should know better. He's gotta be crackin'. Arabs think we all infidel dogs. If they like ya, they'll call you friend, or abu John, or abu Fred. *Abu* means 'father of.' But ya don't have to worry about that because ya ain't a daddy. Or they might call you bin Jimmy, if yer daddy is named Jimmy. They might call ya sheikh, which means ya are the head of something, like a family or a tribe. But I've never heard them call a Christian brother. The Muslim brotherhood is strictly a religion thang that we ain't invited to. Yep, Adbullah is gone clear mad."

"Maybe I misheard him." But then Stephen felt again the warmth in his heart. "Still, I think he said 'brother.' "

"Well, that beats my hide. Ya learn something new each day about these Mohammedans. Really they ain't bad folks, just really confused about the Lord. From what Daddy taught me, and from what the Good Book says, the Mohammedans got a lot of things backward. Still, there's one thing I can't figger. That's Isaiah 11:11. That verse just don't make no sense to me. Yep, 11:11. It's an odd number with an odder message. Them people in that verse are all Muslims."

That's interesting, Stephen thought to himself. *That verse must be of particular importance for the people in the ancient times if Nephi included it in the Book of Mormon,*[1] *and it had to be of paramount significance for the last days if Moroni quoted the verse to Joseph Smith.*[2] Just then the Ford passed through the gates of the CALTOC compounds.

"That one's yer hut over yonder. You'll share it with four other guys, but ya got your own room."

A couple of teenage Saudi boys in sandals ran over to help unload the pickup. "These young broncos are our houseboys. Ya don't need to pay 'em. The company gives jobs to these poor folks whenever they can. Them poor Arabs are hard workers. They will do anything ya ask of 'em."

Once the boys had Stephen's trunks in his quarters, he thanked Timmy for his help and arranged to meet him for dinner in the mess hall. As soon as Timmy left the room, Stephen reached for the trunk that contained his four most valuable possessions: the picture of his fiancée, a faded picture of his parents, his Book of Mormon, and his Bible. He fetched the Bible even before he turned on the air conditioner. He had to dissect Isaiah 11:11 and what it had to do with the Muslims. He opened the Bible to Isaiah, found chapter eleven, and pointed his finger to verse eleven. As he started reading, Stephen realized it was a message for those living in the last days. Isaiah was far more than a prophet; he was a great seer, and here was his description of the gathering of the house of Israel in the last days.

> And it shall come to pass in that day, that the Lord shall set his hand again the second time to recover the remnant of his people, which shall be left, from Assyria, and from Egypt, and from Pathros, and from Cush, and from Elam, and from Shinar, and from Hamath, and from the islands of the sea.[3]

One by one, Stephen located these ancient city states on his Old Testament map. *Yes, there's no doubt about it. Today these are all Muslim countries,* Stephen thought. But didn't this verse refer to the Lord's people that were held captive by the Assyrians? These were some of the very lands that once made up the great Assyrian empire, where the tribes of Israel had been held captive.[4] It could mean that some of the tribes never left the areas that they were scattered to by the Assyrians.[5]

Stephen read the preceding verses in chapter eleven that led up to the discussion of the great gathering in verse eleven. Isaiah also described a "young lion and the fatling together; and a little child would lead them" (Isaiah 11:6). The scriptures went on to say that "the lion shall eat straw" (Isaiah 11:7) and the "sucking child shall play on the hole of the asp" (Isaiah 11:8). It couldn't be any clearer to Stephen. Isaiah was writing about the gathering at the beginning of the Millennium. Stephen was beginning to wonder if the pre-Millennial gathering of the Lord's people would actually come from people who lived in today's Muslim nations.

Stephen read on. "The earth shall be full of the knowledge of the Lord, as the waters cover the sea" (Isaiah 11:9). *Aha,* he thought, *sounds like someday people will be able to take a device and find any information they want from anywhere they want at anytime they want. Like somehow surfing a sea of information like the Hawaiians surf the waves.*

He continued reading in verse ten. "A root of Jesse, which shall stand for an ensign of the people; to it shall the Gentiles seek."

Stephen remembered learning on his mission that this verse foretells the gospel being restored in the latter days.[6] Therefore, Isaiah is definitely writing about a gathering in the last days.

Perhaps, he questioned, *those to be gathered will not be Muslims, but small pockets of Jews that are still living in those countries.* Stephen read on and discovered that in verse twelve Isaiah described the second stage of the great gathering of the "dispersed of Judah," which he knew was to be the gathering of the Jews to Jerusalem in preparation for the Second Coming.

If the Jews were the second stages of the gathering, then they would not be the people to be gathered with the first wave. Stephen read verse eleven again. This time his eyes stopped on the words *recover the remnant.*

The remnant! That's got to be part of the code. So who are they? Then it hit him: General Moroni. Stephen reminded himself that Moroni had identified explicitly who the remnant are. Stephen returned to his trunk and took out his Book of Mormon.

It's somewhere in here. So often, he reminded himself, *it takes the Book of Mormon to decode the Bible.* He turned the pages until he found the red-shaded verse he was looking for: Alma 46:23.

> Moroni said unto them: Behold, we are a remnant of the seed of Jacob; yea, we are a remnant of the seed of Joseph, whose coat was rent by his brethren into many pieces.

"That is it!" Markham exclaimed aloud. "Joseph's seed consisted of two of the twelve tribes of Israel, Manasseh and his younger brother Ephraim. The Old Testament refers to the two royal tribes of Israel as simply Ephraim. However, if only the remnant is to be gathered in the first wave, then it meant that the Apocrypha was correct in stating that the tribes of Ephraim had separated themselves from the other lost tribes who went on to the land northward."[7]

Wait a minute! he caught himself thinking. *Is this crazy or what? How can the royal tribe of Ephraim be part of the Islamic nations? They don't even believe Jesus is the Christ.* Stepping back, he shook his head as if trying to wake himself up.

What a day it had been. Stephen couldn't believe he had only been in Arabia a couple of hours, and already he was thinking backward. *The Jews are the good guys,* he reminded himself. *The Muslims are the bad guys.* He was now confused. He wondered again, *How could the house of Joseph, the father of the tribes of Ephraim and Manasseh, not be Christians? The Muslims believe in a religion that teaches that Jesus is not the Son of God.*

Then again, during his mission he had read that the house of Joseph would need to be taught about the Lord Jesus Christ when they were to be gathered in the last days. Stephen quickly flipped through 3 Nephi until he found the verses he was looking for:

> Yea, and surely shall he again bring a remnant of the seed of Joseph to the knowledge of the Lord their God. And as surely as the Lord liveth, will he gather in from the four quarters of the earth all the remnant of the seed of Jacob, who are scattered abroad upon all the face of the earth. (3 Nephi 5:23–24)

Stephen realized that if he was to understand Isaiah's code, it would be through the Book of Mormon. He figured it was one of the reasons Nephi quoted Isaiah so often in his own record. The Book of Mormon had already opened Stephen's mind to Biblical interpretations that the day before would have seemed as foreign to him as the land he had just arrived in. *Could it be true,* he pondered, *that the remnant, the tribes of Ephraim and Manasseh, would be gathered from the countries that are today Muslim, including, it seems, people from Saudi Arabia? Is this the reason I felt a special closeness with the old man at the customs house? Could he be my Ephraimite brother?*

Stephen returned to Isaiah and read the next verse describing the gathering of Israel in the last days.

> The envy also of Ephraim shall depart, and the adversaries of Judah shall be cut off: Ephraim shall not envy Judah, and Judah shall not vex Ephraim. (Isaiah 11:13)

It's all starting to make sense now, he mused. *Until the Lord comes a second time and stops all the vexing, there's going to be a lot of hatred between Ephraim and Judah. So who do the Arabs hate in the last days? The Jews! Likewise, who do the Jews hate today? The Arabs! Boy, did Isaiah get it right about the last days!* He remembered Isaiah 9:21: "Ephraim, Manasseh: and they together shall be against Judah."

What have I gotten myself into? Stephen finally flipped on the air cooler and lay down on his bed to ponder questions he had never thought of before. *Are some of these Arabs members of the tribes of Ephraim and Manasseh? Have they mixed with the seed of Abraham's first son, Ishmael? Are the Arabs my brothers?*

The cool air refreshed his thoughts. *Why not? Why wouldn't the tribe of Ephraim join with their cousins, the descendants of Ishmael?*

The tribe of Ephraim possibly had closer cultural and ethnic ties with Ishmael than they had with their cousins from Israel.

Indeed, Ephraim and Ishmael shared the same patriarchal lineage of Father Abraham, and both had Egyptian mothers. Perhaps they had already mixed together by the time of Lehi. According to ancient Semitic customs, cousins married cousins. Lehi's children probably married their cousins, the children of a man named Ishmael. *Since no decent Israeli parent would name their child Ishmael, doesn't this imply that he must have been an Arab? That would suggest that Lehi had Arab bloodlines as well,* Stephen pondered.

Finally, Stephen wondered if there was some divine plan that brought him to Arabia in search of oil. *If we discover oil in Arabia,* he thought, *will God make the toothless porter, the customs man, and the rest of these impoverished people outrageously rich? Is oil the living waters spoken of in the Doctrine and Covenants? Will the Arabs someday emigrate to America and inherit the land of Joseph?*[8]

Stephen was startled to find another applicable verse of scripture:

> And in the barren deserts there shall come forth pools of living water; and the parched ground shall no more longer be a thirsty land. And they shall bring forth their rich treasures unto the children of Ephraim, my servants. . . .
>
> And the boundaries of the everlasting hills shall tremble at their presence. . . .
>
> Behold, this is the blessing of the everlasting God upon the tribes of Israel, and the richer blessing upon the head of Ephraim and his fellows. (Doctrine and Covenants 133:29, 31, 34)

Notes

1. 2 Nephi 21:11.
2. Joseph Smith—History 1:40.
3. Ezekiel 38:13 is a collaborating verse linking tribes of Israel with Arabia: "Sheba, and Dedan, and the merchants of Tarshish, with all the young lions thereof, shall say unto thee, Art thou come to take a spoil? hast thou gathered thy company to take a prey? to carry away silver and gold, to take away cattle and goods, to take a great spoil?" Sheba is found in southwest Saudi Arabia (see LDS Bible Dictionary), Dedan is in northwest Arabia (LDS Bible map, "The Ancient World at the Time of the Patriarchs"), and Tarshish (possibly a port in southern Arabia along the Indian Ocean shoreline) certainly has great wealth in the last days. Elder Bruce R. McConkie said of this verse, "Gog and Magog shall confiscate the wealth of Israel" (Bruce R. McConkie, *The Millennial Messiah* [Salt Lake City: Deseret Book, 1982], 481–82).

4. 2 Kings 17:6.

5. Joseph Fielding Smith wrote, "The ten tribes were taken by force out of the land the Lord gave them. Many of them mixed with the peoples among who they were scattered. A large portion, however, departed in one body into the north and disappeared from the rest of the world" (Joseph Fielding Smith, *The Way to Perfection: Short Discourses on Gospel Themes*, 8th ed. [Salt Lake City: Genealogical Society of Utah, 1949], 130).

6. Doctrine and Covenants 113:1–8.

7. "Elder George Reynolds has stated, the Israelites of the tribe of Ephraim were 'so characteristically . . . rebellious and backsliding,' that some of them 'turned aside from the main body' of the ten tribes as it traveled northwards. For the writer Baruch, in the Aprocrypha, has stated that there were eventually only 'nine and a half tribes, which were across the river Ephrates' and who became lost to the rest of mankind" (R. Clayton Brough, *The Lost Tribes* [Bountiful, UT: Horizon Publishers, 1979], 37).

8. Ether 13:63; Nephi 20:22.

Chapter 4

The Deep End of the Desert

Neither a wise man nor a brave man lies down on the tracks of history to wait for the train of the future to run over him.

Dwight D. Eisenhower

Stephen Markham
Mid-October 1936
CALTOC Camp—Dhahran Saudi Arabia

Stephen had been in Arabia less than two months when he was called into the office of Mr. Bennigar, CALTOC's chief geologist in Arabia. Stephen had waited anxiously for this day, realizing that the chief would be appointing him to his first field assignment on a surveying team. These were the first days of fall, and it was finally starting to feel like it. The scorching summer heat had broken enough to be bearable without taking constant refuge in an air-conditioned building. The break in the temperature was the sign the oil company was waiting for to renew its search for Arabia's elusive oil.

"How are you settling into Arabia, Markham?"

"Well . . . to be truthful, sir, I wake up each morning still feeling like I've been bucked off a horse and landed on my head on the dark side of the moon."

"Listen, Stephen, I've been here two years, and I still get that feeling every now and then. You cannot deny it, the Arabs are different and they're not going to change. You just have to get by at their speed and do things their way. Stephen, the best way to learn Arabic and to understand the Arab mind is to jump in headfirst, cold turkey. Sink or swim! Do you think you're ready for the deep end of Arabia?"

"How deep is deep, sir?"

"You're a religious boy from Utah, right?"

"Uh, yes . . ."

"Have you ever heard of the land of Midian?"

"Of course, it's where Jethro was a priest. It's the land where Moses went after he fled Egypt."

"Well, how would you like to be a modern-day Moses? Because that's where we're sending you."

"Why not?" Stephen replied.

"The British did some preliminary surveying in Midian before the Great War. Among the Brits was a young archaeologist named T. E. Lawrence. Actually, the whole lot of them were surveying part-time and spying on the Turks full-time. The Turks had been Germany's allies and used to control Arabia. Anyway, the Brits felt the area was promising for oil and gas, but they never finished their survey. That'll be your job. Finding oil in Midian is a long shot, but we need to know one way or the other. So take all the time you need.

It is a large area, so we figure you'll be there for the duration of your first two-year contract."

"What surveying crew will I be assigned to?"

"You are the crew. You will work alone and report to me by mail. We'll send Ahmed bin Al-Hajri with you as your translator. He's from a Bedouin tribe in the area. Besides being your ambassador to the tribes, he is to teach you Arabic. Besides that, we want Ahmed to keep you alive. As long as you're with Ahmed and have a letter of permission from the emir of Tabuk, the prince over the area, you'll be safe. But just in case, you do know how to use a rifle, don't you?"

"I can shoot a deer from three hundred yards if that's what you mean. Do you really think I'll need a rifle?"

"No, but we'll issue both of you rifles just in case. Besides, where you're going, the tribesmen won't respect a man unless he carries a gun. There haven't been very many foreigners living up there, and the government says there hasn't been any trouble for westerners traveling in that area. Besides, if you like hunting, I hear there are plenty of Ibex in the mountains of Midian."

Stephen wasn't sure about the deal. "I came here to find oil, not to have a shoot-out with a Bedouin raiding party."

"Don't worry, Stephen. If the emir of Tabuk thinks you need protection, he'll assign some soldiers to watch over you. All you'll need to do is feed them and keep them supplied with cigarettes. You know, Stephen, that's the reason we're here and the Brits aren't. British Petroleum was here first, but when CALTOC first met with the king, he asked the Californians if American troops would be required to protect their workers. Apparently he had never done business with an American corporation. The CALTOC man replied, 'What? We're not with a government. We expect your Arab soldiers to protect us.' The King is no fool. The next day the Brits were gone and we were in."

"I'll pass on hosting a private army in my camp. So it's only Ahmed and me and a couple of rifles?"

"That's right. I guess you deserve to know why I selected you for this isolated assignment. Timmy Cullerson tells me you're a cowboy from southern Utah, and that during high school you paid your own way through life by taking care of your grandpa's cattle."

"That's right, but what's it got to do with Midian, Moses, and oil?"

"I bet that during the summers you spent weeks alone working cattle in the high pastures of those red sandstone mountains."

"Yes, but how would you know that?"

"Geologists get around. I've been through southern Utah looking for oil. Nice country. I grew up on a cattle ranch in western Texas.

Look, Markham, it's going to be tough up there as the only American. But just look around the mess hall at the geologists they recruited for me. The company expects me to survey this giant desert and, heck, except you, every one of the American recruits is a city boy. They're book smart, but they complain like old hags about the living conditions right here at the CALTOC camp. They wouldn't last a week in Midian. You're different. You don't complain, you treat the Saudis as equals, and there's an inner toughness about you. Perhaps it's because you know how to work alone, or maybe it's something you picked up while knocking doors on your mission. Stephen, I thought about it for a long time. We need to survey Midian, and you're the only man who I think can stick it out."

"Well it sounds like a challenge, and I appreciate the confidence you have in me, but having to work in a remote area . . . Is there any extra money in it for me?"

"Did you forget we're in the middle of a depression? No money, but then again, look on bright side. You'll be on your own. Think of it—no boss and no headaches! Start work when you want and end work when you want. Just get the survey completed before your contract is up. I'll give you the freedom you need to get the job done, but whatever you do, remember who you are. Don't let those religious long beards catch you at a weak moment. Anyway, just be sure you keep your head on your shoulders and stay out of trouble with the Bedouin. I'll make sure they send you with a short-wave radio and generator. That way you can stay in tune with the real world."

"You don't have to worry about me. I'm a dyed-in-the-wool Mormon, and my Grandpa taught me to shave every day. And just to be on the safe side, I won't take my Stetson off my head."

"That sounds like a good idea. Listen to the British Broadcasting Company news every night, and if the BBC reports that war has broken out in Europe, get your butt back here as fast as you can. We hear that there might be Germans floating around northern Arabia."

"So now it's Bedouin and Germans? Are you sure there's no extra money available for this assignment? I plan on getting married in two years, and I could use all the extra money I can earn. I can handle the danger, but I hate being poor."

"Okay, Markham, it's worth it to us. I will get you a pay code increase, but you'll need to get the job done alone. Like I said, finding oil in Midian is a real long shot, and we can't allocate more than one geologist to a nominal region. Believe me; Arabia is sitting on oil. We just need to find it. Once we start striking big oil, we need to recover it, starting with the fields with the largest reserves. Prospects for finding large reserves of oil and gas west of Tabuk are slim, but it is possible. It's your job to survey the area and let us know its potential for further exploration. That's what we need you to tell us—whether or not the area's geological formations are favorable for oil and gas."

Stephen's excitement over his first assignment was dampened by the real possibility he would be living in a primitive environment and surrounded by hot-tempered tribesmen and German enemy infantry. "Is there a CALTOC camp in Midian?" he asked.

"Nope, none at all, Markham. Welcome to the life of a geologist. No hotels and no company camp. We will get you a Bedouin tent and keep you well supplied. Along with your paycheck, we'll send up a truckload of supplies each month. The truck will arrive on the first day of each month, and you can give the driver your monthly survey reports and a list of the supplies you're low on. Find big oil, Stephen, and we'll build you a city up there with grocery stores, movie theaters, and a soda fountain. Just find oil, and the company will make the world your oyster."

"I'll try my best, sir, but like you said, Midian sounds like deep desert. How will my mail get to me?" Stephen wondered just how long it would take to receive his precious letters from Jan.

"Sorry, but the supply truck will be your mailman. It'll just take a few weeks longer. I know you have a sweetheart, Stephen, but remember: love letters are like wine. The longer you wait for one, the finer the bouquet. We'll keep your mail safe and sound and send it up with the supply truck."

Stephen was not impressed by finely-aged wine or long-awaited love letters. He could go a lifetime without wine, but each week that passed without hearing from Jan seemed like an eternity. All the same, he didn't take long to decide to accept the assignment. He knew he was the junior man in camp, and he could tell from Chief Bennigar's body language that he had already decided it would be Midian and its Bedouin wilds for Stephen. Otherwise, as punishment for not taking the assignment, he knew Bennigar would assign him to some grunt job doing the documentation for a local crew of senior geologists. Having once known the freedom of roaming the open ranges of southern Utah, the ex-cowboy wanted nothing to do with a paper-pushing desk job. Besides, it was the Depression, and nothing scared the young oilman more than the possibility of losing his job and not being able to marry Jan. *What's the difference?* he surmised. *It's all strange to me. How much crazier could it get on the dark side of the moon?* Stephen smiled. "When do I leave?"

"That's the spirit, Markham. You'll leave as soon as we can arrange a meeting for you with Sami bin Bandar. We need to request a letter of introduction for you to the emir of Tabuk. Of course, the letter must also ask the emir to give you permission to survey the land of Midian."

"So who is this Sami bin whatever?"

"You haven't heard of him? You will. He's the emir of Al-Hasa and the rest of the eastern province of Saudi Arabia. King Abdulaziz authorized him to oversee the operations of the CALTOC oil concession. We need to ask him to request permission for you to survey from Jamal Al-Murri, the emir of Tabuk, the prince responsible for the Midian area. But I'm warning you to be polite and not to offend Sami bin Bandar. You might want to take a couple of extra toes along when you meet him."

"Toes?"

"Yes, he's a tough but fair man. That's what the people admire here, a strong man who will bring down the law on violators but, at the same time, is honest and fair. The king trusts him. His father, a relative to the king, was one of the fourteen men who helped Abdulaziz attack the Masmak Fort Riyadh. His father was the one who killed Ajlan, the Al Rashid emir, during the battle. That incredibly bold raid brought the Saudi tribe and King Abdulaziz bin Saud to power. From that day on, the king's Saudi tribe warriors and his allied Wahhabi Islamic fundamentalist army expanded his kingdom to what it is today. In 1913, they captured the Ibrahim Fort in Al-Hasa. To reward his loyal cousin, Abdulaziz made bin Bandar's father the emir of Al-Hasa, the title he passed down to his son."

"So why bring spare toes?"

"As I said, Sami bin Bandar is tough but fair. A man was once brought before him for meddling with another man's property. He was caught with another man's bag. The man said he found the bag of rice along the road. The emir asked him how he knew it was a bag of rice. The man said he kicked the bag with his toe, and it felt like rice inside. Bin Bandar ordered the man to be taken outside and have the toe that kicked the rice cut off. It was to punish him for meddling with someone else's property."

Chapter 5

The True Believer

Don't stop unless you are afraid of the consequences.

Arabian proverb

Stephen Markham
Late-October 1936
Al-Hasa City, Saudi Arabia

Stephen and his translator, Ahmed bin Al-Hajri, drove to Al-Hasa in one of the company's Ford sedans. The oasis city was a three-hour drive south of Al-Khobar along a rough gravel road. The crude highway tried to stay free from the soft sands, but at times the going got tough and Stephen had to gear down and keep the RPMs revving high. This was especially true each time the gravel road had to traverse one of the small dunes. If the sedan became stuck in sand, they would need to lower the tire pressure and pray that they could make it the rest of the way without overheating the deflated tires and finding themselves in even worse trouble.

To say the least, the terrain was bleak. The tan sand stretched for miles with just a spattering of desert brush, an occasional low lying sand dune, or a distant limestone outcrop. The small limestone mesas were called *jebels*, and as unimpressive as they might be, the little hills broke up the mundane desert landscape. Fortunately, an occasional herd of camels could be seen grazing near the road.

Eastern Arabia's mind-numbing landscape resulted from its once having been a seabed. Over the millennia, the Arabian seismic plates had pushed eastward against India. The result was the Himalayas and the exposing of the eastern Arabian seafloor.

Entering the town of Al-Hasa, Stephen felt like they had been driving in a time machine and stopped somewhere in Old Testament times. Everywhere he looked there were mud walls, two-story mud-brick houses, long-bearded Arabs riding on donkey carts rolling slowing down narrow streets, and women covered head to foot in their traditional black abiyas. Camels were hitched to posts next to shops. Despite their monochromatic color, the dry mud walls, minarets, Arabian arches, and geometric patterns gave the city a mysterious outer shell. Indeed, Al-Hasa was a living window into a distant past.

Outside the city walls, date groves spread as far as the eye could see. Ahmed told Stephen the Al-Hasa area was the largest true oasis on earth. Millions of gallons of pure. fresh water rose to the surface each day at several large springs. The oasis was like a fairy tale, a green garden at the edge of the scorching desert called the Empty Quarter. It was a city that in 1936 seemed to have been lost in time. Around every corner Stephen expected to confront Ali Baba and his forty thieves.

"This place seems ancient to me," Stephen said to Ahmed as they pulled the Ford up to Ibrahim's fort. Thirty-foot mud walls surrounded the fortress that now functioned as the palace of Emir Sami bin Bandar. The uninformed would not have expected that the crumbling mud fortress was the capital of eastern Arabia and the administrative offices of a promising oil concession.

"This is a very old and famous city in the Middle East," Ahmed explained. "Inside the grounds of the emir's palace is a mosque that has the world's largest dome made entirely from mud brick. The dates from the oasis are the best in the world. Their famed fruit is called the khalas date. There are more than a hundred different varieties of date palms, and each type has a different quality of fruit, depending on where it grows. The water, soil, and summer temperatures all affect the flavor of a date. The best of them all, in my opinion, are Al-Hasa's khalas dates."

The two CALTOC men got out of their sedan and walked to the gate of the fort. Ahmed presented their documents and explained to the guards the reason they had come for an audience with the emir. After looking over the CALTOC documents, the guard indicated that they could pass and directed them to the waiting room outside the emir's receiving hall.

As the two men walked toward the hall, Stephen asked, "The people here, are they Sunni or Shiite Muslims?"

"They are a mixture, but the original settlers here were not from the Arabian Peninsula. They came here thousands of years ago as refugees from the Assyrian Empire. They fled Assyria when it fell to the Babylonian army."

"That's when the ten lost tribes left Assyria," Stephen could not help but say aloud.

"Who are the ten lost tribes?" Ahmed asked.

"They were ten of the twelve tribes of Israel. They were taken captive from Palestine into Assyria but were later freed when the Medes defeated the empire. Most scholars believe they were lost in a land northward, but you say these people here were refugees from Assyria?"

"Yes, they were. There are other villages in Arabia that were settled by Jews. There's even a village between here and Riyadh called Judah."

"No, the lost tribes were not Jews; they were the tribes of the other sons of Israel."

"Well," Ahmed tried to explain, "there are two kinds of Arabs, those from the south and those from the north. They all claim to be the direct descendants of Ishmael, the first son of Ibrahim, the man you know as Abraham, peace and blessings be upon him. But the pure Arabs are the southerners from the grand tribe of Qathan. However, even the Qathanis were here before Ishmael, so they are only partially Ishmaelites. Yet they probably have the strongest bloodlines linking them to Ishmael. The northern Arabs are called Adnanites. From their bloodlines came the great Prophet Mohammed, peace and blessings be upon him. However, they are known to have mixed their seed with tribes from Syria, Iraq, and Iran."

"So it is possible that the Assyrian refugees who settled this city could have been part of the ten lost tribes? Perhaps even Ephraim and Manasseh?" Stephen asked.

"This I don't know. But if you say so, Mr. Stephen, why not? Besides, that was long ago. Since the time of Adam and Eve, the people in this oasis have been marrying and trading with people throughout the Gulf. What difference does it make today if these people are partly descended from some lost tribes?"

Once inside the emir's palace, Stephen and Ahmed waited in the sitting room for what seemed forever. On entering the room, Ahmed had reminded Stephen to take off his cowboy boots and leave them among the dozens of sandals that had been carefully lined up against the wall by those visiting the emir. Like the tall Utahn in an Arabian palace, Stephen's boots stood out among the sandals.

Stephen passed the time by carefully studying the colorful floor rugs and the tapestries that covered the walls of the waiting room. Each rug was a bold array of red, black, orange, white, and brown yarn. Each seemed like an exact copy of rugs made by the native tribes of South and Central America, Mexico, and even the Navajos and Hopi Indians of the American Southwest. He realized that the peculiar similarity between the Old and New World patterns couldn't be a mere coincidence. There had to be a connection between Lehi's descendants in the Americas and the Arab weavers. Stephen tried to mentally wrestle some conclusions from the answers Ahmed had given him.

What difference does it make, he thought, *if today some of these people in Al-Hasa are the descendants of Ephraim and Manasseh?* Yet every logical thought led to the same outcome—it would be incredibly profound if some of the people in Arabia constituted the mother tree of the house of Joseph, especially the tribe of Ephraim, the tribe that had the royal birthright to rule in Zion, according to 1 Chronicles 5:1–2 and Jeremiah 31:9. Indeed, Ephraim was the only tribe with the honor to have its name made equivalent to the kingdom of Israel.[1]

After waiting for over two hours, they were finally ushered into Emir Saud's receiving hall. The large hall was the formal greeting room where host and guests sit on rugs and lean on large pillows. Stephen wondered why, with all the emir's wealth, he preferred not to have one of those newly invented air-conditioning machines.

Accompanying the emir were a dozen or so advisors. A young translator, who was probably trained in English in one of CALTOC's training programs, sat beside him.

First came the ritualized Arabic greeting. The emir said nothing more to the American. In fact, he paid no attention to Stephen, indicating by his gestures that he was annoyed that CALTOC would send a young man and not a company elder to ask a favor of him. The age of a man means a great deal to Arabs, and a person of Stephen's age, who is not the sheikh of a tribe by birthright, had no right sitting with senior members of the community, let alone the regional emir.

For another hour, the emir ignored Stephen and talked at length with his advisors. Finally, a slave brought in a large bowl of dates and offered them to the two guests. Stephen took one, placed it in his mouth and immediately realized he was eating his first khalas date. *Oh*, he thought, *this is sweeter than any candy I've ever enjoyed. It must have come from Lehi's tree of life.*

A few minutes later, a servant entered holding a tray with tiny cups for traditional Arabian coffee. Regardless of a guest's social status, an Arab host is obligated by tradition to offer the brewed cardamom and coffee bean drink. Following the slave with the cups was another servant. This one poured coffee from a long-spouted bronze pot. As always, he poured with the right hand. The emir was served first. Then the serving continued until the last person in the room was offered coffee—and that was the cowboy from Utah. Stephen had only been in Arabia a short time, but he knew he had been insulted by the emir. He knew that the Arabs, who pride themselves on their hospitality, always make it a point to serve their guest before they serve themselves or their friends. By tradition, the last person to be served should have been the host.

Stephen could feel the pressure all the way to his toes. He was thinking just how much he cherished those ten little extensions at the end of his feet. Apparently, he had already insulted the emir by just being here, and now he had to either drink the emir's coffee or face the consequences of insulting him again.

Just as the slave was about to pour coffee into his cup, Stephen reached out his hand, palm down, indicating that he did not want the emir's coffee.

Immediately, the emir rose to his feet, waved his arms, and started shouting at the American in Arabic. Stephen wiggled his toes for what he thought might be the last time.

The angry emir turned to his interpreter and requested an immediate explanation.

The nervous young translator tried to compose himself and asked in a high-pitched voice, "The emir would like to know why you rejected the coffee he offered you in friendship."

Fortunately, Stephen had plenty of practice turning down coffee during his mission. "Your honor, I ask your forgiveness. I am very sorry. I desire very much to accept your gift, but I can't. I believe Allah does not wish me to take into my body a substance that might harm it. In my faith, drinking coffee, tea, or alcohol is forbidden. It is haram. Again, I beg your forgiveness."

The emir listened carefully as the nervous translator tried to explain what Stephen had just said. Since it was hard to listen and be upset at the same time, the emir seemed to take on a settled demeanor. Besides, much of his outrage had been for show only. Still, as the translator finished his explanation, the emir stroked his beard with his fingers as he took in this new information. He then told his interrupter to ask Stephen what religion he held so strongly that prohibited things like alcohol, tea, and coffee.

Stephen then explained that he was a Christian and that his people were called the Mormons.

"Mormon!" The emir smiled and laughed. He then instructed his advisors in Arabic to give "Al-Mormon" whatever it was he came for. "Anyone who believes so strongly in God that he will offend me must be a trustworthy person. I like this American, but it is a good thing he does not know that it is also forbidden for Muslims to drink tea and coffee. Remember, our forefathers used to take Muslims who were found drinking coffee and put them in bags and throw them in the sea."[2] The emir then said, "Salaam aleikumm" and left the room, having finished that day's business.

"What was all that about?" Stephen asked Ahmed.

"You're a very lucky man, Mr. Stephen. You are probably the first American to insult the emir and still get what you wanted. The emir thinks you are a Mormon."

"I am a Mormon."

"Not that kind. He thinks you are a true believer."

"I am a true believer in my faith."

"Not your faith, Mr. Stephen," Ahmed insisted. "A true believer of Islam. You see the word *Mormon*[3] in Arabic means a 'true believer in Allah,' one who lives all the rules and does righteous deeds."

Stephen smiled. "Really?"

Notes

1. See LDS Bible Dictionary, sv. "Kingdom of Israel."

2. Abdul Rahman bin Zayd Al Swaida, *Arabian Coffee and What Was Said About It in Poetry* (Riyadh: Information Ministry Number 4694/M, Hijra calender 1410), 31.

3. There are many ways to spell *Mormon* (true believer) in Arabic. The most common are *Momen* or *Moumen*. In spoken Arabic, it is hardly possible to distinguish it from the English pronunciation of *Mormon*. *Al-Momen* means "the Momen" or "of the Momens."

Chapter 6

My First Real Job

The Arabs are a race which produces its best only under conditions of extreme hardship and deteriorates progressively as living conditions become easier.

Wilfred Treiger, *Arabian Sands*, 1959

Jake Sorensen
Summer 1989
Moon Crest Magazine Unit—PAMMCO Oil Company
Week Two of Ten-week Internship

I was excited Saturday morning when I got to my cubbyhole of an office at PAMMCO and found a nameplate with my name on it. The Saudi workweek runs from Saturday to Wednesday. I wasn't sure what my rough-edged, house-building dad thought of my first office job, but I was pretty darn proud of myself for having a desk job at the world's largest oil company. I even had a window with a view from the fourth floor of PAMMCO's east engineering tower.

There was no way I was going to start the day's work without asking Abdulrahman Al-Dossary a few questions about that hard-to-believe story I heard that weekend at the Commissary Inn. Like me, Abdulrahman was an intern but certainly a rose of a different color. He was a Saudi and received a full PAMMCO salary. In addition to that, all his expenses were paid while he studied at the University of Arizona. From the pictures he showed me of his blonde girlfriend sitting in his BMW convertible in Tucson, it appeared to me that he must be taking a full academic load in leisure studies. I was certain he was taking the lowest possible number of credit hours to maintain and extend his company scholarship. I gathered from our short acquaintance that all Abdulrahman had to do to keep his job was get some kind of a report card from the States and show up each summer and act like a pious Muslim at work. Still, as lowly as my station in life must have seemed to Abdulrahman, he treated me as if I were his superior. It had something to do with the respect Saudis held for the Americans who helped them discover oil and brought change to their nation. Besides, one could not help but like Abdulrahman. He seemed to have a double dose of that Saudi charm that makes his countrymen such good diplomats.

Half an hour later, I heard, "Salaam aleikumm." It was Abdulrahman greeting me as he finally dragged himself into work.

"Same to you," I said. "You're late again. You must be having a good time getting back in contact with all your Saudi friends."

"Right on! I just got back from Bahrain three hours ago. Let me tell you, the Russian babes over there are foxes. Just had enough time this morning to go to the Mosque for sunrise prayer, grab a couple hours of sleep, and come to work."

"Sounds like your life is a little out of control. How do you manage?" I asked.

"It's crazy all right, but I have to get in all the fun I can. I'm getting married next summer and then it's all over. Good-bye wild life. My parents let me do what I want now, but once I marry, alas, I'll have to toe the line. You know what I mean? I'll have to grow a long beard and become a religious freak. That's our culture, and I'll accept my fate; it's the way we do things here."

"Hey, can you help me with a few questions?"

"Sure. What's up?"

"I heard a story about a Bedouin called Al-Mormon. What is a Mormon in Arabic?"

"It's what I am not, but what I will become once I marry. A Mormon is a true believer. If you see an Arab downing Jack Daniels at a disco in Bahrain, he's not a Mormon."

"So a strict practitioner of Islam is a Mormon?" I inquired.

"Yes, I guess you could think of it that way. He lives all the rules of Islam and pays his religious tithes, called *Zakah*."

"How do you spell *Mormon* in Roman characters?" I asked.

"That all depends. When English speakers try to write Arabic words, they come up with ten different ways to spell the same word. You've seen it on our highway signs. Each road sign has a different spelling for the same street. It's a miracle westerners can find their way around our towns. I've seen Mormon spelled, M-o-u-m-o-n, M-o-m-e-n, and even M-o-r-m-o-n."

"Is it a common name?"

"Sort of. There are two or three tribes with that name. There are several Al-Mormons working here in this building. Why are you so interested in a Bedouin named Al-Mormon? There nothing unusual about a Bedouin having that name."

"Well, this Al-Mormon is supposed to be an American living in the desert with the Bedouin. Do you think there's any credence to such a story?"

"No way, dude. Look, most of us city Arabs couldn't survive in the desert more than a day or two without heading back to the city for a pizza. I doubt an American could survive out there. Besides, why in the world would an American want to live like a goat in the desert?"

"I see what you mean. Thanks."

"No problem, man. Anytime."

At first, I thought Al-Mormon would be a hot story, but it turns out that there are Al-Mormons all over Arabia. They are the tribes of the true believers. Abdulrahman's answers were not encouraging, but before throwing out the baby with the bathwater, I thought I would give the story of the White Bedouin one last chance.

When I got back to my room that evening, I reached for my Book of Mormon. I wanted to know just what the name Mormon meant. The Arabs have a word to describe a true believer, yet as often as I had called myself one, I had no idea what the name Mormon meant. I even served a mission for the Mormon Church. Now I was glad no one had asked me what the name meant.

I thumbed through the book, looking for the name's origin. I found that the earliest use of the name was found in the eighteenth chapter of Mosiah. Mormon, I discovered was the name of a place associated with believers. Around 148 BC, many people believed the words of Alma. Mormon was where the believers hid from the wicked King Noah. Although the king didn't know where the place was located, he referred to it as Mormon because it was where the believers congregated. It was the place those who believed went to hear the words of Alma. It was the place Alma taught the believers. *Bingo,* I thought. *Seventeen of the first eighteen chapters in the Book of Mormon take place in Arabia. Here's another witness of the book's truthfulness. We know that some of the characters in the Book of Mormon were written in Arabic, and one of them seems to have been the very name of the book—Mormon, the believers![1]*

As I fell asleep that night I thought of the lonely American sitting in a tent and feeling inspired to go out and help two rough oil workers who were barely hanging onto dear life in the desert. I pictured a white Bedouin risking his life to save total strangers. I was humbled to know that a man who earned a meager living as a nomadic herdsman would pay the medical expenses for men he would never meet again. I was proud to think that he might be a Mormon. I could not give up on the story. For some reason I felt that Al-Mormon had to be a real person. But was he a Muslim Mormon or an LDS Mormon?

Notes

1. See Joseph Smith—History 1:64. Joseph Smith is reported to have said that the name Mormon meant "more good."

Chapter 7

Castle of the Lost Tribes

There is a time for departure, even when there's no certain place to go.

Tennessee Williams

Stephen Markham
October 1936
Leaving the CALTOC camp

The Ford pickup was loaded to the hilt, and all Stephen had to do was top off the gas tank and fill two barrels with gasoline before starting up the road that led north toward the Jordanian border. Stephen and Ahmed would need to drive for two days along the graded dirt road before they would turn west and cross the entire breadth of northern Arabia. Their destination was Midian, the land of Moses.

"Brother, you can't leave town without saying adios," Timmy Cullerson's voice bellowed out.

"Partner, there is no way I would leave without saying goodbye to you," Stephen replied. The two men had become good friends during the two months since the Utahn arrived. Stephen was a regular at Timmy's Bible classes and enjoyed the unique approach Timmy had to teaching the Word. Stephen knew that Timmy was off course on a few doctrinal points, but the Texan's colorful oil-field language mixed with his father's Southern-style preaching made the Bible classes a lot more flamboyant than most of the Sunday School lessons back home. Besides, who could blame good old Timmy for wandering a little off the chosen path? He was leading Bible discussions made up of four Baptists, a Pentecostal, two Catholics, an Episcopalian, and a Mormon returned missionary.

"I'll miss your preaching, Brother Timmy, and I'll miss your wildcatter tales even more. Is it proper for a Baptist to tell such outlandish stories?"

"Them ain't lies. And ya'll remember to watch out for them six-foot lizards out dere in the desert. They can knock a man over with a flip of deir tail. I heard that if ya get enough of them together, they can down a camel and eat it for lunch."

"Do they wear little slippers so they can sneak up on the camels?"

"No, but dem lizards share deir underground dens with cobras. If that lizard don't get ya, his denmate will."

"My good friend, I promise I'll sleep with one eye open."

"Here's some readin' for ya while you're out dere under God's stars. Just a bunch of books the fellas left behind when they took off from these parts. Dere's an English Qur'an in dere. An imam thought he could convert me by givin' me deir holy book. Got no need for it.

Perhaps you can digest it." With that, Timmy gave Stephen a stack of books and a letter he picked up from the mail house. "Ya almost left town without dis here letter from ya gal."

Stephen took the letter and couldn't hold back a broad smile. "I checked my box this morning, but there wasn't anything in it."

"Ya ol' rustler, haven't I taught ya anyding?" Timmy grinned back. "Old Al-Jameel in the mail room, he sits on da mail until he gets the feeling it's time to work. That might be today, might be next week. His mail sacks might sit dere fer days. I reckon he figures if it's taken a month just to get here, what's the hurry? I went back dere and made him check fer ya."

"Thanks so much, Timmy. You're a cowboy's best friend. I'll read Jan's letter a dozen times on the way to Midian."

After the friends shook hands in parting, Stephen and Ahmed got in their 1935 Ford pickup and drove to the camp's fueling pumps. From there they headed north into the desert.

Ahmed took the first driving shift. Stephen carefully opened Jan's letter. It was the second precious love letter he had received from Jan since arriving in Arabia. His large fingers took care to leave the envelope as much intact as possible. Jan's rice paper envelope would be her love letter's sheath, knowing very well he would be opening and reading the letter over and over again.

His patience paid off. As he finally extracted Jan's letter, he felt the thrill of a lover's anticipation. He could feel his heart beating as his eyes rushed to read his sweetheart's handwriting.

> *Dear Stephen,*
>
> *Two years is a very long time. I need you to know Verlan Jacobs returned from his mission three weeks ago. That was eight weeks after you left for Arabia. We started talking at my cousin's wedding. I wrote you about it. I was the maid of honor.*
>
> *It's just too long. Too long. I've already waited while you were in Texas looking for work. That didn't work out, and now you're halfway around the world. Verlan has a job delivering groceries for his uncle's store and our families are good friends. I'm sorry, Stephen, but please don't write anymore. God be with you.*
>
> *Your friend,*
> *Jan Roberts*

Stephen's stomach knotted and his heart almost stopped.

"Stop! Please, please stop the truck!" Stephen abruptly said to Ahmed.

Ahmed slammed on the breaks, and the round-bodied Ford came to an abrupt halt. Not waiting for the dust to settle, Stephen stepped out of the truck and ran into the desert a hundred feet or so. Ahmed looked on in amazement as the brokenhearted American finally stopped. Stephen screamed to the heavens, "No! No! No . . ." Then the cowboy started kicking the desert brush, as if he wanted to propel each bush to the moon. The fit lasted only a minute or two. Before the pickup's dust cloud had fully dissipated, Stephen was slowly walking back to the truck.

"Sorry, Ahmed. We can continue."

"Are you okay, Al-Mormon?" Ahmed had started calling Stephen by the title the emir of Al-Hasa had branded him with. "Is my driving making you sick?"

"No, of course not, Ahmed. I'm fine and so is your driving."

Ahmed turned the key to start the motor. He put the truck in gear and started up the road again. The truck hadn't moved fifty feet before Stephen put Jan's letter back in it's envelope, ripped it to pieces, and threw it out the window. Like confetti, the letter flickered away in the wind as bitter tears rolled down his cheeks. Since leaving his mission, life had been a hard road for Stephen to follow. His dreams of a happy life had centered around Jan and his faith that she would honor their engagement while he went abroad to work for the means they needed to get started. Now even Jan was gone. At that moment, he felt hopeless. Would he ever know what it was like to have a real family again? Trying to count his blessings, he needed only the fingers of one hand. He had a job in a land were he could not speak the language. He had a rifle to help him stay alive on his first assignment. He had his unproven skills as a geologist. As long as no religious zealot found his scriptures, he had guidance of the Word. Finally, he had his faith in the Lord; no one could take that away.

As a faithful Muslim, Ahmed knew it was his responsibility to comfort his companion. "Was it the letter?" Ahmed asked after watching Stephen tear it apart and fling it out the window.

"Yes, the woman I was going to marry has decided to marry someone else."

"Oh. That's good. It's God's will," Ahmed said. "That's why we marry our first cousins and have our parents arrange our marriages. Was that woman your cousin? If so, she not only dishonored herself, she dishonored her parents and your parents."

"No, Ahmed, she was not my cousin."

"That explains it. You should never marry a girl who is not your cousin. Otherwise, how would you know if she will get along with your family? If not your own uncle and aunt, who will care for her while you're away looking for oil? Our people have a saying, 'Only a fool does not marry his cousin.' "

"I think marrying your first cousin is illegal in the United States. Besides, the only unmarried cousin I have is only fourteen years old."

"Fourteen, that is a good thing. That's a very good age for marriage. My wife was fourteen and I was sixteen when we got married. We are very happy. How did this other man meet her? Didn't your woman cover herself up with an abiya?"

"Sorry, Ahmed, but American women don't wear black coverings over their bodies."

"They should. It is a good thing. Your woman was immodest. An abiya is a signal to men not to talk with that woman. It shows men that the woman is no longer a girl and should not be looked upon by men, except her husband, father, and brothers. If your woman had worn her abiya, this thing would never have happened. But still, it is a good thing."

"Well, maybe I should send an abiya to Verlan Jacobs so he can cover up my ex-fiancée. I, for one, certainly don't want to see her face again!"

"What's an ex-fiancée, Al-Mormon?"

"It's a fiancée who is no longer a fiancée," Stephen said as he shook his head in disgust at what Jan had done to him.

Ahmed kept pushing Stephen to talk. "What?" he questioned. "What is a fiancée?"

"I thought it was someone who promises to marry you and agrees not to flirt with anyone else. If I ever have a fiancée again, I will cover her with one of those abiyas and lock her in a vault."

"What's a flirt, boss?"

"A flirt is an American girl over fourteen years old, who is not your cousin, who removes her engagement ring, takes off her abiya and veil, and is a dishonorable maid of honor."

"What's a maid of honor, boss?"

"Sorry again, Ahmed. I'm just sorry right now. Very, very sorry. I don't want to talk right now."

"Okay, boss, but remember this was a no-good woman, and it is good she left you. It is a good thing."

"Sure. And why do you Muslims keep saying everything is good, and everything is the will of Allah?"

"Because it is a good thing, boss. We like telling this story to our children. Once upon a time there was a king and his faithful chief servant. The servant was a good Muslim. He was known to be cheerful and always thanked God for every event, whether good or bad. Alhamdellah: 'thank God; It's a good thing'," he would say.

"One day the king decided to take a trip and have his chief servant accompany him. Just before they were to leave on the journey, the king accidentally cut off part of his little finger. 'Alhamdellah,' the servant said. 'It is a good thing.' The chief servant's apparent insensitivity outraged the king, so he had his loyal servant put in prison.

"While on his journey, the king had to pass through a dark jungle. Deep in the jungle, primitive savages attacked the royal party. The king's guards were killed, and the king was taken hostage. The savages gathered firewood to burn the king alive. Just as they were about to sacrifice the king to their pagan god, the savages noticed that a part of his finger was missing. Sacrificing such an imperfect offering would only offend their god, so they let the king go free.

"When the king returned from his journey, he immediately freed this chief servant from prison. 'Forgive me, Forgive me,' the king said to his chief servant. 'You were right. If I had not cut off part of my finger, I would have been burned at the stake. Will you ever forgive me?'

" 'Alhamdellah,' the servant said once again. 'Thank God you threw me into prison. It was a good thing.'

"The king shook his head, 'How could it have been a good thing that I put you in prison?'

"The servant replied, 'If you had not put me in jail, I would have been with you in the jungle, and the savages would have sacrificed me in your place.'

"So you see, boss, Alhamdellah. It is a good thing this immodest woman became your ex-fiancée."

Stephen looked at the Arab beside him and then cracked a one-sided smile. "*Shukran*" (thank you), he said, "for the story, partner."

The pickup continued north, but Stephen felt no better.

The dust cloud that trailed their lonely pickup truck across the desert marked the course the sad-hearted cowboy and his Arab guide had taken. It took Stephen and Ahmed two days to reach the turnoff for the city of Tabuk. Since opening Jan's letter, Stephen hadn't noticed much of the landscape. If he had, he would have seen the same boring scenery that surrounded the CALTOC camp in Al-Khobar. The sandy flatlands looked like the floor of an ocean.

At one point, a herd of thousands of camels crossed the road in front of them. They watched the camels pass before them. The creatures looked like a great school of tuna and seemed to move with one mind. Ahmed explained to the American that the Bedouin drive their herds from lands north of Arabia to the far south of the peninsula. They do it to follow the seasonal foliage that grows after the rains. He said that the Bedouin often wander as far north as Syria and as far south as Oman. The Bedouin nomads do not recognize international borders. What they do respect, he added, are the tribal lands where they have relatives or areas where they trade with the local tribe for permission to graze their camels. To the Bedouin, nations and international borders are alien concepts created by foreigners, namely the British and French.

The two oilmen were traveling by day and sleeping under the stars at night. The turnoff to Tabuk was seven hundred miles north of the CALTOC camp and three hundred miles short of the Transjordanian border. The turnoff took them from one gravel road onto another. This one headed west toward the sunset. Except for a severe broken heart, the trip had been uneventful. Since the flat terrain was uninspiring, Stephen started counting the desert wildlife they occasionally spooked as they passed. Most often he spotted rabbits. But there were also desert cats and dhabs, the seemingly peaceful two-foot lizards Timmy had warned him could down a man.

From the turnoff, they still needed to travel six hundred miles across the northern width of Arabia to reach the land of Midian. After a half-day's drive into their westward trek, the two men entered a fertile area that Ahmed called Wadi Jouf. Surrounded by palm groves and olive orchards, they found the city of Dumah.[1] It was an oasis of far smaller size and distinction than Al-Hasa, but it had enough water to support a sizable community and a few square miles of farmland. The terrain remained featureless except for a few small limestone mesas like Stephen had seen with Ahmed on their way to Al-Hasa.

As they drove into Dumah, Stephen noticed a huge mud tower projecting upward from the palm trees on the north side of the city.

"What is that strange looking structure?" he asked Ahmed.

"That's the very old palace, Al-Mormon. It is an old fort. Its walls are over two hundred feet tall. The people of Dumah have been attacked many times but were only defeated once. They built it above a cliff, so it was very hard to penetrate."

"Was it built by the Muslims?"

"Oh no, it's very, very old. It has stood since long before Mohammed's time."

Ahmed suggested they get something to eat before the Islamic prayer call, but Stephen insisted that they explore the fort first. Ahmed didn't share Stephen's enthusiasm. Like most Muslims, he felt that any history before the time of Mohammed was of no real significance. The Muslims referred to times before Mohammed as the dark ages of their millennial history.

Reaching the fort, Stephen got out of the truck and stood in amazement. Here was a well preserved fortress that looked as if it had been built by the crusaders. Yet Ahmed said that it was of great antiquity. Stephen climbed the steps of two long stone staircases before reaching the gate that led into the inner courtyard. Meanwhile, Ahmed sat in the shade next to the truck, still wondering why the American would postpone lunch just to see an old mud fort.

As he climbed the stairs, Stephen heard the tapping of hammers. Someone was either tearing down or restoring the fortress. He walked past several crumbling stone walls that appeared to have once formed rooms of the inner court. He came upon two men and a woman. The cowboy greeted them and learned that they spoke English. They were Italian archaeologists from the University of Pisa.

Stephen couldn't wait to learn what they knew about the history of the fort. Since they were Italian, he figured the old fort must have had some tie to their nation's legacy. "Is this fort part of the system of Roman garrisons that used to protect the empire's eastern frontier?"

"No," one of the men said, "the Romans didn't reach this far east until six centuries after this fort was built. Don't you know, young man, that this town was settled by Dumah, the great-grandson of Abraham spoken of in Genesis 25:14? This was a Hebrew settlement. I don't mean that Jews lived here. What I mean is that they were Arab Hebrews, being Hebrews because they were from Abraham's seed. But Dumah didn't build this fortress. It was built by people who migrated here from Assyria. As you can see, this is Assyrian architecture and it was built in that era."

Stephen had no idea what Assyrian ruins looked like. Still, he was amazed by what the Italian said. "Are you serious? That's nearly three thousand years ago. Weren't the Assyrians farther north than the Arabian Peninsula?"

"You're right there, young man," the woman answered. "That's the puzzling thing about this fortress. It is of Assyrian style and was built in their day. However, the Assyrians did not build it."

"Then who built it?" Stephen asked.

"Have you heard of the lost tribes of Israel?" she replied with her own question.

"Sure."

"Good. From the inscriptions we read on this wall, an ancient stonecutter wrote that this castle was built by the prince of the tribe of Manasseh of the house of Joseph."[2]

Notes

1. See Dumah in the LDS Bible maps of northwest Arabia (Genesis 25:14).
2. See Amir 'Abd Al-Rahman bin Ahmad Al-Sudairi, *The Desert Frontier of Arabia*, arabic edition (London: Stacey International, 1995).

Chapter 8

Evil Dominions

How desperate a thing it were, to be abandoned in the midst
of the wilderness of Arabia; where we dread to meet with
unknown mankind more than with wild beasts!

Charles Doughty, *Travels in Arabia Deserts*, 1888

Stephen Markham
October 1936
Nafud Desert

To reach the land called Midian with its tall mountains and sandy valleys, Stephen and Ahmed still had to navigate their Ford pickup across the great Nafud, Arabia's second-largest sand desert. The Nafud is not as vast as the famous Empty Quarter, but its millions of small sand dunes have their own vicious ways of killing those who enter their grip.

The morning they started across the Nafud dunes, the American was surprised when the Saudi translator ate no breakfast. "Not feeling well?" he asked.

"Yes and no," Ahmed replied.

"What do you mean?"

"Yes, I don't feel good anytime I enter the Nafud. It is a sea of sand where the genies rule. No, I know I don't need to worry because Allah will protect us, for I am fasting."

"I thought Muslims only fast during the month of Ramadan?" Stephen said.

"That is not quite exact. We fast whenever we feel we need a special blessing from Allah. If we have a sick family member or need to overcome a temptation, we fast."

"So you're fasting today because you're afraid of ghosts?"

"Of course. Don't you believe in genies?"

"Not really. I believe in evil spirits, but I have never seen one. How about you, ever seen a genie?"

"No, I haven't. But the Qur'an tells us that some genies are good and others are evil. The sand dunes are full of evil ones."

"How do you know, if you've never seen one?"

"The old men in our tribe have seen them."

"And you take their word for it?"

"Of course. We respect our elders. Besides, each year people die in the Nafud. Some are experienced caravaners who had traveled for years in the dunes. Yet they enter the Nafud and are never seen alive again."

"That doesn't mean they were killed by a ghost. Perhaps bandits murdered them," Markham suggested.

"I have seen with my own eyes a few of the bodies that have been found in the sand dunes. What happened to them must have been the handiwork of the devil."

"You might be surprised what can happen to flesh after it has been lying around in a hot place. I've found dead cattle in Utah. Within two or three days, the flies and vultures can sheer off the soft flesh and leave a filmy slime over the entire carcass."

"You're not making me feel any better," Ahmed protested.

"Sorry. I just think you should not blame everything strange that happens on the devil. In Utah, some of the farmers thought those dead cattle had been mutilated by aliens. Can you believe that?"

"Think what you want, Al-Mormon," the Arab said. "Some of the bodies I saw were of people I once knew. What happened to them was not the work of maggots. You drive, while I fast and recite the Al Fatihah from the Qur'an for both of us."

The road through the Nafud twisted its way through the sand dunes. At times it simply disappeared beneath sand drifts. When this happened, the two men had to stop the truck and set out on foot to find where the road reappeared from beneath the sands again. Next, they had to determine what would be the best way to get the truck through the sand drifts to where the road reappeared. Each of these detours was a challenge. The Nafud's short dunes ran north to south with soft slip faces on the east—the side they needed to climb. Even lowering the pressure in the tires did not always help. Time after time, the truck would sink axle-deep in the soft sand. To free the Ford, they dug away the sand with shovels. Next, they placed twelve-inch rubber belts between the tires and the sand. They geared down and lugged the truck free, at least for a few more feet. The going was tough, and progress was measured in feet.

The second day in the Nafud was just like the first. Ahmed was still nervous. The Bedouin was fasting again and continually mumbling the Al Fatihah under his breath. Ahmed was not exactly starving. An Islamic fast allows the faithful to eat and drink between sunset and sunrise.

Stephen blocked out Ahmed's endless reciting by humming to himself his adaptation of the hymn "There Is Sunshine in My Soul Today." What other song would a Mormon cowboy sing on a cloudless day in Arabia?

In the early afternoon, they found themselves, once again, bogged down in the deep sand. The roadway was nowhere in sight. Ahmed went ahead to scout the course forward to the place where the road reappeared. In the meantime, Stephen got out the shovel and started digging the sand away from the truck's axles. It was back-breaking, frustrating work. As soon as his shovel lifted away a load of sand, millions of grains tumbled back into the hole he had just formed. Stephen was starting to think that an invisible wizard was re-encasing the truck in sand as fast as he was freeing it.

While Stephen was preoccupied with the seemingly futile exercise of digging away the sand, he heard a sudden, odd rumbling sound in the distance. He looked up and could hardly believe his eyes. On the horizon to the northwest was a massive wall of dust heading straight at him. He knew what it was. The old timers at CALTOC had warned him about the *shawals*, but this was the first sandstorm he had seen. And it was coming his way. He had only a few minutes before the giant tumbling clouds of sand would reach him. There was little he could do. He sprang to his feet and rolled up the windows of the truck. He called for Ahmed but heard nothing in return. He reached for the supplies in the back of the truck and took out a canvas tarp he hoped he could use to cover the provisions. His heart raced as the storm approached. The sound of the storm became deafening, and the wind started whipping the tarp in all directions. He took a quick look to the west, and the sight stunned him. The storm was thousands of feet tall and spread as far as his eyes could see. The giant cloud churned like the sides of a tornado. The announcement of its coming rivaled the thunder of a thousand locomotives. For a moment, Stephen found himself lost in the majesty of what was about to swallow him and his truck.

An ecliptic shadow fell over the truck. The walls of the storm had blocked out the rays of the sun. Suddenly, Stephen felt an impending doom. He realized he had only a few seconds before the storm hit. He tried feverishly to tie the tarp over the supplies. His mind was fixed on their fate in the desert without their supplies. If the sandstorm didn't kill them, odds were that the desert would. It was too late—a powerful gust of wind whipped the tarp from his hands. Then it hit. The sand whirled about, blasting Stephen's body in all directions. The sky darkened as if it were nightfall. He felt like he was being sandblasted. The larger grains of sand felt like the sting of a bee. He closed his eyes to protect them from the sand. What he needed most was air to breathe. He was choking on the thick sandy air and was starting to feel dizzy. In desperation, he pulled out the tail of his shirt and bent over so he could hold it against his mouth, but as soon as he did, the air cleared and he was able to inhale without difficulty.

He remained bent over for a few moments while his head cleared. He was trying to find the door to the cab when he noticed the air had completely cleared of dust. He opened his eyes and noticed that the light had reappeared. He looked up in wonder at the miracle surrounding him.

To his amazement, there was a cylinder of complete calm within the giant sandstorm. It was as if he was in the eye of a hurricane. Towering walls of sand encircled him, swirling around him and stretching as high as he could see. The walls of the storm were no more than twenty feet from where he stood, yet he felt not the faintest breeze. Nothing was moving inside the eerie cylinder. He seemed to be safe within the unnatural calm, but just beyond the funnel's wall, he could see nothing but blasting clouds of thick, whirling sand.

Stephen looked at his arms and legs. He was completely covered with a thick layer of dust. He shook his head and sent up large puffs of dust. He was just about to fall to his knees and pray for his life and that of Ahmed, when straight through the whirling walls of sand walked a man dressed in black. The man's demeanor was casual, his smile broad, and his countenance that of a kindly friend.

What's going on? Stephen wondered. *Who is this character?* The man stopped a few feet in front of the American. He was tall, muscular, and strikingly handsome. He had light skin, black hair, and shining dark eyes. He was the human equivalent of a Spanish bull.

"Salaam aleikumm," the man greeted Stephen.

For a moment Stephen couldn't respond. He tried to gather his thoughts, but his mind was having difficulty making sense of what his eyes were seeing. The man wore shiny black Persian-style trousers that appeared to be made from fine silk, a black shirt with black pearls for buttons, and a dashing black head scarf that trailed down his side like a costume of a character from one of the tales of the Arabian Nights. Gold chains adorned his neck, and a magnificent sword rested by his side just below a black sash. Suddenly, cold-blooded fear raised the hair on Stephen's arms. He noticed that the stranger's clothes and body had not a trace of dust on them. The American's knees weakened as the man addressed him in perfect American English.

"I say, good friend, peace be with you."

"And peace to you," Stephen replied in a weak voice. He was still caked in dust and trying to pull his senses together.

"As you can see, friend, this is no place for you. Arabia is a dangerous land. If this sandstorm doesn't kill you, the tribesman in the north will. They are fierce and extremely suspicious of strangers. Go back. Believe me; there is no oil in this land. No prize for the Christian exploiters. Go back to CALTOC and tell them your work here is fruitless. I know each inch of the land of Midian and, believe me, there is no oil."

Stephen just stood there, unable to speak.

"Dear Stephen, don't you realize that you're lost? Go home. Go back to America. There is still time to win back Jan's heart. She wants you to return. She still loves you. You must forgive her. Like any woman, she needs her man by her side. Go to her; you still have time. Go to her! Leave this land of drought and scorpions. Take beautiful Jan back in your arms and claim her for yourself."

"Who are you? How do you know these things?" Stephen finally uttered with a choked voice.

"I am your friend, and I only wish the best for you. I am rich and powerful, but I have come out of my way to help you before it's too late."

"Too late for what?" Stephen choked up as he asked.

"Too late to turn back, to return to America and to the woman you love," the handsome stranger said in a most sincere voice. "And before it's too late to save these Arabs from the destruction that oil will bring to their lives."

"I thought I was here to help these people. Why would discovering oil destroy them?"

"You Americans think of oil as a blessing from the deep. However, with oil money, the Arabs will buy up banks, companies, and nations. They will become a spoiled, lazy, and deceiving lot. They will soon stop listening to me. It will be the end."

Stephen said nothing but tried to concentrate on the thoughts that were forming in his mind. Blessings of the deep? Where had he heard that before? "They'll stop listening to me . . ." *This man must have some control over people,* Stephen reasoned. *How does he know my name and where I work? How does he know my fiancée left me? He couldn't be God . . .*

"Are you the devil?" Stephen probed.

"My goodness, no. As I said, I am your friend. I come here to guide you, and you think I am the devil. I am a messenger sent to save you."

Just then a still small voice from within reminded Stephen of the blessing received by Ephraim, son of Joseph. With that thought, the strangest words came from the young Mormon's mouth. "Joseph's brethren said, 'Shalt thou indeed reign over us? or shalt thou indeed have dominion over us?' (Genesis 37:8)."

As Stephen recited the words of Genesis, the stranger's demeanor suddenly darkened. "You putrid Mormon, you think the tribe of Joseph shall rule this land again? Never! This is my land, my sea, my Arabia, and my world!" the black clad stranger yelled in anger. He then stretched his hand out toward the American. Suddenly, the wind started whirling and his black clothing began blowing in the wind.

Stephen took a step back as his mind raced to find the right words to counter the attack. Blessing of the deep. Joseph, the beloved son of Israel. Ephraim and his son, Manasseh. What events had brought Stephen here to search for oil? What did it all mean?

Taking a step toward Stephen, the stranger drew his sword. He pointed it at Stephen and demanded, "Go now, my friend. I came in peace and brotherhood to warn you, but you're not listening. Leave this instant, or I will kill you myself. What is your answer, you dog?"

Rather than answer him, Stephen kept speaking aloud his thoughts. "Joseph's seed was blessed to rule Israel. The remnant, which is the house of Joseph, shall be redeemed by God from the Muslim nations. God the Almighty promised to bless Joseph's seed with 'blessings of heaven above, blessings of the deep that lieth under.' " Stephen quoted Genesis 49:25.

"Shut your mouth, you infidel dog! Stop using those lying words," the man shouted.

The Mormon kept pondering aloud. "The riches from the oil I am searching for will be used to redeem the seed of Joseph and help them rule the house of Israel again. Then they will rule the world, under the Son."

"Don't use that vile name, you fool! You think you know the words of the prophets? All that reading you did on your mission won't help you now. Look around you, you worthless spit. You recite the words of dead prophets. Where is your invisible God now? Can't you see he has forsaken you?"

"My Father will never forsake me. You are an evil spirit."

"Surely you're joking. Evil! I'm here to help you. Just look at yourself, you piece of Mormon dung. You are lost in a sandstorm halfway around the world from your home. Ha! You have no home. Your parents are dead. Even your grandfather died on you, and now your Bedouin interpreter is dead. As soon as the tribesmen find you, they will skin you alive. Ha, ha! Your God hasn't forsaken you? You fool, after giving everything you had for two years as a missionary, your God rewards you by sending you to this miserable desert." The dark one stopped just long enough to laugh with full pleasure. "You can't find a job in America, and you don't have enough money to marry that harlot of yours. Even that fool-headed girl is smart enough to drop a nobody like you."

It was spiritual warfare, and Stephen had heard enough. "She's not a harlot!" he yelled back. "And my Father has not forsaken me.

I know it, and I know your thoughts. The Spirit fills my mind. I command you to leave and to take your evil storm with you."

"You think you can command me, the great Al-Dajja?"

"In the name of my master, the Son and Savior, Jesus Christ, I command you to leave."

A hot wind blasted Stephen and sent a sickening odor deep into his nose. He could not breathe, and he collapsed to his knees. He looked up at the handsome personage and noticed something dripping from his right eye. Then . . . then . . .

"Wake up, boss. Wake up, Al-Mormon."

It was the voice of Ahmed. Stephen felt his Arab companion shaking him awake. "Are you okay, Mr. Stephen? That was the worst sandstorm I have ever seen. Even I, a Bedouin, got lost and feared I would die. Alhamdallah, thanks to God, I was fasting so Allah preserved our lives."

Stephen felt something heavy on him and he realized that he was half buried in sand. Grains of sand were stinging his eyes, and he had to clear his mouth of sandy mud before he could sit up and try to speak. "Ahmed, my good friend, I thought you were dead."

"No, boss, but we almost got buried alive by the storm. You must have lost consciousness."

"Has the storm passed? Are we safe?"

"Yes, Al-Mormon, the storm is gone, and we'll soon be safe in the land of my tribe."

Thank goodness, Stephen thought, *that evil spirit was only a bad dream.*

Notes

1. The Al Fatihah is the first section of the Qur'an, and comes from *fatihah*, the Arabic word meaning "opening." All devoted Muslims memorize the Qur'an. If they are in danger or need protection from temptation or an evil spirit, many Muslims will recite the Al Fatihah.

Chapter 9

Pitching a Tent in the Valley of Lehi

The Wild Arabs . . . will traverse burning sands barefoot to receive the last breath of some kind relation or friend, . . . teach their children at the earliest period resignation and fortitude, and . . . always keep alive a spirit of emulation amongst them! They are the boldest people in the world, yet are endued with a tenderness quite poetic, and their kindness extends to the brute creation by which they are surrounded. For myself I have the greatest affection and confidence in these people; besides, I admire their diamond eyes, their fine teeth, and the grace and agility (without capers) which is peculiar to them alone.

Hester Stanhope, *Memoirs of Lady Hester Stanhope*, 1845

Stephen Markham
October 1936
Entering the Land of Midian

After the sandstorm and Stephen's blackout experience, entering the ancient city of Tabuk seemed uneventful. The city, Stephen thought, had probably never looked better (or different, for that matter). Small rolling sand dunes on the east and rocky barren mountains on the west encircled Tabuk. Within the city were small fields of wheat and orchards of olives, oranges, dates, and other fruit. Like Al-Khobar, the entire city was made of mud bricks. Its buildings stood side by side along narrow dirt walkways. Every so often, there were overhanging walkways between the second floors of the buildings to allow women to pass between houses without being seen. To protect women from the glaring eyes of men, the windows were covered with lattice, which the Arabs also found useful to cool the air inside their homes. There were no signs of streetlights or any other form of electricity.

Since the local traffic consisted exclusively of camels, horses, and donkey carts, the oilmen drove slowly so as not to spook the animals. Although it seemed stuck in antiquity, Tabuk was still the largest city in the northernmost regions of Saudi Arabia. Ahmed explained that the city was known for its abundant water and a climate tame enough to grow many varieties of fruit, vegetables, and grain.

Ahmed was from the region of which Tabuk was the capital city. He provided Stephen with a long version of the town's history, including the name of every sheikh that had somehow distinguished himself in battle or exhibited some remarkable feat of hospitality. Stephen decided to put to memory the important points. Tabuk was a major halt on the ancient frankincense trail that started in Damascus and ran south through Arabia. In antiquity it became rich by trading provisions and fresh camels to the caravaners. Today it was one of the poorest regions in all of Arabia. The local emir was all-powerful over the welfare of the people who dwelled in the small towns and desert valleys of his realm, but most important to Stephen, the emir was not fond of foreigners. Ahmed explained that, luckily, the emir dreamed of discovering oil in Midian and the prospect that his tribe would have the wealth necessary to return to its lost days of glory. Stephen and CALTOC were important parts of this dream.

Stephen wanted to present his papers to the emir and get out of town as soon as possible. The cowboy always felt more comfortable in the countryside, and he was itching to continue west to the mountains near the Gulf of Aqaba, where he could start his survey. However, Ahmed had another idea. He insisted that they find a restaurant for lunch, a local Mondi eatery, a place that specializes in rice cooked with chicken or mutton. Mondi rice is cooked in the broth and grease of the meat, drenching the rice in more oil than Stephen would probably discover in all of Midian. The grease allowed the rice to be squeezed together in the right hand. The idea was to form a small ball of rice and then pop it into the mouth—no silverware needed. Since arriving in Arabia, Stephen had grown fond of the Yemeni dish. Ahmed agreed that a heavy lunch would maintain them during the hours they would need to wait in line for the emir to see them.

In the short time Stephen had been in Arabia, he had almost mastered the Arab way of eating. However, he did not agree with Ahmed that the food tasted better when eaten with the fingers. Furthermore, he didn't understand why he would not offend the emir when he later honored him with a greasy handshake. Washing up in such eateries was a simple matter of wiping your hands on a towel that had been used by every other customer that week, an unhealthy substitute for soap and hot water.

After lunch Stephen was ready to see the emir of Tabuk, but Ahmed told him it was now too late. The emir would be sleeping after lunch and his majlis (court) would not be open until that evening. It was the eager American versus the Arab notion of time, and there was no way Stephen could ever win the battle. "What do we do for the next six hours?" Stephen asked.

"No problem, boss. I have an uncle who lives here in Tabuk. We will sleep in his garden."

Stephen just nodded.

The heavy lunch and long nap proved to be a wise investment. The traditional evening meeting with the emir of Tabuk was a long, drawn-out saga. There were fourteen other people sitting on pillows in the emir's meeting room. All were eagerly waiting their turns to seek his favor. In one corner was a small wood fire with a teapot next to it. The smoke vented up the corner walls, eventually finding its way out small open windows high on the walls. Everyone sat waiting to talk to the emir, but the prince was tensely focused on playing a game of chess with a friend. No one seemed to be in a hurry. And why should they be? Nothing had changed in Tabuk in the last thousand years.

Finally, the game was completed, and the emir's assistant asked the guests, one after another, to come over and sit before the prince.

Apparently, the frontier prince wanted to impress his people by making the foreigner wait. Stephen recognized the pattern from his visit to Al-Hasa and realized he and Ahmed would be the last to leave the prince's majilis that night.

It was nearing midnight when the cowboy and his translator sat across from the leader of the northwestmost tribes of Saudi Arabia. After the formal greetings, Ahmed explained the nature of their request and handed the introduction letter from Emir Al-Hasa asking his permission to have the American survey Midian for oil. The emir took the paper, read it with a look of utmost indifference, and then had his assistant read it. Ignoring Stephen and Ahmed, the emir and his assistant privately discussed the matter for no more than a minute.

The emir then turned to Ahmed and told him that the CALTOC oilman could start looking for oil, but he would later talk to King Abdulaziz in Riyadh as to how much of the oil would belong to the people of Tabuk. He then pointed to Stephen and said to Ahmed, "You are from the beni Murri tribe. You are one of us. I know your father well. The Ameriki can survey anywhere he wants in the land of Midian, but as you know, he is forbidden to visit the beni Ibrahim or their land. He is in your trust. You know what I am referring to. Go now. Peace be with you."

Ahmed did not translate for Stephen the confidential reminder the emir had given him. It was a confidence that was not to be written. And its trust was not to be violated.

The next morning Stephen and Ahmed drove west from Tabuk into the rocky foothills of the Hejaz Mountains, where the land of Midian began. Beyond the rugged hill was a flat plateau of red sand. Every couple of miles, they passed below towering sandstone cliffs and hoodoos that reminded Stephen of the canyon lands back in southern Utah. After several hours, they could see the majestic granite mountains of Midian to the west. As a geologist, Stephen recognized that the sharply peaked mountains were young formations according to the geological timetable. He knew these granite monsters had been formed by upheavals of the earth's crust.

Spreading to the west was a long flat wadi (valley) that continued thirty miles until it plunged into the Gulf of Aqaba of the Red Sea. "Let's find a well in this area and set up camp," Stephen decided. "Midian is a beautiful land. No wonder Jethro lived here. What do you call this valley?" Stephen asked Ahmed.

"This is Wadi Lehi."[1]

"The valley of Lehi. Next you'll tell me there is a city called Nephi in Arabia."

"Yes, you are right, Al-Mormon. There is a city of Nephi in central Arabia. Lehi and Nephi are Arab names. Nephi[2] was the eleventh son of Ishmael."

No wonder I feel at home here, Stephen thought. It looks like Utah, and it sounds like Utah.

Notes

1. Barbara Toy, The Highway of the Three Kings: Arabia from South to North (London: John Murray, 1968), 19.
2. The most common spelling of the name of the eleventh son of Ishmael is Nafis, the Latin pronunciation of Nephi with an added s. There are many people in Arabia called Nafi or Nephi, including an entire tribe of Nafi.

Chapter 10

My Toothache of Opportunity

There are only two ways to live your life. One is as though nothing is a miracle. The other is as though everything is a miracle.

Albert Einstein

Jake Sorensen

Summer 1989
PAMMCO World Headquarters—Dhahran, Saudi Arabia
Week Three of Ten-week Internship

My summer internship was almost a third over, and I had not found one credible clue that the White Bedouin had ever existed. There were over fifty thousand people working for the world's largest oil company, and it appeared to me that not one of them had heard of a white Bedouin. I was beginning to believe that Hank's account of the Empty Quarter massacre was a well-rehearsed prank played by two seasoned roughnecks on gullible newcomers like me. That was until I paid an unpleasant visit to the PAMMCO dental clinic.

One of my wisdom teeth was finding the cruelest means possible to let me know it had arrived. Going to the dentist was no longer an option; it was a necessity. Sharp pain was ringing out from the core of my tooth, and I could not take it a minute longer. I made the short walk from the PAMMCO office tower to the company's Central Dental Clinic. The clinic was located across the street from the state-of-the-art PAMMCO hospital and was no more than four hundred yards from the office towers.

"The camp" is what the old timers from the CALTOC days still called PAMMCO's private city. Believe me, PAMMCO's camp is the furthest thing from a tent city. The dental clinic itself is three stories high and has enough space for a few dozen dentists, labs, and private offices. There are over three thousand western-style housing and apartment units, wide and spacious avenues like those found in Utah. The camp also boasts an accredited American school district, its own police and fire departments, several parks, scores of tennis and squash courts, a chilled Olympic-size swimming pool, horse stables, an eighteen-hole golf course, a drama theater, a library complex, and a little league baseball program that consistently sends its champions to play in the Little League World Series. Of course, PAMMCO's huge oil revenues pay for all the incongruous amenities.

My appointment was with Dr. Hamilton Richards, a Brit from Wales. I was in no condition to talk, but Dr. Richards turned out to be a first-class chatterbox. After nearly driving me crazy with what seemed like an endless stream of meaningless questions about who I was and why I was here, the talkative dentist finally had my mouth in a position where all I could do was grunt. This didn't slow him down one bit. He just continued on with a detailed monologue of his last week's affairs. He rattled on about how he had been sent to the city of Tabuk in the northwest part of Saudi Arabia. He explained how PAMMCO had a small dental clinic there to serve the employees in that part of the kingdom. He complained about the service on the national airline, Saudia. The hotel they put him in was supposed to have been a five-star, but the water in the pool was not cooled, and on and on he rambled. I was on the verge of asking him to knock me out with some laughing gas when he began talking about what had happened to him the day before he returned to Dhahran. I got so excited I just about jumped from the chair and grabbed the first Boeing headed to Tabuk.

"I tell you," the doctor began, "the most bizarre thing happened at the clinic. I was in a conference room explaining a new procedure to two Saudi dentists. I was just about finished, when we heard people shouting in the lobby. I tried to carry on with my presentation, but the shouting outside the room got louder and more intense. Finally, the receptionist came in and asked if one of the Saudi dentists could see a patient without an appointment. She said that an entire family of Bedouin came into the clinic and demanded that a dentist help their father. The flustered receptionist had asked the Bedouin's sons if they or their father were PAMMCO employees. The sons said no, but explained how long ago their father had worked as an oilman. They proclaimed that they were Saudis and demanded that the oil company give their elderly father dental treatment. The old man, the receptionist said, was sitting on the floor surrounded by women and children while the sons stood by the counter pounding their fists and demanding immediate attention.

" 'Can't you see our father is in pain?' they shouted. 'Treat him immediately or we will call the emir of Tabuk.' When the receptionist asked them for their documents, they said, 'We are Bedouin. We are nomads. We do not need documents.'

" 'Please, doctor,' the receptionist pleaded, 'will you take a look at their father? His sons are large men, and I am afraid they will get violent. They're straight out of the desert. They are all carrying guns and knives in their belts.'

"One of the Saudi dentists apologized for his countrymen's behavior. 'So, Dr. Richards, you see how crazy some Arabs can be, especially when it comes to caring for their beloved parents.' He stepped out of the conference room only to return in two or three minutes. 'Please, Dr. Richards, these crazy Bedouin won't have anything to do with a Saudi dentist. They say they came to the PAMMCO clinic because they want their father to be treated by a western medicine man. They don't speak a word of English, but I would appreciate it if you could handle the old man.'

"*What the heck,* I thought. *The Bedouin have already disturbed my presentation.* I agreed and proceeded to the lobby. The place was in chaos. The Bedouin men were screaming at the receptionist and waiving money in her face. I tried to calm them down and asked, for myself, if any of the sons spoke English. They didn't understand a word I said. Then, with the help of an old woman, the elderly Bedouin father got to his feet. As he steadied his stance, the old man looked at me and said in perfect American English, 'I have an infected tooth. I would appreciate it if you could give me a shot of antibiotics.'

"Was I ever stunned! Can you believe it? Here was this elderly man, an American grandpa at that, with a long white beard, dressed from head to foot in authentic Bedouin garb and surrounded by his family of nomads. To top it off, he had light blue eyes.

"The old man's family looked as shocked as I did. They just stood there with their mouths wide open as if they'd just seen Jesus walking on water. One little girl looked at the old man and asked him something in Arabic. I asked the Saudi dentist what the little girl had said. The dentist replied that she had said, 'Grandpa, how is it that you can talk to an English man?'

"The old man wouldn't tell me anything about his identity. He was very polite but tight-lipped. I decided to stop asking him questions, figuring that he must have been a WWII deserter who took up with the Bedouin."

When my mouth was free again, I asked Dr. Richards with my half-deadened mouth, "Did the American Bedouin tell you his name?"

"No, he only used his familiar name, Abu Yousif, or father of Joseph."

I left Dr. Richards's dentist chair realizing that I had probably just been treated by the same dentist who a few days before had helped the White Bedouin, the one called Al-Mormon.

In a dentist chair that morning, I learned a lesson that only comes to journalists through experience. Every time a new lead emerges, it carries with it more questions. If Al-Mormon lived in northern Arabia, what was he doing in the Empty Quarter in southern Arabia the day he saved Willy and Hank? Could there be two white Bedouin? There are over two thousand hellish miles separating the city of Tabuk in the northwest and the Empty Quarter. However, the odds seemed next to impossible that there could be two long-lost Americans roaming the Arabian wilderness.

Chapter 11

The Land of Moses

Now Moses kept the flock of Jethro his father in law, the priest of Midian: and he led the flock to the backside of the desert, and came to the mountain of God, even to Horeb [Sinai].

Exodus 3:1

Stephen Markham
Christmas Eve 1937
Al-Bada' Midian

Surveying Midian for oil deposits was slow and discouraging. Stephen and Ahmed started at Wadi Lehi and worked their way west to the southern end of the Gulf of Aqaba. Oil exploration had come a long way since amateurs started looking for seeping gas and oil. Stephen was working in a land that reminded him of the Old Testament, but he knew his geology and how to sniff out oil. Before coming to Arabia, he had already cut two notches in his belt for the successful wells he had prospected in Texas. Just two years out of college, he knew how to use the latest technologies to hunt down the elusive black gold.

His survey of Midian would have gone a lot faster and perhaps would have been more fruitful if he had one of the new seismographic machines that could reflect sound waves through the earth's crust to a depth of 2,500 feet. That was the surest way to find the subterranean salt domes that harbor pools of oil. Each month he requested a seismograph and an operating crew. When the next month's supply truck arrived, it always included a letter promising that he would get one soon. He never did. It was becoming even clearer to the cowboy that Midian was not a top priority for the managers back at headquarters. It was no secret. Every PAMMCO geologist, including Stephen, knew that huge oil deposits were waiting to be found somewhere beneath geological features of eastern Saudi Arabia, not its far northwest.

Without a seismograph, Stephen filled his days applying three other proven methods of detecting subterranean salt domes. In each new area, he would first use a torsion balance to check for abnormal levels of gravity. Since rocks have different densities, the gravitational forces they exert also vary. Stephen knew that if light rocks were close to the surface, the gravitational force they exerted would be less than that of heavier rocks. The key was to find very light rocks that hinted of a salt dome. So far, Midian's subterranean rocks measured only heavy.

To confirm the gravity measurements, Stephen would test rocks for magnetism. Most oil pools occur in sedimentary rocks that are nonmagnetic. Igneous and metamorphic rock rarely contain oil and are highly magnetic. Using a field balance, Stephen could measure rocks beneath the earth's surface for their invisible magnetism. This was not difficult, just meticulous, and everything Stephen did had to be logged.

Stephen had one last geophysical technique: old fashioned stratigraphy. The method consisted of drawing correlations by mapping out the exposed fossils, rock hardness or softness, composition, distribution, and succession of rock strata. He then used sample logs and drilling tables to compare his findings to fields where oil had been found. Again, hiking around all day and hammering rocks was not hard for an ex-ranch hand, and besides, Stephen enjoyed the work. It was outdoors, and it made him feel like a private detective trying to solve a mystery. Where did God hide his oil?

On winter nights, ice formed on their tents. Twice they experienced a light snow. During the summer, the temperature rose to 115 degrees. The spring and fall brought sandstorms, which triggered memories of the demon Stephen convinced himself he had imagined in the Nafud dunes. They had been working in Midian for fourteen months and so far had found no geological evidence of big oil. Stephen wondered why CALTOC kept the survey going. He had only eight months left on his two-year contract, so perhaps the company figured Midian and Markham were both lost causes, so why transfer him this late in his contract? That was fine with Stephen, for he had fallen in love again, this time with the land of Midian and the Bedouin tribes that lived there.

Instead of treating him with hostility, Stephen became the topic of tribal curiosity. The Bedouin families competed to host the American at their camps—all the tribes of Midian that is, except the tribe due north of their camp, the beni Ibrahim, the tribe ruled by its emir, Sheikh Ibrahim Al-Ibrahim.

The two oilmen often spent their weekends visiting the camp of Ahmed's tribe. Ahmed and his family taught Stephen to read, write, and speak Arabic. The oilmen were now using Arabic as their working language. Not a workday passed without the two of them being visited by Bedouin tribesmen. Usually the encounters began with a group of nomads riding up on their camels and inviting the geologist and his translator to their tents for "Mormon tea." News passes quickly among the tribes, and it seemed that everyone knew that Stephen was a Christian but a different sort of one. He did not bother their women. He did not drink alcohol. He did not smoke. He refused their tea and coffee. He rode a horse like an Arabian warrior. And he wore a strange hat.

In Stephen's honor, each tribe had created their own brand of tea for the American. The odd recipe usually consisted of some mixture of warmed goat's milk, cardamom, and sugar. Each tribe added its own odds and ends to the brew. Actually, Stephen did not like these Mormon tea concoctions, but the Bedouin were so proud that they finally found something they could serve the American that Stephen could not refuse their offerings. Each time he was presented a cup, he looked at it, smiled, and thought to himself, *Open the hatch, torpedoes away.*

In the high desert of Wadi Lehi, the night sky was full of stars. Once a week, between the end of work and first starlight, Stephen would take the Remington rifle CALTOC issued him and go into the mountains to hunt. His favorite target was the ibex, the long-horned mountain sheep of Arabia. While in the mountains, he would often put down his gun and sit on a rock. At these times, he would either think of how it could have been with Jan, or in more recent days, he would think of the words of the Book of Mormon prophet Enos. At times Stephen engaged in long oral prayers. They were prayers one would not expect from someone of Stephen's age and circumstances. His prayers did not ask Heavenly Father for the typical wish list: a partner to take to the temple, a house, a car, and a dependable job back in the States. His scriptures had become his best friend in the desert, and the more he read them, the more he wanted to understand their meaning and their mysteries. The young Mormon prayed for spiritual enlightenment.

While reading the Book of Mormon one evening by the light of a flickering campfire, an old Bedouin appeared within the outer glow of the firelight. The man stood there staring at Stephen like a wolf silently stalking sheep. Stephen put down his scriptures and walked over to greet him. The Bedouin said nothing, just stood there watching. "What can I do for you? What do you want?" Stephen asked the Bedouin in Arabic.

The old man gave no reply as Stephen drew closer. Instead, he looked at the tall white man. Then he turned and walked away.

Forty-five minutes later, another Bedouin appeared on the perimeter of the campfire's light. Again, Stephen greeted his visitor, but the man didn't respond. Again, Stephen approached the man and stood before him. "Who are you?" he asked.

The man's eyes swept over Stephen from head to foot, then scanned him over again. Finally, he replied, "I am Yacob of the beni Ibrahim tribe. I was told the oilman was a Mormon. I just wanted to see what one looks like." And with that, the man turned and walked back into the night. This odd encounter was the first but not the last time he would deal with the elusive beni Ibrahim tribe.

Other strange events occasionally occurred, and Stephen was beginning to wonder, again, about the people of Arabia and a possible relationship they might have with the Mormons of Utah.

Tomorrow would be Christmas Day, his second in Midian. Last year's sacred holiday had been miserable for Stephen. Back then, he was the only Christian he knew of in all of Midian. He had spent the entire twenty-fifth of December thinking about how unfortunate he was being an orphan so far from his homeland. Visions of Christmas lights, presents, and his lost love had danced before his eyes. By now, Jan was probably married and a mother with twin babies under her Christmas tree.

This year, he would spend Christmas Eve looking to the north and pondering the same starlit sky that Joseph, Mary, and the baby Jesus had witnessed. Bethlehem was only two hundred and fifty miles away, and living among nomadic herdsmen with their camels and sheep made the original nativity seem closer to his heart than ever.

Stephen looked forward to the next day. He was going to a simple, but greatly appreciated, Christmas celebration. He had been invited by two German archaeologists to the village of Al-Bada' to commemorate the Savior's birth. The Deutschlanders were the only westerners he had encountered since coming to Midian, and they, like him, had grown fond of the village's Mondi restaurant, a small five-table eatery. Greasy rice and chicken would have to do in lieu of a roast goose and red cabbage for the Germans and turkey and dressing for Stephen. Instead of family members, it would be a Christmas lunch with two archaeologists who would probably be the American's war enemies before the next Christmas came around.

Talk of war was thick on the BBC airwaves, and the Axis powers were already approaching the Turks to join them in turning the Middle East into a battle ground. Stephen was certain the Germans were actually spies, but he wasn't about to confront his friends over the matter and risk losing his only western acquaintances. *All the same*, Stephen thought, *the Lord taught us to love our enemies, and besides, we're not at war yet*. He felt inside his heart that these were two good men.

Stephen had met the Germans the month before while out surveying. They were nice enough to invite him to join them in celebrating the Lord's birthday. The Germans made Stephen laugh. They were a Bavarian version of Laurel and Hardy. Gerhard was the lean, serious type, and Klaus was a sturdy, fun-loving German with a mustache that made him look like a tanned replica of

Kaiser Wilhelm. The first day he met them, Stephen knew that he would keep his promise to have Christmas with them, even if by then Germany and America were at war.

Stephen gave Ahmed a few days off for Christmas. Before leaving camp to visit the Germans, Stephen packed a bag of ibex jerky as a gift for the two Europeans and another bag of dried meat for Ahmed's family. Wearing his cowboy hat and boots and his best shirt and pants, Stephen hopped in the truck with Ahmed and started driving east to the tent of Ahmed's family, some twenty miles from their own camp.

Stephen and Ahmed's father had quickly taken to each other, and each time they met, there was an exchange of gifts. This time, Stephen received a gift of dried dates, and Ahmed's father received a large bag of ibex jerky. After the traditional greeting of rubbing noses, Stephen got back in the truck and drove to Midian. The trip took him back west thirty miles, then another twenty miles northwest up the Valley I'fal to the small village of Al-Bada'.

Given his lonely circumstances, Christmas lunch with Klaus and Gerhard was a holiday delight. Their Mondi dinner was first rate for a wilderness outpost. The only complaint came from the Germans, wishing now and then for a good German beer to wash down the grease. Klaus concluded with a laugh, "Christmas would be perfect if we just had a keg of dark German beer."

Stephen presented his gifts of ibex jerky to Klaus and Gerhard, announcing it as what Buffalo Bill used to do with all those buffalos he buffaloed. At the sight of the meat, hefty Klaus burst out with joy, "Primo! I bet this is as good as blood pudding!" Gerhard just kept turning the dried meat in his hand as if trying to figure out what to do with it. "Do you boil it until it turns back into real food?" he asked.

"I've never tried cooking it with sauerkraut," Stephen noted. "Try it straight, without cabbage."

Meanwhile, Klaus was already munching away on the jerky. "Billy Buffalo must have been a Bavarian. *Das ist ser gut!*"

In return, Klaus handed Stephen a small ancient-looking bowl of earthen pottery. "It is from here, the town of Midian. I uncovered it at Jethro's well. Maybe it was the perfume bottle of one of Jethro's daughters," Klaus said. He followed with a hearty laugh.

"You mean to tell me that Jethro's well is here in this little village?" asked the surprised Mormon.

Gerhard replied, "The wells are just down the dirt road to the south a couple of hundred meters and off a little to the left. You passed it as you drove into the village."

"Are you sure it's Jethro's well?"

"Just ask anybody in the village about the old name of this town. Even on old Arabic maps it is shown as the village of Midian,[1] the Biblical town where Jethro was the priest. On modern Arabic maps, this town has two names, Zuqaib, which translates to Jethro, and Al-Bada'."[2]

"Holy tannenbaums!" the cowboy hollered. "Hot dog! I'm celebrating Christmas where Moses and Jethro once lived."

"What you mean by hot dog?" the serious Gerhard asked.

"Sorry, that's an American expression we use when we get excited. It's like a bratwurst."

"Americans get excited over a bratwurst? Here, this is what I get excited about," Gerhard said. "Take it; it's yours. Merry Christmas."

Gerhard handed Stephen a gold ring. Its twisted design looked very old, and it appeared to have been an earring. "I found this in Wadi Musa. Musa is the Arabia name for Moses. The valley is about ten miles to the north of here. It is an important discovery because we know the Israelites took with them the gold of Egypt, and this is evidence that Wadi Musa could have been a campsite of the children of Israel on their way to Mount Sinai."

Stephen was touched by the kindness of the Germans and astonished by the information they were giving him. He had been surveying in Midian for over a year and had not had the least thought to look for what was on the Earth's surface—the historical evidence of the Exodus! His whole attention was focused on subterranean rock formations that might encase oil. That would now change. "So you believe Mount Sinai is in Midian? I thought it was located in the Sinai Peninsula."

"Of course it is in Arabia," Klaus said. "Jethro lived here, right here. Look at any Bible map of the ancient patriarchs, and you'll see that the town of Midian was located here in this little village. Moses was eighty years old when he went back to Egypt to free the Hebrews. Jethro was his father-in-law and a priest. Jethro must have been even older than Moses. After Moses crossed the Red Sea, the elderly Jethro traveled to visit his camp. The priest was probably over one hundred years old by then. How far do you think Jethro could have traveled by foot or on camelback?"

Gerhard interrupted. "That's why we think Moses camped with the children of Israel in Wadi Musa. The trail to it is flat and easy going. It's only ten miles from here, and the elderly Jethro could have made a trip over that distance."

"So where do you think the Hebrews crossed the Red Sea?"

"That's an easy thing to figure out," Klaus said. "It had to have been at the Straits of Tiran at the southern end of the Gulf of Aqaba. The book of Exodus says the children of Israel crossed the Red Sea in one night. The Red Sea proper is one hundred and fifty miles wide and seven thousand feet deep. Any halfwit would realize that it was not possible for the Hebrews to make such a journey in a single night. However, the Straits of Tiran are an entirely different matter. They are only ten miles across and only six hundred feet deep. There are even two islands that help bridge the straits. You see, *mein freund*, it is shallow because there is an underground mountain range that bridges the entire length of the straits. If Moses crossed the Red Sea, it was at Tiran. Besides, as you know, the straits are just forty miles from here, and we're eating dinner where Jethro lived. Makes sense, yah?"

"Yah, you're right," Stephen surmised. "So where is Mount Sinai?"

"We don't know," Gerhard said. "That's our goal. We came here to find it. The Apostle Paul taught that Mount Sinai was in Arabia.[3] Paul traveled to Arabia to prepare for his mission, and we are certain he visited the actual mountain of Moses and was taught there by the Lord, just like Moses was. Otherwise, why would Paul have come to Arabia, and how could he have known that Mount Sinai was in Arabia unless he actually saw it with his own eyes?"

Stephen interrupted. "Okay, Mount Sinai is in Arabia, so it can't be far from here because Moses was tending to Jethro's sheep when he saw the burning bush."

"*Ser gut*," Gerdard continued. "However, as you know, the Bedouin in this area will travel great distances in search of grazing land for their animals. They move from camp to camp with their sheep and goats. Moses would have done the same thing. The prophet probably knew the valleys of Midian like the back of his hand. From the Biblical and Qur'anic accounts, it appears that Mount Sinai is a short distance northeast of here. You see, Moses wrote that he was on the backside of the desert when he saw the burning bush.[4] From this village, the backside of the desert would be on the east side of the mountains to our east. You know the terrain, Stephen. We are here in Wadi I'fal. This valley runs north to south, with the shoreline mountains on the west and the Jebel Al-Lawz Mountain Range on the east. When the Arabs refer to inland, away from the sea, they speak of going into the desert. Thus, we would expect the backside of the desert to be in the mountains farther in the desert or more inland. That would point to the Jebel Al-Lawz Mountains that lie to the east of Jethro's village."

"That makes sense," Stephen agreed.

The logical German continued. "The front side of the desert would be the side of the mountains facing the place where Moses lived in this village of Midian. Thus, the back side of the mountain, the place where Moses spoke to God, is on the east side of the mountains."

"Great, so let's go and see what we can find on the east side of the mountains," Stephen suggested excitedly.

"The trouble is we can't. Of course that's where we would start looking, but the emir of Tabuk only gave us permission to conduct archaeological digs from the shoreline of the Gulf of Aqaba to Wadi I'fal. He forbids us from going farther east. He told us it was for our own protection, for the beni Ibrahim tribe is hostile and will kill anyone found trespassing on their lands."

"That's interesting," Stephen said. "No one told me the beni Ibrahim were bad tempered. I have permission to survey all of Midian. When I get up that way, I'll look for your mountain. But what should I look for?"

Klaus spoke up. "You'll know if you find it. Absolutely! Remember, the children of Israel camped there for several months, and the Bible says they made several sizeable monuments. Remember, time stands still in the desert. We are sure those monuments are still there. This desert is hot and dry, and if Mount Sinai is here, its monuments are preserved better than Buffalo Bill's jerky. If you do get up there, start by looking for a small brook, at least a stream that would flow during the rainy season. The children of Israel needed water, and we know Mount Sinai had a brook because Deuteronomy 9:21 describes it. Next to the stream look for a monument made of uncut stones. Moses needed water to wash the sacrifices, and we know from the Bible that Moses built an altar from unhewn stones."[5]

"What else should I look for?" Stephen inquired.

"There should be something resembling the altar to the golden calf. Making the idol was a big event, so we would suspect that there could still be evidence that the idol's altar had once existed there. If so, you will find the altar of the golden calf within sight of Mount Sinai.[6] This altar will have been carved by stone cutters and will possess images of a false god. And remember, Stephen, the image of the calf will not be a North American buffalo or a cowboy riding a Brahma bull. It will have the image of an Egyptian calf like the ones you would find on an Egyptian monument."

Scholarly Gerhard felt Klaus was getting somewhat sacrilegious in his description of the sacred mountain. He stoically completed the list.

"A qualified candidate for the mountain of God should have boundary markers.[7] Moses was told to construct markers so that the people would not intrude on the mountain's holy soil. Beware, if you find the mountain, remember even Moses was told to take off his shoes."

Stephen asked for a short pause. The list of archaeological evidences was becoming too long to remember, so he took out a pen and started a list. A minute later he asked Gerhard to continue.

"You need to find twelve pillars, one for each tribe.[8] You'll also have to survey the mountain and see if there is a cave."[9]

"Right," Stephen nodded. "Elijah stayed in a cave on Mount Sinai." Stephen realized that discovering a cave might be harder than it first sounded because Mount Sinai was described in the scriptures as an "exceedingly high" mountain.[10]

Gerhard continued, "There must be room at the base of the mountain for a large encampment of people. I estimate that there must have been somewhere between one and three million Israelites camped next to the mountain.[11] That's probably more people than live in your entire state of Utah. The campsite was in a location where the children of Israel could see the presence of God on the mountain."[12]

Klaus's bubbly personality couldn't be contained any longer. "If there were millions of people, do you think they kept their sheep in their tents? They camped by the mountain for months, and this would have required there to have been an area where they could find food for their animals for a sustained period. That's a lot of lamb chops and camel steaks to keep on four legs. I don't think the beasts ate manna, so there had to be miles and miles of grazing land for their animals."

"Okay," Stephen said as he assessed the final list. "It's been over three thousand years since Moses and the children of Israel camped at the mountain. What makes you think all the monuments would not have been removed by the Arabs?"

As if reciting a pet theory, Gerhard jumped in to answer Stephen's question. "Moses might have left Mount Sinai, but God did not. It is still a sacred mountain. Before Solomon built the great temple in Jerusalem, each year the children of Israel would send a delegation to the mountain to make sacrifices. The Israelite pilgrimage to Sinai lasted for five hundred years. Moses fasted forty days on the mountain. Elijah fasted forty days when he went to Mount Sinai, and we suspect that when our Lord Jesus Christ fasted forty days in preparing for his mission, the wilderness he wandered in must have taken him to Mount Sinai. Recall that the Spirit led our Lord to an 'exceeding high mountain' described in Matthew 4:8.[13]

"The last person we know to have visited the mountain was Paul. Even the Muslims believe that Allah will call Christ at his Second Coming to take the faithful Muslims to Mount Sinai,[14] where they will enter new covenants. You see, *mein freund*, Mount Sinai was dedicated by Moses to be a holy temple. Even though the Israelites eventually built a temple in Jerusalem, Mount Sinai continues to be a sacred place for making covenants.[15] The mountain is still a temple of God, a place where man can connect with the powers of heaven. We doubt if anyone would dare desecrate God's mountain. Everyone here must know where the mountain is, but no one will tell us. It is their great secret. They're probably afraid we will desecrate their sacred mountain or misuse its special powers."

"Do you know the purpose of temples?" Stephen asked the archaeologists.

"Of course, to make offerings and pray and pay tribute. And to obtain God's priesthoods and special powers."

"I mean, do you understand the reason the children of Israel made offerings and why they entered covenants?"

"Of course, young man," Gerhard said with a tone of defensiveness. "We are archaeologists, Bible experts, and Germany's leading scholars on Mount Sinai. There were several kinds of offerings made at Mount Sinai: one for thanksgiving, one for remission of sins, and so on."

"Yes," Stephen said, "but Sinai, like the temple in Jerusalem, contained a special room, a Holy of Holies, the place where God stands and confers with his prophets face to face. It is a place where only authorized priests can officiate and where unclean feet should not trod. If you remember, the children of Israel were forbidden to step foot on the mountain. If it is still a temple, do you think it is safe to go there?"

"Like Gerhard said, we are Bible scholars," Klaus inserted, "not Bible fools. All that talk about burning bushes, pillars of fire, and the finger of God is figurative. You don't really believe those things really happened, do you?"

"Yes, I do," Stephen said. "In my church, we have temples, and within their walls the Lord has appeared, along with his angels."

The rest of the afternoon was spent discussing the restoration of the gospel and Latter-day Saint temples. As he shared his beliefs, Stephen felt the sweet spirit of Christmas, the very presence of the Spirit of Christ. What better gift could he have given his friends than to share with them the same gospel the Christ child brought to the earth? Stephen was not sure if the Spirit penetrated his scholarly German friends. However, they respectfully listened to the young American as he explained the story of the Prophet Joseph Smith, the returning of the keys of temple work by Elijah in the latter days, and the work of perfecting the Saints in preparation for the Second Coming.

Just before sunset, Stephen and his two German friends took a short walk outside the village to a large well. It was approximately twelve feet wide and eighty feet deep. A beautiful young girl was drawing pure water from the old well. "What do you call this fountain?" Stephen asked her in Arabic.

She smiled. "You don't know? This is Prophet Jethro's well, peace and prayers be upon him." She then pointed to a hill a quarter of a mile to the west. "And there," she said, "are the caves of Moses. That is where Prophet Moses lived."

"And where can I find Mount Sinai?" Gerhard asked.

The girl smiled and walked away.

"See what I mean?" Gerhard said. "They suddenly clam up when it comes to Mount Sinai."

But Stephen understood why the girl would not reveal the location of a sacred temple, even if it were only a granite mountain of boulders. He also understood that the motives of the Germans for finding the sanctuary where God manifests his powers might not be as innocent as they claimed. Still, the Germans had transformed a simple wilderness supper into a Christmas holiday he would never forget.

Moses and Elijah walked here, and so did Paul. Stephen wondered if this was also the very wilderness that Jesus Christ walked, in preparation for his earthly mission. Did he come to Mount Sinai and find Satan waiting for him? Was it at the top of sacred Mount Sinai that Christ commanded Satan to leave its holy grounds?

Notes

1. Al-Ansary, Abdul-Rahman, Sa'as A. Al-Rashid, Ali Ibrahim Ghabban, Abdullah Al-Saud, Khalid Mohammed Eskoubi, Majeed Khan, *Al-Bid'*, (Riyadh: Ministry of Education, Kingdom of Saudi Arabia, 2002), 17–18.

2. See Farsi road maps of Tabuk region.

3. Galatians 4:25.

4. Exodus 3:1–2.

5. Exodus 20:24–26; 24:4.

6. Exodus 32:17–19.

7. Exodus 19:23.

8. Exodus 24:4.

9. 1 Kings 19:8–9.

10. Moses 1:1.

11. Exodus 12:37.

12. Exodus 19:17–18.

13. See Joseph Smith Translation.

14. Imam Abu Zakariya Yahya Bin Sharaf an-Nawawi, comp., *Hadeeth of Prophet Mohammed, Riyadh-Us-Saleheen,* vol. 2, S.M. Madni Abbasi, trans. (Riyadh: International Islamic Publishing House, no date), 873.

15. Lynn and Hope Hilton, *Discovering Lehi* (Springville, UT: Cedar Fort, 1996), 60.

Chapter 12

The Second Coming to Mount Sinai

Where is he that is born King of the Jews? For we have seen his star in the east, and are come to worship him.

Matthew 2:2

Stephen Markham
Christmas Night 1937
Surveying Camp—Midian

Driving back to his isolated camp was as tricky as ever. The Ford pickup slid this way and that way through the soft sand. Stephen kept the truck in low gear and its motor's RPMs revving. A year earlier he could hardly have made it a mile through such driving conditions, but after fourteen months in the desert, Stephen could manage the drive at night while humming Christmas carols. Desert survival was now second nature to him. He chuckled at the thought that he was being slowly transformed into a Bedouin. On he drove, singing his own adaptation of a Christmas classic.

Jingle bells, Jingle bells,
Jingle all the way,
Oh what fun it is to slide around in a land full of sand.

The carol included an entirely new set of characters such as a one-humped camel, a jolly German, a skinny Prussian scholar, and an old man with a long white beard selling rice and chicken.

Reaching camp, Stephen lit an oil lamp. His mind was still excited about what he had seen in the small village of Al-Bada'. He could not sleep, so the young Mormon took his scriptures from his tent and placed them on the camp table beside the lamp. He then retrieved the English copies of the Qur'an and the Hadeeth he'd found in the bag of books Timmy Cullerson gave him when he left the CALTOC camp. He placed the Islamic text next to his Bible. The Hadeeth is an Islamic sacred book that recounts the sayings and actions of the beloved Prophet Mohammed.

Under Christmas stars, Stephen started his daily survey of the word of God. He probed the pages of his Book of Mormon and Bible for all the references he could find on Midian. He found a reference that seemed strange to him. The Nephites had named one of their lands in the New World Midian.[1] *Why?* he wondered. *Why would the Nephites have used the name of an Arabian land for one of their own areas?*

Next, the cowboy opened his Bible and thumbed through the letters of Paul. He wondered if the apostle had actually come to Midian. Was Sinai actually in Arabia? Speeding through the epistles, he discovered pay dirt in the book of Galatians. Stephen read that Paul had stayed in Arabia and Damascus for three years![2]

Stephen was now certain that Paul knew Midian and Mount Sinai like the back of his hand. Three chapters later he found what he was looking for. Paul, an apostle of the Lord, had studied in Arabia and stated clearly that Mount Sinai was indeed in Arabia and not in the Sinai Peninsula of Egypt.[3]

Stephen read on and discovered verses that gave him insights for understanding the Arabs and their religion.

> For it is written, that Abraham had two sons, the one by the bondmaid [Hagar, the handmaid of Sarah and the mother of the Arab nation], the other by a freewoman [Sarah, the mother of the house of Israel]. But he who was of the bondwoman was born after the flesh; but he of the freewoman was by promise. Which things are an allegory: for these are the two covenants; the one from Mount Sinai, which gendereth to bondage, which is Agar [Hagar, a bondsmaid]. For this Agar is Mount Sinai in Arabia. (Galatians 4:22–25)

What does all this mean? the American pondered. If the house of Joseph, the tribes of Ephraim and Manasseh, were living among the Arabs today, they would still be subject to the covenant of bondage. The Muslims believe their Qur'an includes the restoration of the law of Moses, which was given to Moses on Mount Sinai.[4] Would this mean that the main tribes of Ephraim and Manasseh still did not have the higher law or a testimony of Jesus Christ? Were they non-Christians?

Stephen's mind was churning out ideas in high gear. *When will the Muslims receive a witness of Christ?* he questioned. *They still practice animal sacrifices.* He turned to Doctrine and Covenants section thirteen. The very first verse said, "Upon you my fellow servants, in the name of Messiah I confer the Priesthood of Aaron." Of course, Aaron was the brother of Moses and presided over the priests of the tribe of Levi at Mount Sinai. The tribe of Levi administered the ordinances of the lower priesthood and the covenants the tribes of Israel made with God. Stephen read on, "This shall never be taken again from the earth, until the sons of Levi do offer again an offering unto the Lord in righteousness."

Stephen's mind generated even more questions. *Could this be the reason the Muslims believe that in the last days God will command Jesus Christ to take the righteous to Mount Sinai?* Certainly, the descendants of the priests of Levi would still be living among the tribes of Ephraim and Manasseh in Arabia. And why would Jesus Christ gather the

Muslims to Mount Sinai? *That's easy enough to answer,* he thought. *The Doctrine and Covenants states that they will make a sacrifice to the Lord, even an offering in righteousness.*

Wait just a minute. Stephen stopped his rushing train of thought. *Where is this all leading?* It would mean that at the beginning of the Second Coming, Christ would appear to the Muslims at Mount Sinai, right here in Midian.

Stephen did not need to open the Doctrince and Covenants. He knew very well what it said about the coming of the Lord. "For a trump shall sound both long and loud, even as upon Mount Sinai, and all the earth shall quake" (Doctrine and Covenants 29:13). What the Mormon didn't know was that the Qur'an talks about the same event. "The trumpet will be blown, and we shall collect them all together" (Qur'an 18:99).

Notes

1. Alma 24:5.
2. Galatians 1:15–18.
3. Galatians 4:19.
4. Qur'an 20:80.

Chapter 13

The Devil's Donkey

To the north-east across the great Arabian desert live other Jews, possible descendants of the "ten lost tribes of Israel" who have maintained their freedom through their fighting abilities.

Wolfgang von Weisl, *London Evening Standard*, 1928

Jake Sorensen
Summer 1989
Al-Dossary Hunting Camp
Week Five of Ten-week Internship

I woke to the powerful rumbling of five Toyota Land Cruisers. Abdulrahman shook me awake and said we must start the hunt at the morning's first light.

"Come, Jake. The rabbits feed at dawn, and we must hunt before the sand becomes so hot it burst our tires."

To be honest, it already felt so hot that I thought my butt was blistering right there in bed. We were camped on the edge of the Empty Quarter in July. It was still dark, and it felt like it was already over one hundred degrees. It would top 140 degrees by noon, and I had to remind myself again why I was here in the first place.

After the story about the White Bedouin and the evil phantom of the Empty Quarter, I could hardly refuse my workmate's offer to go falcon hunting there with this cousins. Abdulrahman Al-Dossary might be a pampered city Arab, but like most city Arabs, he had an uncle or two with Bedouin bloodlines, and for some reason, the mega rich Arabs still find time to train falcons just as their ancestor did in the days of the pharaohs.

When Abdulrahman first invited me to go camping in the Empty Quarter, I was concerned to say the least. I asked Abdulrahman if he had ever heard of evil spirits living in the sand dunes. My officemate just laughed. "You're an American, and you're afraid of genies?" With that reply, I had no choice but to defend my manhood and accept the invitation.

The Al-Dossary hunting camp consisted of just two tents for sleeping and another tent that functioned as a kitchen. The camp was located among a landscape of small sand dunes. To reach it, we drove south from Dhahran, through the bustling city of Hofuf, and then we drove along the highway to Qatar and the United Arab Emirates. Four hours past Hofuf, we left the highway and turned due south. We followed a graded dirt road that had been forged deep into the Empty Quarter by PAMMCO. The road was rough and at times covered by streams of drifting sand. I figured it was all an oil-hungry geologist needed to follow in the footsteps of old Willy and Hank.

Two hours down the graded road, we reached the Al-Dossary camp. Even this outpost was still not in the heart of the dreaded

Empty Quarter, where Hank claimed he met the anti-Christ. It was merely a tamer tentacle of the deadly desert. The small dunes that surrounded the camp were covered with desert bushes Abdulrahman called *dekaka*, a hard and brittle brush that resembled sagebrush back in Utah. Here and there were small patches of hay-like grass and, if I believed Abdulrahman and his cousins, lots of rabbit holes. It seemed next to impossible for any game, however small, to live in this sandy wasteland. When I challenged my officemate on this matter, he quickly assured me that there was plenty of life in the sands. "So watch where you step," he declared. "It's summertime, so this place is crawling with venomous vipers and scorpions." If that was not creepy enough, just before we went to bed, one of the Al-Dossary cousins, Ali, told me to close the tent door tight so that camel spiders could not find their way into the tent and into our flesh.

To a modest degree, I was starting to appreciate the harsh conditions that had hardened the faces of Willy and Hank. "What's a camel spider?" I asked with a good measure of alarm.

Perhaps Ali should not have answered my questions in such detail. "They're not really spiders," he explained. "They look like giant spiders, but they are of the scorpion family. Their scorpion cousins are their favorite food. If one of those large black scorpions crosses the path of a camel spider, it doesn't have a chance."

"How big are they?"

"The largest can be the size of a man's palm, but they're mostly legs. That makes them very fast. The nasty end of a camel spider is their large jaws. They can crush the shell of a scorpion and rip through the leathery skin of a camel. If one crawls on you while you sleep, it could disfigure your face by morning."

"Wouldn't its bite wake you up?"

"Legend has it that it first injects a chemical that numbs its victims. Allah gave the camel spider its own anesthetizing needle. As children, we heard stories of how British soldiers fighting in Arabia during World War I would get drunk and pass out in the desert. When they woke in the morning, their noses were missing."

"Do you believe those stories?" I asked Ali.

"I am not sure. Maybe our fathers and uncles were just trying to scare us away from alcohol. All the same, close the tent door all the way."

It was nice to wake in the morning and find my nose still attached to my face. There was no time for a real breakfast; we needed to get the falcon and head into the desert before it became too hot. I enjoyed a handful of dates and some *laban,* the sour buttermilk-like drink the Arabs used to temper the sweetness of the dates. My Arab hosts ate their dates with a yellow tea blended with a hefty dose of sugar. Boosted by the carbohydrates, we were wired for what would be the ride of my life.

Ali was the falconer. He would ride in the lead Land Cruiser with his bird of prey resting on a leather strap on his arm. With a blindfold over its eyes, the fierce-looking falcon stayed remarkably calm during our wild search for its prey.

Before getting in the trucks, my Arab companions bent down and let air out of the truck's tires. I wasn't sure that was wise. The sand would be scorching hot, and lowering the tire pressure would only add more friction to the rubber. It took only a few minutes to figure out why they did it. Abdulrahman asked me to ride shotgun in the Land Cruiser he drove. As we left camp, he pointed to southeast at some huge red sand dunes. The red mountains of sand must have been twenty miles away and appeared to tower several hundred feet in the air.

"Those are the red dunes," Abdulrahman remarked. "The red dunes lie on the border of Saudi Arabia and the United Arab Emirates. You can drive on those sands."

He then pointed southwest in the direction of some less impressive dunes. "See those white dunes?" he said. "The Bedouin call them the dunes of death. The red dunes are hard and firm, so you can read their contours easily. You can depend on the red sands. The white dunes are soft and treacherous. It is very easy to get stuck in the white sands. Their white color is inviting, but like a spider's web, it is a trap. Each year people are found dead in the white dunes, even experienced Bedouin hunters lose their way and die."

"So why are we headed that way?"

"Don't worry, Jake. We're going to hunt right here where the rabbits live." Those were some of the last audible words I heard that morning. Abdulrahman turned up the tape deck to maximum volume and from then on all I could hear was high-energy Gulf music—drums of all sizes, violins, lutes, and some gal singing about *Abibi, Abibi* (boyfriend, boyfriend) and something about Allah. It was all packed into the rhythm of a lively Arabian war dance.

And war it was. All of a sudden, the lead Land Cruiser took off like a cookie thief dashing from his mother's kitchen. The Land Cruiser roared right up the back of a small dune and flew over its edge. The truck came crashing down on the soft side of the dune. I thought they were crazy, but I perked up when I realized that Saudi rabbit hunting was more of a follow-the-leader ride of terror than a serious hunt for game. We were the third truck, and Abdulrahman had to prove that he could get more air than the first two. He gunned the pedal, and up and over we went. "Hang on," he warned. All I could do was lock my jaws, hoping to save my teeth when we landed.

Mr. Toad's Wild Ride had just begun. The lead daredevil drove up the face of a fifty-foot dune and then turned sideways and crossed the entire face of the sand dune. I could not believe his truck didn't roll over and tumble down the face of the dune. It was as if it defied gravity. *Oh crap!* I thought. *Here we go!* Abdulrahman roared up the face of the dune. Then he turned at a right angle and drove across the entire width of the dune. If I hadn't worn my seat belt and held the door handle, I would have landed in Abdulrahman's lap. We had to be tipped at a forty-degree angle.

"Having fun?" Abdulrahman asked.

"Right on! But at this angle, why don't we roll over?"

"The soft sand on the slip face holds us up. That's why we lower the tires. It gives us more surface area for the soft sands to hold on to us. You can go over the back on these dunes and drop straight off the top and down the steep slip face. You don't even need to use your brakes. The sand grabs the tires and brings you safely down the dune."

"Say what you want, but you guys are loco driving like this. Don't you ever roll over?"

"Sure, the young Arab men make it a form of chicken, like teenagers do in the U.S. We try to out-do each other, not drive at each other. Sometimes we roll our trucks over and our parents get mad. Sometimes someone is killed, but *inshalah*, it was God's will. All the young Saudi men do it, at least until they get married and have to report to their wives. It's a national sport. We call it dune busting. It's also a very good way to shake out a rabbit."

Hearing how God's will had terminated some of the dunes busters, I was even more uncomfortable. The next maneuver was a series of jerky turns along the rim of the smaller dunes. The lead driver headed across the top edge of the dune and then quickly dropped down the face of the dune before hitting the gas peddle hard to get the truck back on the top of the dune. We repeated the maneuver again before our stomachs recovered. Both times I was certain we would tumble down the face of the dune if, for some reason, we lost power. The stunt reminded me of surfers riding along the face of a wave and swinging their boards back on top of the wave's crest before dropping down into the curling tube.

I was close to losing what little breakfast I had eaten when the lead truck stopped and Ali hopped out with his falcon. Untying the bird's blindfold, Ali lifted his arm, and the bird took off like a rocket.

"Da Rabbit, da Rabbit!" Abdulrahman cried out, doing his best imitation of Taz, the Looney Tunes' Tasmanian devil. It was just another of those strange paradoxes that one finds in Arabia—boys who learned English watching American cartoons yet practice the age-old art of falcon hunting.

Ali jumped back in the lead truck and off they went in pursuit of the bird. It was a mad dash by all of the trucks to follow the bird. Over dunes and through the dekaka brush they sped after the bird while trying to avoid hitting the other trucks. During the chase, I was amazed that there were no collisions. The drivers seemed to be watching the bird chase the rabbit and nothing else.

We repeated this wild technique for finding rabbits a dozen times. Once it spotted a rabbit, the falcon took no more than five minutes to catch its prize. After each conquest, the bird politely turned over his catch for a token of raw meat. By ten o'clock, we had nine rabbits and a growing desire to get back to the shade of the tents.

Arabs seem to have a built-in talent for sleeping through the hottest afternoons. I had no such skill and spent six sweltering hours trying to doze off. I kept wondering how anyone could rest in such hellish heat. When the sun finally went down, the young Arab men rose for sunset prayer. They spread a rug and lined up toward Mecca. After their group prayer, I was in for yet another surprise. One of Abdulrahman's cousins stacked wood for a large fire. The camp had two four-burner propane stoves. I wondered why they wanted to cook the rabbits on an open fire.

I decided to ask why a fire was necessary on such a hot evening. "What's with the fire?" I asked.

"The fire is not for cooking. It's a friendship fire," came the reply. "It is the way of the desert. If you have a successful hunt, you certainly want to share your food with those who are not so fortunate. It pleases Allah, and it make us feel good to share what God has provided us."

"So the fire is a signal?"

"Yes, in the desert a fire can be seen for many miles, especially a large one like this. If a Bedouin family sees the fire, they will know we have meat and will come to be our guests."

"But what if we had caught only one rabbit? There are sixteen of us."

"It doesn't matter. Even if we had only a small bird to eat and we were starving, we would prefer to share the tiny meal with everyone within the light of our fire."

I didn't respond. I just watched as the boys started the fire. I wondered how living with the hardships of the desert and applying the teachings of Mohammed had given the Arabs a sense of nobility that was not found in the West.

Like clockwork, just as the rabbits and a large pot of rice were finished cooking, two Nissan pickups drove up to our camp. There were three men in each of the small cabs and a couple of younger Bedouin sitting in the back. As they greeted their Al-Dossary hosts, each man embraced those of the other party and rubbed noses as if they were long lost friends. As I later learned, the Bedouin and the Al-Dossary cousins had never met before. It was just the way of the desert.

My portion of rabbit meat was smaller than I had anticipated, but it was a meal I will not soon forget. Certainly, the joy of sharing what you have with strangers is more satisfying than the finest feast. It also gave me an opportunity to meet some genuine Bedouin who knew how to survive on the edges of the Empty Quarter.

Fortunately for me, one of the Bedouin was Fadh Al-Hajri. He was a real oddity, a nomad who spoke English. Through his tribal connections, he had been given a job at PAMMCO as a security guard. After working from nine to five for two years, he yearned to return to the freedom of the nomads. He said he never felt at home in a PAMMCO uniform, patrolling a housing unit. "Where could I keep my camels and goats?" he explained.

As the sky darkened, the air cooled, and it even felt good to sit around what remained of the friendship fire. It was not long before I told Fadh what was on my mind.

"Fadh, have you heard of a ghost called the White Bedouin?"

"Ghost? Are you kidding? Anyway, I have never heard of a genie story by that name."

I was beginning to expect that answer, so I persisted. I was learning that an investigative reporter has to be willing to ask many dumb-sounding questions to get one good lead.

"Well, have you ever heard of a real man that goes by the name Al-Mormon?"

"There are many Arabs named Al-Mormon. There is even a large tribe that calls itself the true believers."

I had heard that before and decided to stop my questioning. However, Fadh was not finished. "Perhaps you mean the old camel trader. He has fair skin and calls himself Al-Mormon."

I was squatted on the rugs like the others, but I nearly toppled over. "Yes," I said, "he has skin like a Caucasian. What can you tell me about this trader?"

"I have never met him, but my father has traded with him. My father says he is an honest man and breeds the fastest camels."

"Is he an American?"

"Now that's a question for the wind. My father thinks he is a half-breed Bedouin. Besides, if he were an American, my father would know it. You see, my father speaks only Bedouin Arabic, and I have never heard of an American who could speak Bedu Arabic."

"Does he live near here?"

"No one lives in the Rub Al-Khali, just around it edges. If he were from here, I would know him. I think he comes from the north and brings his camels to sell to the emirate tribes in Dubai and Abu Dhabi. It is a very profitable business, and many camel merchants come here from the north."

"Could he be from Tabuk?" I asked.

"I don't know. Like I told you, I have never met the man. It's possible though. There are many Bedouin tribes in northwest Arabia, and their camels are legendary."

"Is that all you can tell me about the man?"

"I am sorry. Alas, I know no more."

The course of the conversation turned back to typical Arabian subjects: How is your tribe related to mine? Do you know so and so? When do you think the rains will come?

Suddenly, the Arabic chatter stopped, and the Bedouin Fadh turned to me and said, "I remember one more thing my father told me about the fair-skinned camel trader. He said that he was so honest that he drove away the bad genie from the Empty Quarter."

"What do you mean by 'drove him away?' Was there an evil genie in the Empty Quarter?"

"Of course not. Our old people are superstitious. They had no electricity or telephones, only their old genie tales. Since they did not understand how things worked, they were afraid of everything. I'll give you an example, so you know what I mean. When the religious leader of our tribe first saw a bicycle, he called it the devil's donkey."

"You're kidding!"

"No, I'm serious. He really thought he had seen the devil's donkey. Even when the wind changed direction, our parents believed it had to have been either the will of God or an evil spirit. My generation drives trucks and flies in planes. We understand that there is a scientific explanation for all natural events. So my generation doesn't believe in ghosts, and none of us has ever seen a genie. When my father was young, everything happened because of ghosts, but today genies are only found in the stories of the old men. Yet to this day, my father believes that there was once a very evil spirit in the Empty Quarter, but it has gone away."

"He believes it left because of the old camel trader?" I asked.

"As I told you, my father is superstitious. My father probably believes the appearance of a white Bedouin is a good sign from Allah. So when we no longer experienced genies, he put two and two together and gave credit to the fair-skinned camel trader for ousting the evil genie. In reality, the evil genie is no longer in the Empty Quarter because he never existed."

"Do you think it would be possible to meet the old camel trader?"

"Not now. The traders bring their camels south when the rains come. Perhaps in November or December you'll find the old man in one of the camel markets in southern Arabia. But believe me, if you ever find him, he'll be a Bedouin, not an American. No American could survive in this desert, even if he has magic over the ghosts."

Chapter 14

Ephraimites: We Are All Arabs!

People only see what they are prepared to see.

Ralph Waldo Emerson

Stephen Markham

January 1938
Wadi Ifal, surveying site south of Al-Bada'

If Jan could only see Stephen now, she would never take him back. But that did not matter anymore. Besides, who was the oilman supposed to impress out here in a land that had never made it out of the Dark Ages? Stephen's beard now measured somewhere over three inches. On the cooler days of winter, he wore a strange native garb. From a distance, he was starting to take on the image of a pale Bedouin. Under his cowboy hat, he wore a red and white gutra headdress to protect his head and neck from the sun and cold wind. Draped over his shoulders was a full-length camel-hair coat, which the Bedouin lined with sheepskin. Working alone on the windy Ifal plain, Stephen blended well into the Arabian wilderness. The only parts of his gear that stood out were his surveying instruments, his Ford pickup truck, and his Stetson.

Today, he was working eighteen miles southwest of his base camp. He was about a dozen miles from the Gulf of Aqaba to the west and an equal distance from the Red Sea to the south. Stephen made a lonely figure on the wide wadi plain, especially since he was now working without the aid of Ahmed. The week after Christmas his translator had been reassigned back to the CALTOC main camp at Khobar. Stephen was already conversational in Arabic. Since exploration efforts were accelerating in the eastern province, CALTOC needed to steadily increase the number of its American oil workers. The new recruits sorely needed the young Bedouin's translation skills, so Stephen found himself living a solitary life.

He would just have to tough it out alone in a land full of myths and exotic tales. This did not bother him that much. Since his parents' death, Stephen had lived a somewhat solitary life on his grandfather's ranch. His grandfather was a good, hardworking man, but he never had more than a few words to say to him. So Stephen felt he could handle the isolation. Besides, he only had another six months left on his contract.

When he saw a growing dust trail headed his way, he knew it must be the comical Germans. Klaus and Gerhard arrived in their truck a few minutes later and announced their arrival by honking their horn and waving their hats. "*Wie gates? Wie gates es ennen?*" the jolly Klaus yelled out. "How are you doing?"

"*Ist gut,*" Stephen replied. "So what brings the two distinguished archaeologists in search of the local cowboy?"

Klaus spoke up first. "I ate all my ibex jerky you gave me for Christmas. It was *ser ser gut*! You don't want to trade some German language lessons for some jerky, do you?"

"Nah, the only Germans in these parts are you two guys, and you speak English. On your way back to Al-Bada', stop by my camp and take all the jerky you want. It's in a wooden box beside my camp table. And you, Gerhard, what brought you all the way out here?"

"I just needed someone to talk to besides Klaus the pipe organ. I love his belly laughs, but he could talk the whiskers off a cat."

"So let's talk archaeology," Stephen suggested. "Have you found Mount Sinai?"

"No yet," said Gerdard. "We're busy at a dig near Jethro's well. However, we're running out of time. We need to find the mountain soon, or our sponsor will withdraw his support. If that happens, we will be on our way back to Germany. We are working on a plan to sneak into the beni Ibrahim lands at night. As soon as it warms up a little, we are thinking about climbing over the mountains in the dark. Are you interested in joining us?"

"What's the hurry?" Stephen asked. "Give me time to catch up with my work and I'll find the mountain for you. I have permission to survey anywhere in Midian."

"Thank you, but like I said, our sponsor is an impatient man. We have received word that he will only support our research in Midian another three months. It's locate the mountain or pack up."

"Well, good luck. By the way, I'm working on a theory I'd like your opinion on."

"What ya dinking, mein Mormon Freund?" Klaus joined in. "You always have such curious ideas."

"Well, you're archaeologists, and maybe you can tell me something about the history of the tribes of Arabia. While I was in Al-Hasa I was told that the people who first settled the oasis came from Assyria. They were refugees from Assyria after the fall of Nineveh. I think some of the Arabs are from the lost tribes of Joseph. You know, the tribes of Ephraim and Manasseh. However, this doesn't seem right. Aren't the Arabs the sons of Ishmael?"

"Yesser, yesser. All der men with rags on their heads are the sons of Ishmael." Klaus laughed at himself. "Just ask them Ishmaelites. They'll tell you so."

"You know better than that," Gerhard interrupted. "Certainly some of the lost tribes could have found their way to Arabia. To begin with, not all Arabs are descendants of Ishmael. There were people living in Arabia long before Ishmael, and many other groups came here. It's kind of like you Anglo-Americans thinking that you're the real Americans because the English colonists formed the United States by revolting against their motherland. However, there were people living there before your ancestors arrived by ship from the British Isles. African slaves arrived shortly after the British. After the Revolutionary War, other groups came, like the Irish, Chinese, Italians, and our people from Germany. Yet, if you read an American history book, it reads as if the only real Americans are the descendants of the British."

Stephen listened intently as Gerhard continued the discussion. "Like I said, Arabia was populated long before Ishmael's time. The descendants of Ham, the son of Noah, populated the southeast shoreline of Yemen. The Arabs pronounce Ham's name as Yam, the root of the word *Yemen*. The word for *north* in Arabic is *Shem*, after Noah's first son. The Arabs believe Shem's people settled in the northern towns of Arabia. The people on the east coast of southern Arabia are believed to have settled there when the languages were confused. Joktan had thirteen children and eventually left Babel to settle in what is called Dhofar or Sephar in Oman.[1] To this day, the tribesmen along that coast refer to Joktan as their Great Father.[2]

"So you see, Stephen, there were many tribes already settled in Arabia when Abraham left Ishmael and Ishmael's mother, Hagar, at Mecca.[3] But then again, the book of Genesis tells us that other descendants of Abraham settled in Arabia about the same time as Ishmael. These would include Ishmael's half-brother, Midian, who settled Al-Bada', the village where we are living. The Arabian cities of Dedan and Seba were founded by Ishmael's nephews.[4] Later, Jewish tribes came to Arabia to settle in Khaybar in the north and Yemen in the south.

"If that's not mixing up the bloodlines of Arabia enough, think of this: the Arab tribes are divided into two super-tribes, the Qahtan in the south and the Adnan in the north. The southern tribes believe they are the pure Arabs and have more of the blood of Ishmael in their veins than the northern Adnanites, who have intermarried with tribes from northern areas. Adnan was also a descendant of Abraham, but there were forty fathers between Adnan and the great patriarch. In search of pasture and fertile lands, the Adnanites spread out of Mecca to Madinah, Dedan, Khaibar, Hail, Dumah in northern Arabia; to the Euphrates River areas of Kuwait and Basra; and throughout the borders of Iraq.[5]

"Since Al-Hasa is close to Kuwait and Iraq, it is quite possible the Adnanites migrated there and mixed with the town's founders, the remnant of Ephraim and Manasseh. If the Adnanite Arabs spread to Al-Hasa, I believe they would have naturally intermarried with Ephraim and Manasseh's tribes. And why not? They had the same basic religion, and both groups where descendants of Abraham. The same natural mixing would have taken place as the Arab tribes settled in communities in Syria and Iraq, where other Ephraimite groups continued to live after the fall of Assyria.

"Ethnically, the Arabs would have blended well with the tribes of Ephraim and Manasseh. Both the Arabs and the tribes of the sons of Joseph were half-breeds. Their common father was Abraham, and they both had Egyptian mothers. As I see it, your theory would be in harmony with history of the tribes of Arabia, Jordan, Syria, and Iraq."

"I always knew the Arabs were a bunch of half-baked cakes," Klaus said.

"What do you mean by that?" Stephen asked.

"Der Bible, good man. It claims that the tribe of Ephraim would mix its seed with the seed of all the nations.[6] Your theory makes sense in that Ephraim's blood is mixed into the Arab's. Not only have they mixed their blood with the Hebrew tribes of northern Arabia and Iraq, but, believe me, no group of people has wandered around the world mixing things up like the Arabs have. Therefore, if they are Ephraimites, then they have certainly fathered many little Ephramites around the globe. Arabs have been sailing to China since the time of Sinbad the Sailor. They colonized Indonesia and the Philippines. The Moguls in India have Arab bloodlines, just like all the nations of eastern Africa.

"The Arabs were the great missionaries of Islam. They took the sword of Islam and colonized all of northern Africa and then crossed over to Spain. For seven hundred years, the Arabs occupied Spain and Portugal. Finally, Isabel and Ferdinand drove the ruling Arab families from the kingdom of Andalusia in southern Spain. However, the Christian rulers did not exile the Arab commoners. Most were converted by force to Catholicism and never left Spain. That same year, Columbus sailed to the New World, and Isabel and Ferdinand introduced the Spanish Inquisition. For the Arab Muslims still in Spain, it was convert, leave town, or be burned at the stake. A convenient solution for many young Arabs was to jump aboard the first ships leaving port for the New World. That's the reason the ships of Spanish conquistadors were filled mostly with Arabs. The Arab migrants to the New World took wives from the native inhabitants and spread their seed throughout the Americas."

Stephen could hold off no longer. "Just a minute, Klaus. You mean to tell me that the Spanish who settled the Americans were actually Moorish Arabs?"

"That's right. You Americans need to revise your history with a good sprinkling of truth. Name any ship that sailed from Spain to places as far spread as Argentina and California, and you'll find that if it left from a port in southern Spain, it was packed full of Spanish Arabs fleeing Spain."

Now Stephen's mind was traveling at light speed. He remembered how the Book of Mormon said those who would come to the Americas after Columbus were fleeing from captivity.[7] "Thanks, my friends. You've really helped me understand the genealogy of the Arabs. But from what I read in the Bible, Ephraim would practice idolatry and be forced to leave the land of Israel. Remember the words of Hosea that state that Ephraim would be driven out of the promised land into a 'wilderness, and set her like a dry land, and slay her with thirst' (Hosea 2:3)?"

" 'A dry land and slay her with thirst.' Sure sounds like Arabia to me. It's the most hellish desert on God's earth," Klaus intervened with a loud laugh. "Arabia is a wilderness; you can't find a beer anywhere in this place to quench your thirst."

That evening Stephen sat by the campfire and thought of what Gerhard and Klaus had said. If it were true, then the seed of Joseph, through Ephraim and the Arabs, would have mixed with the people of Latin America and the seven thousand "Isles of the Sea" called the Philippines. If that were true, then the people of those nations would be of the house of Joseph and would be receptive to the gospel in the last days. *Oh well*, Stephen thought. *The Germans are probably wrong. Any Mormon knows that there are no Latter-day Saints in Latin America and the Philippines . . . are there?*[8]

ᴺotes

1. Genesis 10:30.
2. Al-Shahri and Ali Ahmad, *The Language of Aad* (Dhofar Salalah: self published, 2000), 30–35. Also see Rev. Charles Forster, B.D., *The Historical Geography of Arabia*, vol. 1 (London: Darf Publishers, 1984), 126–27.
3. Galatians 4:22–25.
4. Genesis 25:1–3.
5. Al-Mubarakpuri, Saifur Rahman, *Al-Raheeq Al-Makhtum* (*The Sealed Nectar*), 9–10.
6. Hosea 7:8.
7. 1 Nephi 13:12–13, 16.
8. In 1936 there were few members of the LDS Church in Latin America and the Philippines. Today, nearly half of the members of the Church live in those areas, and the members are not so much from the indigenous population, but from the Spanish and mixed-Spanish bloodlines.

Chapter 15

An Invitation to Die

To glance at the genuine son of the desert is to take the romance
out of him for ever.

Mark Twain, *The Innocents Abroad*, 1869

Stephen Markham
January 1938
Lands of the beni Ibrahim

Stephen had heard enough. Gerhard and Klaus had him convinced that Mount Sinai was to be found only forty to fifty miles due north of his camp, and his study of the scriptures convinced him that the mountain was still an extremely important temple for Mormons, other Christians, Muslims, and, of course, the Jews. His first day off, he packed a lunch and drove north along the back side of the mountains.

The trek was without road, but the going wasn't all that bad. Every so often, he passed over patches of soft sand, but for the most part, the terrain along the east side of the Jebel Al-Lawz Mountains was level and hard. He followed the flat valleys that ran north and south between the mountains. He noticed that the farther north he traveled, the taller the mountains became. By the time he was as far north as Al-Bada', he estimated that the mountains were over seven thousand feet high and still rising in elevation as he continued north.

The landscape was picturesque and peaceful. Granite mountains towered skyward to the north, while wind-carved sandstone cliffs formed the valleys' eastern borders. In each valley, he passed a Bedouin tent or two. He respected the privacy of the tribal people and avoided passing too close. He knew the Bedouin women didn't cover themselves with abiyas and veils like the town Arabs, but he understood from his many visits to their camps that the Bedouin still protected the privacy of their women. He hadn't passed these particular camps before, and he wondered if the children who stopped and stared at his truck in the distance had ever seen a motorized vehicle. *What peaceful lives these Bedouin have*, he thought. However, he knew the history of this land bore witness that the people who lived here had once lived more stressful lives. Jeremiah called the Arabs notorious highway robbers. The Bedouin not only raided the caravans passing along the incense route, but when times got difficult, they would raid the camps of neighboring tribes. He passed shepherds carrying nothing more than walking sticks for protection, even though the Bedouin told him they had killed the last lions in Midian no more than ten years before.

Learning about the lions of Midian gave Stephen a new appreciation for the real suffering Nephi experienced at the hands of his wicked brothers. Nephi wrote that they traveled in the wilderness three days before camping next to a river of water. The river emptied into the Red Sea.[1] Stephen calculated that the Valley of Lemuel must be in Midian, somewhere on the shoreline of the Gulf of Aqaba.[2] He recalled how Nephi wrote that on returning from Jerusalem with Ishmael's family, his brothers became angry with him. They beat him until Nephi bled, bound him in cords, and sought to kill him by leaving him in the wilderness to be devoured by wild beasts.[3] Stephen tried to put himself in Nephi's shoes that night, being bound and left in the dark wilderness. Did Nephi hear the roar of Midian's lions, the howl of its wolves, and the laughter of hyenas in the distance? *Man!* Stephen thought. *Nephi must have been frightened stiff. I'm sure glad the lions are gone.*

Stephen had traveled almost thirty-five miles due north when he noticed a tall, sharply peaked mountain about five miles northwest. It was a distinguished-looking mountain, standing out among lower mountains with more rounded peaks. However, the feature that got his attention was the mountain's unusually dark-colored peak.

Stephen stopped, took out his binoculars, and stepped out of the truck to get a closer look. The mountain's lower slopes were a lighter color that matched the granite of its neighboring peaks. The upper slopes were a blackish color, as if a fire had burned them.[4] *I bet that's our mountain*, he thought.

He scanned the lower slopes again and saw what he thought could be a large cave. Still, he was a long way off; it could have been just the shadow of an overhanging cliff face.

He could feel his heartbeat quicken, as he asked himself if that was the temple of Sinai. There was only one way to know for sure. He would have to drive over and see if he could find the monuments that were described in the Bible. Suddenly, he heard a shot from a rifle and saw at least a dozen armed men riding their camels into the valley from the north. As the camels galloped toward him, he wondered what he should do. These guys didn't look friendly, and since Stephen had no road to follow, the camels could easily outrun his truck. As the men closed in, Stephen said a prayer for protection. Showing no fear, he walked to the front of the truck to await the arrival of what appeared to be a raiding party.

As the gunmen arrived, they circled Stephen with their camels. These were not typical Bedouin. They were taller than most of the Bedouin he had met before, and each looked fit enough to handle a good fight. Their faces were strikingly handsome and their beards neatly trimmed. Whoever they were, they looked like a proud lot, not likely to be outlaws.

"Peace be with you," said the one who appeared to be the leader. "What are you doing here?" he continued in Arabic.

"I am looking for oil," Stephen answered in Arabic. "I have the permission of the emir in Tabuk to survey for oil in Midian.

I can show you my letter from the emir if you'd like."

"That won't be necessary. Papers or no papers, you cannot enter this land without the permission of Al-Ibrahim. He is the sheikh of our tribe and the emir of this valley. He is the only one who can give you permission to enter our lands."

"If Al-Ibrahim is the only one who can tell me I cannot enter his land, who gives you the right to tell me to leave?"

"I am Osama bin Ali bin Ibrahim. I am the oldest nephew of Al-Ibrahim and the captain of his troops. I speak for my uncle."

"Well, partner, I came all the way from the United States of America to look for oil, and I don't think you're going to stop me. If I need Al-Ibrahim's permission then take me to his tent. I'll ask for his permission face to face. I am sure he will agree. I am here at the request of King Abdulaziz Al-Saud."

"My uncle does not work for Abdulaziz. We are his allies, not his servants. There is no reason to meet my uncle. He will not allow a foreign infidel to travel in his lands. Please go no farther north. These are our lands, and they are not to be entered."

Stephen remembered how Timmy Cullerson had told him that there were no laws in Arabia, at least not laws like those in the United States. The law, Timmy explained, was anything that a local leader felt was consistent with his personal interpretation of the Qur'an. "Perhaps your uncle doesn't know why I am here," Stephen ventured. "I'm looking for oil. If I can find it, it will make your people rich."

"My uncle is not interested in the money of an infidel or anyone else. He is a spiritual man and doesn't value material possessions. Now leave, or we'll force you to leave."

"And if I refuse?" Stephen questioned.

The Bedouin leader who called himself Osama was not amused by Stephen's stand. He held up his rifle and said, "We are the beni Ibrahim. If you don't leave our land, I will kill you."

"Take it easy, partner," Stephen said. "I'll consult with the emir in Tabuk and come back to pay your uncle a visit." He then slowly returned to the cab of the truck, took one more look at what could be Mount Sinai, backed up the truck to where he could turn around, and headed back to camp.

Notes

1. 1 Nephi 2:6–8.
2. 1 Nephi 2:9.
3. 1 Nephi 7:16.
4. Exodus 19:18–20.

Chapter 16

The Footsteps of Moses

One of the gladdest moments in human life is the departure upon a distant journey into unknown lands.

Sir Richard Burton, explorer, 1885

Stephen Markham
January 1938
From Tiran to Maqah

The threat on his life by the beni Ibrahim tribe added an entirely new dimension to Stephen's Arabian experience. He had been living on the desert peninsula for over a year and a half, and besides the surreal experience when he'd blacked out during the sandstorm, this was the first time he'd felt a real threat to his well-being. He also realized that it didn't take a genius to know that the beni Ibrahim had something to protect besides rocks and sand. There had to be a sacred shrine in their land, perhaps the most important of all sanctified sites. Stephen believed they were guarding the mountain of God.

Aware of Gerhard's and Klaus's plan to climb over the Jebel Al-Lawz Mountains to search for the Sinai monuments, Stephen would never forgive himself if he didn't warn his friends of the threat of the beni Ibrahim. The American decided not to return to his camp but headed straight for the town of Al-Bada', where the Germans lived.

Fortunately, he found the archaeologists still very much alive, and as the oilman discovered, temporarily distracted from their quest to locate the real Mount Sinai.

"*Danke, fur der warning*," Klaus said, "but you know how the Arabs are. All show but no fight. Give our General Rommel a single tank, and he'll conquer all of northern Arabia in a week. We are Germans. We're not afraid of Bedouin riding camels."

"I would think twice about that. The beni Ibrahim didn't put on much of a performance. It was leave or die, and they weren't your typical Arabs. The ones I saw were a tall and muscular-looking bunch. Neither of you looks like you're ready to compete in the Olympics," Stephen winked, but his concern showed through his joke.

"Dear friend, they must have really scared you. They're just the big bad Arabs," Klaus teased the American. "Like them three pigs and the wolf."

"Laugh all you want," Stephen said, "but think about it. If they believe it's their sacred duty to guard the holiest spot on earth, they might very well put their duty before your blood."

"We do thank you, Stephen," Gerhard said, "but if the beni Ibrahim are guarding God's mountain, wouldn't you think they would observe God's laws? One of those is 'thou shalt not kill.' Besides, we've got something we need to do first. Our university sent us a book written by Sir Richard Burton. You know, that Englishman who searched for the source of the Nile. Sixty years ago, he was right here in Midian. Look at what he wrote." With that, Gerhard handed Stephen their copy of Burton's book, *The Gold-Mines of Midian.*

"Look what it says on pages 219 and 220," Klaus joined in. "Burton received a letter from one Charles Beke, who claimed that he visited a small village on the Gulf of Aqaba named Maqna. Beke discovered that the village was a place of pilgrimage for both Christians and Muslims alike. The villagers told him that pilgrims have been coming there since the Exodus. You see, they believe it is Marah,[1] the first place the children of Israel camped after crossing the Red Sea. Marah was where Moses took the branch of a tree and cured the bitter waters."

"That's nice, but why would my two archaeologist friends think Maqna is possibly a campsite of Moses?" Stephen questioned.

Gerhard took a map off the top of the bookcase and unrolled it on the dining table. "Look, Stephen. Maqna is thirty miles north of Tiran, and that's the place where Moses parted the Red Sea. Once in Arabia, the children of Israel walked three days before they found water. That would be a distance of roughly thirty miles, the distance from Tiran to Maqna."

"So what are we waiting for?" Stephen said.

"Breakfast!" Klaus said with an eager smile. "Spend the night with us, and tomorrow we'll get up and explore Maqna."

By nine o'clock the next morning, the threesome had arrived at the village of Maqna. The twenty-mile drive to the tiny fishing village was over a primitive dirt track. They were lucky it took only three hours. As their truck crested the last hill, they saw below them a storybook village consisting of mud huts with roofs of palm fronds. The village stood next to the bluest waters Stephen had ever seen. To the west, across the waters of the Gulf of Aqaba, he could see the Sinai Peninsula. On the Egyptian side of the gulf, he could see a mountain range. It was a beautiful day, and the scene was spectacular.

The ever-present trail of dust followed them into the village where the three men stopped their truck in front of what appeared to be the only shop in the village. *"Ameriki! Ameriki!"* shouted the children playing soccer in a field next to the small store. Within seconds, the children had mobbed the truck, like a squadron of flies attacking a potato salad in the park. The children climbed on the hood, jumped up and down in the pickup's bed, and even climbed on the top of the cab. Apparently they had never seen pale skins before. To the children, all Caucasians were Americans. The men, the children had been taught in school, had come to their land to make them rich.

Klaus turned out to be the children's favorite "Yankee." In part, the fat German got his large girth by snacking on hard candy. He was seldom found without a small bag of candy, but on this day he would lose a little weight. He gave away every last sweet in his candy bag.

Before long, an elderly Arab yelled for the children to leave the foreigners alone. After waving off the kids, the man welcomed the foreigners to his village. He inquired as to why they had come to his village of less than two hundred people. The westerners started to explain what they were looking for when the old man smiled and said, "Follow me." The old Arab turned and headed out of the village and up a hill above the shoreline community. There couldn't have been a more marked difference from the threatening welcome the beni Ibrahim warrior had given Stephen the day before and the sincere smile of this elderly man.

While following the Arab up the sandy hill, they noticed a small oasis on the right side of the hill. Date palm groves stretched about a quarter of a mile from the top of the hill to the beach below. Despite their guide's age, the three foreigners, especially the portly Klaus, had a difficult time keeping up with him. About two-thirds of the way up the hill, they turned right and entered a palm grove, where they immediately came upon tiny streams of clear water that formed an intricate network of irrigation ditches. The Arab said nothing, just waved the three stragglers farther upstream.

Near the top of the hill, they came to an opening. In the clearing was a shallow pool of water entirely surrounded by a three-foot bank of sand. The pool was about twenty feet across and maybe six inches deep. Cut through the west side of the sand bank was a narrow ditch that directed the water from inside the pool into the irrigation lines that watered the grove. "Here," the old man said. "This is where the pilgrims come to pray toward Jerusalem." He then walked into the pool of water and directed their attention to the narrow ditch that had been dug through the sand to free the water. "This is where Moses cured the bitter waters. When Moses came here, the sand banks trapped the spring water, forming a deep, stagnant pool of bitter water. During the hot months, the torpid pool would have turned green and foul. That's why Moses took a branch from a tree and dug a ditch for the waters to flow out. Once the bitter water was cleared out, the remaining shallow pool of water was fresh and sweet to drink."

"Where does the water come from?" Klaus asked the old man.

"That is the miracle of this place." The man lifted his robe and walked out into the shallow pond. He started counting the springs that bubbled up into the bottom of the pool. One by one, he counted them. "Twelve," he proudly announced. "One for each of the tribes of Israel."

Gerhard shook his head. "Do you know what that means, Stephen?"

"Sure, it's a sign to the children of Israel that the Lord provided these springs for them."

"True, but it means much more. You see, in Judaic symbolism, running water represents life. You recall that the Lord referred to himself as the living waters. Well, these springs have not dried up. You are looking for the tribe of Ephraim, are you not? The fact that these springs are still flowing means that the twelve tribes are still alive. They still exist to this day. Your Ephraim tribe is still somewhere out there, even if it's mixed with Arabs from Iraq to Timbuktu."

"That's what I've been trying to tell you," Stephen said.

"Yes, but do you know why they have mixed with the sons of Ishmael?" Klaus asked.

"How would I know that?"

"Well, all we know for sure is that the Bible tells us they will mix their seed with all nations. But I have a theory as to why they, some of the Ishmaelites, would have intermarried with the Ephraimites, and vice versa."

"Give it a shot," Stephen said. "I'm listening."

"Let's start with what we know. First, in the last days the tribes will be gathered and united. Second, the scattered tribes will be grafted back into the mother tree of the house of Israel. Third, we know that because Jacob's firstborn son, Rueben, sinned, his blessings (including the royal birthright) were given to Joseph's sons Manasseh and Ephraim. Joseph had a dream in which his brothers bowed down to him. Fourth, Jacob switched hands while blessing Joseph's sons, thus giving the royal birthright to Ephraim rather than his older brother, Manasseh. Fifth, we know that Ephraim will mix its blood with all nations. Sixth, we know from Isaiah 11:11 that Ephraim and Manasseh will be gathered from the Arab Muslim nations in the last days, as well as from the isles of the sea. Finally, like a good German family, God's kingdom is a house of order, right?" Klaus looked to Stephen for confirmation.

"That's what the Bible says, except the bit about the Prussian house."

"Well, that's the important part. The kingdom of God will need to be a house of order in the last days. Ephraim and Manasseh will have to stop hating Judah, and Judah must stop hating them. It also means that the patriarchal order will be re-established in the kingdom of God. But you see, the birthright of Abraham has been disputed ever since Abraham dropped Ishmael off in Arabia. You see, the Muslims believe that as Abraham's firstborn, Ishmael, was given the birthright, even if he was born of the handmaiden. Indeed, according to the law of Moses, they are right. Hagar was not a concubine slave; she was Abraham's wife,[2] and therefore, Ishmael was a rightful son, duly entitled to the birthright. Certainly Ishmael was given some kind of birthright, because he was promised that his seed would become a nation.[3] In fact, Ishmael had twelve sons who all became emirs in Arabia."

"You're a little on the long-winded side, Klaus. What's this all got to do with German family order?" Gerhard said with a touch of concern.

"Just this: the Bible gives the right to rule under the Messiah to Ephraim, while the Qur'an gives the same birthright of Abraham's seed to the children of Ishmael. If Abraham's two royal houses have intermarried, the product is a unified birthright."

"However, even with the birthright," Stephen added, "they still couldn't preside over the Lord's kingdom without the priesthood, which means they would have to come to Utah to receive the priesthood."

"Now, what are you mumbling about?" Klaus asked. "More strange Mormon doctrine?"

"That's right," Stephen said. "Modern prophets tell us that Ephraim will come to America with great riches from a barren desert. They will be crowned with glory by those who have the priesthood keys, the restored Church."[4]

"Well, if we're going to share our wildest thoughts, then let me tell you mine," interrupted the scholarly Gerhard. "Not only could the remnants of Joseph and Ishmael intermarry to unify the birthright of Abraham, they could also have a claim on the birthright of Egypt."

"That's too wild for even me," Klaus said. "Explain yourself."

"We know with pretty good certainty that Ephraim and Manasseh were princes of Egypt. Pharaoh made Joseph second in command of all Egypt and gave him Asenath as his wife. She was the daughter of Potipherah, priest of On. In ancient Egypt, the ruling families controlled both the political and religious orders, thus consolidating the major sources of power and ensuring their rule. Undoubtedly, Potipherah was either the brother or son of the pharaoh, thus making Asenath a princess of Egypt.

"Like Ephraim and Manasseh, Ishmael was a half-blooded descendant of Abraham and Hagar, an Egyptian. Hagar was a woman who the Jewish scriptures have very little good to say about. However, Abraham greatly loved Ishmael[5] and undoubtedly loved his mother as well. While the Jews refer to Hagar as the bondwoman, the Qur'an states that she was a princess of Egypt, even the daughter of Pharaoh."

"I see where you're going," Stephen interrupted. "So both Ephraim and Ishmael have a claim to the birthright of Egypt."

"What makes that so interesting is many scholars believe the Egyptians might have been given the priesthood and the temple rights by Abraham.[6] So, God's house of order will be one unified patriarchal hierarchy."

Notes

1. Exodus 15:22.
2. Genesis 16:3.
3. Genesis 21:13.
4. See Doctrine and Covenants 133:29–34.
5. Genesis 17:18; 21:11.
6. See *Faith of an Observer: Conversations with Hugh Nibley,* DVD, directed by Brian R. Capener (Provo, UT: BYU and FARMS, 1985).

Chapter 17

Firm, Steadfast, and Immovable

When my father saw that the waters of the river emptied into the fountain of the Red Sea, he spake unto Laman, saying: O that thou mightest be like unto this river, continually running into the fountain of all righteousness.

1 Nephi 2:9

Stephen Markham
January 1938
The Valley of Lemuel

While Gerhard and Klaus photographed and surveyed the oasis at Maqna, Stephen wandered to a secluded part of the grove, where he knelt down and thanked his Father in Heaven for the opportunity to witness a campsite of the children of Israel and for the knowledge of the restored gospel so he could appreciate the full meaning of this experience.

Even with a geologist helping, it took all day for the archaeologists to properly record the physical features of the sacred site, its flora, and the oral traditions of the villagers. Instead of returning to Al-Bada' that night, they accepted the hospitality of the old villager and spent the evening in his home. They learned from him that the people of the village called the oasis the Waters of Moses.

The next morning, the three men discussed their options. They were hot on the trail of Moses, and it seemed only logical to keep exploring. They reasoned that since Moses led the children of Israel from Tiran to Maqna, he must have been headed north. To the west was the Gulf of Aqaba of the Red Sea. Twenty miles to the east was Al-Bada', the town where Jethro had lived. From the Bible account, they knew that Moses did not take the children of Israel to Jethro's village. Therefore, the Exodus route must have continued north along the shoreline, so that is exactly what Stephen and the Germans did.

After twelve miles, they came to an abrupt barrier. Shoreline mountains rose directly out of the sea. From peaks 2,500 feet above them, the sides of the mountains fell sharply off into the Red Sea. Between the granite walls of the mountains and the sea was a narrow gravel beach no more than twenty feet in width. If the narrow shoreline was Moses's trail, then the three explorers would have to travel it the same way the children of Israel had—on foot.

Leaving their vehicle, the three explorers walked below the towering cliffs for four miles. Rounding the point of one of the shoreline mountains, they were stopped in their tracks. Before them was a breathtaking sight. Here was a Shangri-La-esque beach cove lined with palm trees and framed in a curtain of giant granite cliffs. The aqua blue waters of the gulf led to the opening of a spectacular canyon. The walls that formed the valley were no more than fifty feet apart, and each side towered thousands of feet straight into the sky. "Bravo!" shouted Klaus. "*Wunderball,*" Gerhard softly said in a reverent tone. Stephen simply marveled, "What is this? Look what God has created."

There was no further discussion. They all knew what they would do. The three men picked up the pace and headed for the canyon. As they reached the canyon's mouth, they came to the greatest surprise of all. There was a small stream of pure clear water running out of the canyon and into the Red Sea. "Stop for a moment, please," Stephen requested. "How far are we into Arabia?"

"You mean where Arabia begins at the northern end of the Gulf of Aqaba?" Gerhard asked.

"Yes, that is where the political and geographical wilderness started in the prophet Nephi's time."

"Who?"

"One of the prophets I told you about on Christmas."

"Sorry, I forgot about Nephi. We're about sixty miles south of the Port Aqaba."

"That's what I figured too. It's truly amazing!" Stephen said.

"What are you all excited about, mein freund?" Klaus asked.

"There's not supposed to be a river or stream in all of Saudi Arabia. That's what the CALTOC geologists told me. Yet here is a flowing stream that empties into the Red Sea from a canyon formed by mountains of pure granite. This canyon could be described as firm, steadfast, and immovable."

"What are you mumbling about now, Stephen?" Klaus inquired.

"This desert river is three days' journey by camelback from the frontier that used to divide the civilized world from the Arabian wilderness. Nephi wrote that his family traveled three days into the wilderness. Then they pitched their tents by a river of water."

"So?" Gerhard said with a puzzled look on his face.

"It's mind-boggling," Stephen pronounced. "I'm standing next to the river of Laman. This is the Valley of Lemuel! This was Lehi's home in the wilderness."

Their hike up the canyon was pleasant. The tall canyon walls protected the men from the rays of the sun, and a cool breeze kept the temperature mild. The floor of the canyon was slightly graded uphill, and its gravel bed made a perfect path to walk next to the running water. They stopped several times to drink the sweet water of the little desert river.

As they walked through the valley, Stephen reminded his German friends of the story of Lehi and his family. He explained the reasons the canyon was probably the Valley of Lemuel. He told them how Nephi wrote that they gathered seeds of every kind of fruit and grain in the Valley of Lemuel. Gerhard pointed out that all three varieties of date palms grew in the canyon. They found wild grain growing along the stream. After they paced off three and a half miles, they came to a small grove of tall date palms. They were the largest date palms any of them had ever seen. Hanging just below their fronds were large clusters of the whitish-yellow fruit.[1] At the feet of the palms, they found the source of the small stream—a spring of pure water. Stephen's heart seemed to jump. "What kind of tree represents the tree of life in the Middle East?" he asked.

"The palm tree," Klaus replied. "It has been the sign of victory throughout the Mediterranean region and the icon of the tree of life in Arabia and Iraq."

"Danke," Stephen said and silently tried to recall the images of Lehi's dream: a pathway up a canyon, a river of pure water, and a spring. This valley matched the imagery of Lehi's dream exactly.

A quarter mile later, the canyon's granite walls came to an end. The canyon opened into an upper valley about a quarter of a mile wide and a mile and a half long. They could see that the upper valley contained three large groves of date palms. As they came to the first grove of palms, they noticed that several shallow wells had been dug, yet no one was living in the valley.

Stephen noticed the ruins of an ancient encampment on the north side of the upper canyon. Scattered around the encampment were hundreds of pottery shards. Klaus immediately recognized that the pottery dated to the early Bronze Age, which he said started somewhere between the late second millennium and the mid–first millennium BC. Stephen could only smile, for he knew that period included the days of Lehi.

Gerhard and Klaus weren't half as excited as Stephen about the discovery of the canyon—that is, until they decided to count the wells in the upper valley. Stephen volunteered to count the wells in the grove farthest up the valley. Gerhard took the middle grove, and Klaus, already showing signs of exhaustion, volunteered to count the wells in the grove in which they were standing. Klaus found four wells in his grove, and Gerhard counted five in the middle grove. Nine, they summed, as they anxiously waited for Stephen to report his count. "Could it be?" they prayed.

As Stephen approached, Klaus couldn't wait. "How many wells did you find?" he shouted to Stephen.

"Three," came the reply. And with that Stephen laughed as the two Germans started hollering and dancing around. Stephen thought they must have discovered gold. To the German Bible scholars, it was a discovery far more important than a precious metal or the crude oil Stephen was searching for.

"Stephen, this valley is Elim."

"Great," Stephen replied. "What's Elim?"

"It's the second campsite. We have discovered the second campsite of the children of Israel. Do you remember how Moses described the place they camped after they left Marah? In Exodus 15:27 the prophet wrote, 'And they came to Elim, where were twelve wells of water, and threescore and ten palm trees: and they encamped there by the waters.' "

"Brilliant," Stephen said. "You are set to become two of the greatest archaeologists of our time. All you need to do now is find where Moses struck the rock and water came out. Do you two know why there are twelve wells and seventy palms at Elim?"

"Of course, our good Mormon comrade. Like the Holy Book states, one for each tribe."

"That's only part of the answer. The twelve and seventy represent the priesthood of God, the Twelve Apostles, and the Seventy."

"The seventy what?" Gerhard asked.

"The Quorum of the Seventy. Remember Stephen, my Biblical namesake? He was one of the seven presidents of the Seventy during the meridian of time."

"Oh yes! You Mormons are very interesting. You must tell me more about the Twelve and the Seventy and your Valley of Lemuel. I find it intriguing that your prophet Lehi stayed in the same place as Moses."

"I'll do that, Gerhard. The next time I come to Al-Bada', I will let you borrow my Book of Mormon and Doctrine and Covenants."

Notes

1. Dates are picked when they are a light yellow color, almost white.

Chapter 18

Dead Men Tell No Tales

You can change everything in Saudi Arabia except wasta.

King Abdulaziz bin Saud

Jake Sorensen
Summer 1989
PAMMCO Personnel Records Office—Dhrahan
Week Six of Ten-week Internship

Even if I tried, I could not explain why I was so sure the old man who visited the PAMMCO dental clinic in Tabuk was the white Bedouin who saved Willy and Hank in the Empty Quarter. But the only way to prove my premise was to find out just who the old man was and what relationship he had with PAMMCO.

Getting permission to view confidential personnel files is hard enough in America. It is altogether another matter in a kingdom based on tribal politics. The only way business gets done in Arabia is through a system based on favors or special deals. It is called wasta, and the process dates back to the beginning of recorded history. Being a lowly summer intern meant I had zero wasta or personal influence, and wasta was the only way I could get into the files. Thus, I needed to borrow all the wasta I could muster.

I started my quest by asking for an appointment with my dad's friend Mac Pastore. As a PAMMCO VP, Mac was the only person I knew who could possibly have enough executive wasta to get me permission to see the personnel files. When I asked Mr. Pastore for his help, he seemed perplexed by my desire to research through the old files for the character Al-Mormon. If he had not heard for himself the strange Empty Quarter yarn from the two Irishmen, I am sure he would have dismissed me as a college boy nutcase. But thanks to old Willy and Hank's spooky tale of the gruesome monster and their miraculous rescue by the White Bedouin, Mac seemed to have just enough curiosity to support my expedition into the old personnel files. It didn't hurt my case when I told Mr. Pastore about the visit I had to the talkative dentist who treated an old American Bedouin in Tabuk and the meeting I had around a campfire with a Bedouin whose father had traded camels with a fair-skinned nomad called Al-Mormon.

Fortunately, Mac knew some of the history of the company and steered me to the CALTOC files. He told me that before World War II, the California Arabian Texaco Oil Company did some preliminary surveys of the Midian area west of Tabuk. However, the CALTOC surveyors found little evidence for oil, so the geological exploration was terminated. He explained that after CALTOC discovered the world's largest oil fields near Al-Hasa, four other oil giants joined

CALTOC to form PAMMCO, a joint operating company. Two decades later the Saudi government nationalized the company, and they helped setup OPEC. The rest is history, and the Tabuk area never made it back on PAMMCO's radar screen. Except for some gas fields that were discovered near Tabuk in the seventies, there were always more promising places to exploit, and that, Mac explained, was the way an oil company operated. "I'll see what I can do for you," Mac concluded, "and if you do find anything in the old CALTOC files, let me know."

Thanks to Mac's wasta, three days later I received a memo authorizing me to visit the old CALTOC personnel files. I immediately excused myself and walked over to the personnel department. Once in the records room, it didn't take long to find what I was looking for. There was only one American file for Tabuk that was dated prior to 1950. It belonged to one Stephen Markham. Written on the cover of the file folder was "Place of Origin: Utah." Eureka! He had to be Al-Mormon! I rushed to a desk in the records room and, with great anticipation, I opened the folder and read the inside cover.

Hired: June 1936
Arrival in Saudi Arabia: August 1936
Died: 1938 Tabuk, Kingdom of Saudi Arabia

"Crappers! This is the file of a dead man! Flipping flip, this guy's been dead for fifty-one years!" My hopes for my first major investigative story were crushed. There, staring at me was the death certificate of Stephen Markham. The darn thing was stamped, dated, and sealed by the Saudi Ministry of Health. The only other full sheet of paper in the file was a brief description of his hiring and transfer to Tabuk. Stapled to the inside cover was a small memo noting that all CALTOC records were microfilmed in 1979 and were now in the PAMMCO U.S. Services Company archives in Houston, Texas. Not only had I wasted my own time, I had made Mr. Pastore waste some of his wasta. All I had to show for it was a certified dead man.

"Perhaps Al-Mormon was a ghost," I said aloud.

Chapter 19

Who Do I Call Friend?

I shall allow no man to belittle my soul by making me hate him.

Booker T. Washington

Stephen Markham
January 1938
Surveying Camp in Midian

Stumbling upon the Valley of Lemuel was something Stephen had never dreamed of. All he had tried to do was warn his two friends not to enter the beni Ibrahim lands. He realized that the discovery was no accident; it was a blessing. Witnessing the very place where Lehi and Nephi experienced some of the most important revelations ever recorded was an omen to Stephen that God had not forgotten him.

Stephen knew in his heart that the Lord's handiwork had placed him in the Valley of Lemuel. It was just as apparent to the Utah cowboy that the intuition of the two Germans as to a connection between Mount Sinai and Lehi was no accident either. It was crystal clear to them that the campsite Elim of the Exodus and the Valley of Lemuel of the Book of Mormon were the same place. Before leaving the valley that day, the three explorers found several altars made of unhewn stones. What Stephen could not decide was who the altars belonged to: Moses, Lehi, or some other pilgrim.

On their way back to the village of Al-Bada', Stephen finally felt close enough to his German friends to bring up the question that had to be asked. "Why are you two so eager to find Mount Sinai? CALTOC warned me that there might be German spies operating here. So are you spies?"

Gerhard looked at Klaus, and Klaus at Gerhard, as if wondering how to reply to Stephen's question.

Gerhard started. "Well, we are not spies, at least not the kind you read about in novels. If we tell you why we are in Midian, will you promise to keep it a secret?"

"Of course. You can trust me. You're the only real friends I have. Believe me, I'll keep your confidence."

"Okay. To our knowledge, Germany has no intention of going to war with the Americans. Our nations are friends. The truth is Hitler has sent us here to find the real Mount Sinai!"

"But why would the German government be interested in finding Mount Sinai?"

"Because the other so-called Mount Sinais are frauds. Hitler has already had us survey them."

"Survey them for what?" Stephen asked.

Gerhard continued, "For the altar of Moses. It was the very place where the children of Israel purified themselves before God and became invincible in war. Once the Israelites had entered the covenant with God and exercised faith in the Lord, they could not be defeated in battle. It was at Mount Sinai that the Israelis became a covenant people, and regardless of the odds against them—so long as they remained righteous—no army could defeat them."

Klaus jumped in. "You see, Adolph Hitler is mad. He is preparing for an all-out war. Before he attacks France and Russia, he believes he needs to control Mount Sinai. The Jews, whom Hitler despises, believe they are the chosen people and a superior race. It all started right here at Sinai. The rabbis teach that the Gentiles are inferior because they were not at Mount Sinai. The Jewish Talmud says, 'When the serpent came into Eve he infused filthy lust into her. . . . When Israel stood in Sinai that lust was eliminated, but the lust of idolaters, who did not stand on Sinai, did not cease.' "[1]

"If Hitler hates the Jews, why would he care what the Talmud says?" Stephen asked.

Gerhard started in again, "There are two reasons. First, Hitler believes that if his Nazi soldiers can stand before the altar of Mount Sinai, they cannot be defeated. Second, Hitler is a racist, and he can't stand the thought that the Jews are a pure people and that the German race is somehow inferior. He is sick to the bone. He wants to believe that the Germans are a superior race. However, according to his own distorted view of the scriptures, he cannot make the claim of German superiority until they have entered the same covenant that the Jews did at Mount Sinai. With war about to break out any day now, our orders are to find Mount Sinai within a month. Berlin is very impatient with our efforts."

"Do you really believe that the Germans can become a super race by making a covenant on Mount Sinai?" Stephen asked.

"Of course not," Klaus said. "You know what we think of the Fuhrer: he's a blooming idiot with a deformed mustache. Hitler's religious ideas are satanic. He is outright dangerous. He sees himself as the modern Messiah who will save the world from what he calls 'the incarnate evil of international Jewry.' It is rumored that in 1920 the sicko lashed himself with that silly whip he carries around. Hitler preached that in 'driving out the Jews, I remind myself of Jesus in the temple.' In 1926 he announced that what Christ began he would complete. If that does not make you wonder what is going on in his warped brain, just five years ago he parodied the Lord's Prayer in promising a 'new kingdom will come to earth with the power and the glory. Amen.' He concluded his speech by declaring that if he failed to fulfill his mission, 'you should then crucify me.' "

Stephen was surprised that the Germans revealed their inner

feelings about their dictator. He was starting to think that perhaps the Americans should get involved in the coming war. "So Hitler is convinced that Mount Sinai is the key to his victory over other nations, and that he and his army must empower themselves with the glory of God at the mountain's altar?"

"Yes, Hitler is dead set on finding the real Mount Sinai," Gerhard answered. "He met with us personally and told us that it was imperative to the fatherland that we find Mount Sinai before the end of spring."

"So what are you going to do if you find the holy mountain and its altar?"

"Believe me, Stephen," Klaus continued. "We're taking as much time as we can to find Mount Sinai. Perhaps we are delaying the start of a terrible war. However, not finding the mountain will not stop a madman and a nation that has lost its sense of humanity. If we don't report finding the mountain within a few weeks, we will be ordered back to Berlin and thrown in prison. If we do find the mountain of Moses, we'll probably find ourselves performing some bizarre ordinance on the mountain for the Fuhrer and his top generals and then be resigned to a tank core bound for Leningrad."

"Will you tell Hitler where the mountain is?" Stephen pushed them for an answer.

"We are still debating what to do," Gerhard replied. "As Biblical archaeologists, we are dedicated to the identification of historical sites associated with the prophets. Locating Mount Sinai will help enhance the faith of all the world's believers in the One Supreme God and reinforce humanity's need to live by the commandments that were written there by the finger of God. That would include 'thou shall not kill,' an important message for the German leadership. Klaus wants to find the mountain and then defect to America. I am still indecisive. You see, Stephen, I was born from the womb of my Jewish mother; I am half Jewish. If I flee to America I might save my own skin, but I will doom my Jewish family. If I tell Hitler where he thinks he can possess supernatural powers, I might be able to save my family. On the one hand, I know that God would never allow Hitler to tap into the powers of his priesthood. On the other hand, if Hitler seeks supernatural powers at Mount Sinai, perhaps he can partner himself with the false God, the devil. Where there is great good, there is also great evil."

Stephen remembered well that he had received a deadly warning from the Bedouin who believed it was his duty to keep infidels from reaching Mount Sinai. Perhaps the mountain was already the property of murderous devils.

The following week, Stephen spent every evening searching the scriptures for links between the Book of Mormon and Moses. From its first author, Stephen found evidence that suggested that Nephi and his brothers knew that Moses had once occupied Lehi's camp in the valley that opened upon the Red Sea. The young Nephi used the story of Moses parting the Red Sea to illustrate principles of faith to his older brothers.[2] *Why would Nephi have selected the story of Moses and the Red Sea*, Stephen pondered, *unless they were standing in the place where these events actually happened?*

As Stephen reached chapter eleven of 1 Nephi, his eyes suddenly froze on the words *exceedingly high mountain*. He had read so many times before the great revelation that Nephi received while his family dwelt in the Valley of Lemuel, but he never contemplated what those words might imply. Nephi did not receive his great revelation in the valley. He was led by Spirit of the Lord to an "exceedingly high mountain"[3] where he was enlightened. Who else? he tried to remember, had received a profound revelation on the side of an exceedingly high mountain. Of course, it was Moses![4]

Gerhard and Klaus had already narrowed their search for Mount Sinai down to the Jedel Al-Lawz Mountains on the backside of Al-Bada'. That range, which was only ten miles east of the Valley of Lemuel, included exceedingly high mountains; indeed, the tallest peaks in all of northwest Arabia were there. It was all starting to make sense. Both Moses and Nephi had lived in Midian when they received their greatest revelations, and what other exceedingly high mountain could it have been if not Mount Sinai?

With the discovery of the Valley of Lemuel, Stephen now had the answer to his questions. He realized that the Nephites named one of their lands in the New World after a region in Arabia.[5] Their forefather, Nephi, had lived in Midian. It was the place where he married a daughter of his relative with an Arab name, Ishmael. Midian was where Nephi received the assurance from God that he would be given a promised land. He also received his great revelation upon the heights of Mount Sinai in Midian.

Notes
1. Abdah Zarah 22b.
2. 1 Nephi 4:2; 17:24–26, 30, 42.
3. 1 Nephi 11:1.
4. Moses 1:1.
5. Alma 24:5.

Chapter 20

The Appearance of Al-Ibrahim

Thy tribe, oh Bedouin, springs
From those lost tribes of Kings,
Once Kings in Israel.

Mathilde Blind, "Birds of Passage"

Stephen Markham
February 1938
Wadi Lehi

The American oilman had one foot on the Ford's running board to support the notepad that rested on his knee. He was dutifully recording that morning's surveying notes when he heard the muffled pounding of camels' hooves. He immediately realized that he had company, and it would not be the usual one or two men on camelback. He dropped the pad and pencil onto the seat of the cab and turned to see a small army astride camels galloping toward him. Stephen figured it was not a raiding party, for why would so many warriors be gathered for one lone oil worker? Even the truck was not worth this show of force.

To avoid eating each other's dust, the army of thirty to forty men formed a single line with a central core of four men holding flags, two on each side of the man at the very center. The two innermost flags were the green and white flags of the kingdom of Saudi Arabia. However, Stephen did not recognize the matching crimson and gold outer flags. It was clear that the rider between the waving banners was the chief. The direction the troupe came from was the land of the infamous beni Ibrahim.

The men were dressed in white robes. Their red and white gutra headdresses were wrapped around their lower faces to block out the dust. The chief was dressed in the same fashion, except he wore a bright turban instead of a headdress. His turban's color matched the crimson flags, making the leader a dashing sight atop a huge bull camel. The rest of the men rode female camels, the smaller but faster gender of the animal and the kind Arab warriors used in battle. No guns were in sight, but each warrior had his curved jumbia knife secured in his belt. Whether they were friend or foe, Stephen knew they were coming his way and there was nothing he could do but wait for their arrival.

Stephen lifted his right hand to greet the party, but there was no reciprocal gesture from the riders as they pulled up to the American. Only the man with the turban and two other men dismounted. Stephen recognized one of the men who walked toward him as Osama, the member of the beni Ibrahim tribe who had threatened to kill him if he entered their lands. But he was certainly not the leader of this group, for he and the other man walked three paces behind the man with the vivid crimson turban. Indeed, no one would doubt who was in charge of the party. The leader had a commanding gait, and his eyes took no prisoners. He had a hawkish Arab nose, but it was not out of proportion to his strong facial muscles and high cheekbones. His black leather belt held a golden jumbia, and he stood taller than the six-foot three-inch Stephen. His black beard was handsomely trimmed and highlighted with currents of gray. Stephen thought he was seeing a young Moses and knew right way that he liked the man.

"*Salaam Aleikum,*" Stephen started the ritual greetings as the chief approached.

"*Wa alekium salaam,*" the sheikh replied. He continued in English, "I am Al-Ibrahim, the emir of the beni Ibrahim. I have come to apologize for how you were treated by my tribesmen. We wish Allah will help you prosper in your search for what you call oil."

"Thank you," Stephen replied. "I am honored that you would come to greet me. I am sorry I have no tea or food ready to serve you. As you can see, I am working away from my tent."

Al-Ibrahim motioned, and a rider came forward leading a riderless camel. "No need to apologize, Al-Mormon. Today you are my guest. Leave your truck and ride with us. I will prepare a feast for us. Please join us; we need to talk."

"I would be honored," Stephen replied. However, that meant he would have to ride a camel, something he still had not ventured to try. He knew the Arabs rode sidesaddle, but the Utah cowboy felt more confident straddling the camel that was kneeling on all fours in front of him.

Settling on the wooden camel saddle with a flat pillow for a cushion, Stephen was thinking this was kids' stuff when all of a sudden the camel stood up first with its hind legs, flinging the cowboy forward. The only thing that stopped him from falling straight over the camel's neck was the saddle's notch, which caught Stephen squarely in the crotch. As the sickening feeling rose upward, he realized why the Arabs rode sidesaddle. But Stephen had no time to regain his equilibrium. The camel stood up with its front legs, throwing Stephen backward and reinforcing the lesson he had just received: A camel is not a horse!

The camel had a similar problem. Stephen was no Arab, and he had no idea how to guide the beast using a combination of cane swats, a harness, and leg pressure on the camel's neck. After Stephen's camel had circled twice in the same place, two of the beni Ibrahim tribesmen took mercy on the humbled cowboy and decided to ride beside Stephen. The oilman appreciated the gesture and tipped his cowboy hat to both his escorts. Within five minutes, Stephen had adapted to the stride of the camel and settled in for a ride up the valley to the north. He soon switched to sidesaddle and thought to himself how good it felt to be back in the saddle.

The beni Ibrahim warriors and the lone American rode in a similar order as before. The oilman and his camel were wedged about halfway between the emir in the middle of the group and what appeared to be the youngest member in the party, a teenager riding on the far right. Apparently there was a defined pecking order on both flanks of the emir, and the honored guest fit somewhere in the middle. Within ten minutes the entire group turned west and headed up a rocky canyon with Al-Ibrahim leading the way up a narrow, but well-beaten, camel trail. The camels now formed a single-file line to move up the path. Stephen realized that he didn't have to steer the beast. His camel seemed quite content to simply follow the camel ahead of it. Like an ancient wandering caravan laden with incense and gold, the camel train climbed about a mile before coming to a pleasant little oasis with a pool of spring water and a grassy area no more than a quarter acre in size. Here the men disembarked and shackled the camels.

On the banks of the pond, Stephen noticed wild spearmint growing. The mint smelled refreshing after the dusty camel ride. A little farther up the canyon, he heard the bah-ing of some goats that had been designated for lunch. One by one, the men untied the goats from the bushes they had been secured to and took each animal a few paces from the others. To Stephen's surprise, even Al-Ibrahim took one of the goats. He heard the emir softly utter the traditional prayer of thanks to Allah. Then the emir performed the required Islamic slaughter, cutting the goat's throat and holding the animal gently until all the blood drained from its body. Stephen remembered that eating blood was prohibited in the Old and New Testaments.[1]

Stephen's host then left the goat with one of the men. He took a stick and dug in the sand four shallow earthen pits about three feet in radius and six inches in depth. In the meantime, other beni Ibrahim warriors had gathered branches from dead bushes and piled them in the pits the emir had dug. With some dry grass for kindling, Al-Ibrahim started a fire in each pit.

Being the guest of a Bedouin tribe, Stephen knew that it was out of place to even ask to help, so he sat by the small pool and watched the feast unfold. Al-Ibrahim was obviously all-powerful in the sight of his tribesmen, yet, as if by instinct, the chief took on the role of servant and head cook for his kinsmen and company. The emir seemed to be doing most of the work himself. There was nothing Stephen could do but enjoy the hospitality of Al-Ibrahim, a legacy that had been handed down to the emir by his Bedouin forefathers.

The men hung the slaughtered goats from the branches of an acacia tree. Then they skinned and butchered each animal. The heads were removed and buried. The stomachs and pancreases were removed and left for wild animals to eat. The remaining organs and meat were cut into small pieces and put into large *kapsa* pans (two-and-a-half-foot-wide pans with a depth of about four inches). The pans reminded Stephen of giant pie tins.

As the fire in the pits reduced the dried branches to glowing coals, one of the Bedouin young men placed five teapots on top of the coals in one of the pits and placed traditional *ghi'* bags of yellow tea in the pots. Stephen noticed that a sixth pot was placed next to the others, but no tea was added. Instead, Stephen was greatly relieved when the young man cut some of the wild spearmint and placed it in the last pot. This would be a goat grab (a surprisingly accurate term for the feast they were about to partake of) in compliance with the Word of Wisdom.

Next, the ever-busy Al-Ibrahim took some rock salt from a bag, placed it on a flat rock, and ground it with a smooth stone into small salt crystals. The emir seemed to have endless energy. As he worked, he started chatting with the American. He seemed to have already learned just about everything there was to know about Stephen. He knew where he was from, how long he had worked for the oil company, that he had no real family waiting for him back in America, and even that he was a Christian who other Christians called a Mormon. It was not hard for Stephen to figure out where Al-Ibrahim had gotten his information; it must have been from Ahmed's father. So thorough was the emir's intelligence gathering that he knew both Stephen's real name and the one the emir of Al-Hasa had labeled him with, Al-Mormon.

For Stephen's part, he learned that this noble Bedouin's full name was Ibrahim Yousif bin Al-Mansour bin Al-Ibrahim and that he had four wives and over twenty-five children. He had led the tribe since his father's death, when Al-Ibrahim was still a teenager.

The young man in charge of the teapots presented Stephen with a cup of spearmint tea, confirming that there was little Ahmed's father had not told Al-Ibrahim about his guest. As the cowboy enjoyed the spearmint tea, the men brought Al-Ibrahim the goat meat, now cut into small pieces. The host switched his focus from the conversation to the fires. They were now completely reduced to coals. Using the stick, the emir spread the glowing embers into small circles. The fire had been built from small branches, not large pieces of wood, so the coals had a low temperature. Ibrahim rubbed each piece of meat in the ground salt crystals and then placed the meat directly on the coals. After all the meat had been positioned on the coals, the Bedouin emir turned the kapsa pans upside down and placed them over the meat. Then each kapsa pan was covered with more coals, and the men of the tribe stacked more branches on top of the pans and started the branches on fire. *Quite clever*, Stephen thought, *a wilderness oven that cooks the meat from bottom up and top down.*

On a sandy, level area near the pool of water, the teenage warrior rolled out several Persian carpets. While the meat cooked, one of the older tribesmen sounded the Muslim call to prayer, and one by one the beni Ibrahim men formed into lines facing Mecca. Once the men assembled, the emir led the prayer. Stephen wondered just how far to the south the holy city was. During the pilgrimage weeks, he noticed caravan after caravan, as well as thousands of pilgrims on foot, struggling through the punishing desert on their way to sacred Muslim cities. He figured there must be hundreds of thousands of pilgrims that gathered for the pilgrimage, called the *Hajj*, each year.

As soon as the prayer was finished, the energetic Al-Ibrahim dug five more pits, these being somewhat smaller than the ones used to cook the meat. He ordered that fires be built in the pits. As Stephen watched, Al-Ibrahim took another kapsa pan and started mixing water with a batter that consisted of only white flour and rock salt. The emir worked the dough into what looked like five one-inch-thick pizza crusts. As the flames died low, he put each of the five cakes directly on the coals and covered the sides and top of the each cake with coals from the fire. Buried beneath an oven of embers, each flat bread was left to bake.

Witnessing this sight, Stephen remembered that Elijah was fed the same bread when the Prophet made his pilgrimage to Mount Sinai. In 1 Kings 19:4–6, Stephen had read how the exhausted and hungry prophet "sat down under a juniper tree: and requested for himself that he might die; and said, It is enough; now, O Lord, take away my life; for I am not better than my fathers. And as he lay and slept under a juniper tree, behold, then an angel touched him, and said unto him, Arise and eat. And he looked, and, behold, there was a cake baken on the coals, and a cruse of water at his head."

This Bible story had never made sense to Stephen. Why would a heavenly angel appear and then perform the laborious duties of a Bedouin housewife? Experiencing firsthand Arabian hospitality, he could see how the identity of the person who fed Elijah in the wilderness could be another example of how the Bible has been misinterpreted. Over the centuries, he reasoned, there have been hundreds of translations and transcriptions of the Bible, resulting in numerous errors. In 1 Kings 17:4, the text states that ravens fed the prophet Elijah. This sounded disgusting and was one of those hard-to-believe stories of the Old Testament. Why would the Lord have birds bring food to a prophet while he was traveling in a land where people lived? Having learned Arabic, he knew that the Arabic word for raven is very close to the word for Arab. Indeed, Stephen knew that when writing the two words, only a single dot distinguished them from one another. He was certain that the Bible should read, "I have commanded the Arabs to feed thee there."[2] Stephen was certain that the angel who fed Elijah was an earthly angel, even an Arab Bedouin who had the tradition of baking bread directly on coals. *Perhaps that angel,* Stephen mused, *was an ancestor of Al-Ibrahim, the man who now rules the wilderness around Mount Sinai.*

As the coals faded atop the makeshift goat ovens, Al-Ibrahim recruited the others to help uncover the upside-down kapsa pans. Once they had been exhumed, Al-Ibrahim lifted away each pan to reveal steaming chunks of cooked meat still resting on coals. As if completely oblivious to the heat of the sizzling meat, the emir flipped the pans over and reached down to pick up the perfectly roasted goat meat with his bare hands and place them in the pans.

Next, Al-Ibrahim used a stick to brush away the coals from above and around the sides of each cake of bread. The men took each cake of bread and, using smooth stones, rubbed the cakes until all the black cinders were removed. Once the primitive cleansing was completed, the bread cakes were put on top of an empty flour bag and placed in the center of the rugs alongside the pans of goat meat.

As the tribesmen slowly gathered to the rugs, Al-Ibrahim invited the American to sit next to him. Everyone sat cross-legged on the rugs. There was a teacup for each man, pans full of goat meat, and a flour bag stacked high with freshly baked bread cakes. The only thing that seemed to be missing was utensils.

Placed on the rug between Al-Ibrahim and Stephen was a tin of something very foul looking. It was a mixture of thick goat yogurt, goat fat, and a few goat hairs that somehow found their way into the muck. Al-Ibrahim saw that Stephen was perplexed as to what to do with the mixture, so he smiled, took a piece of bread, and dipped it in the tin. Stephen followed suit but did not smile. It tasted like Crisco, sour milk, and cat whiskers all in one mouthful!

While Stephen was trying to force down the greasy bread, a tribesmen across the rug from him took a piece of goat liver and threw it at him. The liver landed on the rug only inches in front of him. Stephen did not know what to do. A man had just thrown a piece of meat at him! Was it an insult? Not knowing what to do, Stephen ignored the liver. However, the problem didn't go away. A minute later, another man threw a piece of meat at him. Again the meat landed on the rug in front of him. Stephen decided to look to Al-Ibrahim for guidance.

Al-Ibrahim sensed Stephen's dilemma. "The men honor you. When they find a choice piece of meat, they give it to you in a gesture of hospitality."

Stephen thanked the man and then took the goat liver. *Good choice*, Stephen thought. *There's nothing like goat liver to wash away the taste of Crisco yogurt.* But even after the goat liver, his mouth still tasted like he had brushed his teeth with a hairbrush and Brylcream. Fortunately, the goat meat was as delicious as the spread for the bread was foul.

As they ate, Stephen was able to carry on a conversation with Al-Ibrahim. He found the sheikh to be an intelligent man despite his lack of a western-style education.

"So tell me, my American friend, when do you think the war in Europe will break out?" the emir asked.

Stephen was surprised that this nomadic desert chief enjoyed discussing world affairs. "I am not sure, but I pray that America will not get pulled into it. We already had to settle one war for them."

"I fear dark clouds are forming over our world, and America is too influential a nation to stay out of the coming conflict. I pray to Allah that the Arabian desert stays peaceful. I have seen enough warfare in my lifetime just among the Arab tribes. The last thing we need is violence imposed on us from outside. Believe me, the evil one has kept the Arabs fighting each other ever since Adam and Eve. Living in the desert is hard, so the tribes fought over the few areas that are good for grazing sheep and planting crops. This is why I love our King Abdulaziz. He is a strong and fair man who does not tolerate Arabs fighting Arabs. Since he became our king, there has been peace in the desert. From now on, I will pray that America stays out of the war."

"That's also my prayer. I do not believe in killing another man unless I am defending my homeland, and Europe is a heck of a long ways from Utah. However, this Hilter fellow is crazy, and someone needs to stop him. From what I hear on the BBC, Adolph Hitler is no angel."

"Do you have a radio?" the emir asked.

"Yes. It's a CALTOC issued short wave. At night the signal is clear enough I can listen to London."

"That is one thing I need to purchase. Then I could hear the Arabic news from Cairo. But how can you operate it without electric power?"

"I also have a small CALTOC generator, and each month they send me gasoline for the truck and the generator."

"Then you must promise me that you will take careful notes from the British radio and share them with me. I love our life in the desert, but the one thing I miss more than anything is news from the outside world. Please, Mr. Stephen, take notes, and every so often I will meet with you so you can tell me the latest news."

Stephen told the sheikh everything he knew about the problems in Europe. However, the conversation quickly turned to religion and family, the two most important subjects to Mormons and Muslims. They laughed about the challenges and joys the emir faced by being a father of twenty-five and a husband to four wives. The emir asked Stephen if he was married. That gave Stephen a chance to test his theory about how Al-Ibrahim knew so much about him.

"Didn't Abu Ahmed tell you I have no wife?" Stephen replied.

Al-Ibrahim smiled. "I paid my friend Abu Ahmed well for his information. He should have told me how many wives you had."

"How many? I am an American. We can only have one wife."

"But, Al-Mormon, doesn't your religion allow you many wives?"

Stephen was taken aback by what the Bedouin chief said. The wilderness sheikh knew details about the Mormon faith. Stephen remembered the night when the mysterious men came to his camp, just wanting to see what a Mormon looked like. They were Al-Ibrahim's men. "Well, we did practice plural marriage for a short time," Stephen explained.

"Good, then whether you are married or not, you should consider marrying one of my daughters." Apparently Al-Ibrahim had a daughter that was proving hard to place, for he made his new friend a special offer. "You can have my daughter. However, you must marry her our way. You cannot see her until the wedding night," he said with a loud laugh.

Stephen was a risk-taker, evidenced by the fact that he was living alone in Midian, but these odds were just too high. He diverted the question. "I thought Muslim women were not permitted to marry outside of their faith."

"That is correct, and it is best that way." Clearly the sheikh was enjoying himself at the expense of his guest, but Stephen didn't mind.

"So how is it that you know so much about my religion?" Stephen asked.

"I have been waiting for you. I always hoped that I would meet a Mormon before I died. Alhamdellah, Allah has answered my prayers. The coming of the Mormons could mean that the last days are here." Stephen gave a puzzled look. "You see, Al-Mormon, I might live in the desert and sleep on the floor of my tent, but I know about the religions of the world. I have a Christian Bible and I have read the essays of Socrates, Aristotle, and Plato. Not only am I the governor of my people, I am also their imam. I traveled to Cairo several times and spent months studying with the great Sunni ulemas of Alshams University. It was there that I was told about the American Christians who follow the principles of Islam."

"I'm sorry, sir, but I don't think we follow the principles of Islam. Mormons are Christians."

"You are right; you are of the People of the Book. You believe that the Prophet Essa, the man you call Jesus, is the Son of God. However, you behave according to Muslim ways and not the immoral ways of most Christians."

"What do you mean by the People of the Book?"

"When the angel Gabriel recited the chapters of the Qur'an to the Prophet Mohammed, peace and prayers be upon him, he told the Prophet that the People of the Book were the Christians and the Jews. The book, he explained, was the Bible. And you believe in the Bible, don't you?"

"Yes, but only as far as it is translated correctly, and over the centuries, it has become corrupted by many errors in translation."

"As I said, Al-Mormon, you believe the same as we do. The Angel Gabriel told the Prophet that the Bible has had many truths taken from it by wicked men, and that is why the Qur'an was given—to restore what was taken from the Bible. Doesn't your Book of Mormon do the same thing?"

"Yes, we believe it does just that," Stephen replied.

"And, like the Muslims, you believe in plural marriage, fasting, the paying of tithes, and, most important, you believe that there is only one supreme God."

"Yes," Stephen agreed.

"And, like the Muslims, the Mormons prohibit sexual relations outside of marriage. You teach your women to dress modestly. You forbid alcohol, coffee, tea, and the use of tobacco. All these sins are also forbidden in Islam, even though many of our people no longer follow all our principles."

"Sure, but that doesn't mean that Mormons are practicing the ways of Islam."

"You see, Al-Mormon, the word *Islam* means 'to submit yourself to God.' If the Mormons submit their lives to God, they are his servants. I am told that the Mormons do not just talk of religion or attend church once or twice a year. They live their faith, and thus, they submit their lives to God. We believe everyone is born a Muslim and that most people become lost because they live among the unbelievers. The Mormons abide by the divine rules. Be they Christians or not, Mormons are believers—true believers—for they follow Allah's laws. The Qur'an seems to have predicted that the Mormons would appear in the last days, and that is why I am so happy to meet you. The Holy Book states,

> Not all of them are alike:
> Of the People of the Book
> Are a portion that stand
> (For the right): they rehearse
> The Signs of Allah all night long.
> And they prostrate themselves In Adoration.
> They believe in Allah
> And the Last Day;
> They enjoin what is right,
> And forbid what is wrong;
> And they hasten in (all) good works:
> They are in the ranks
> Of the righteous.
> Of the good that they do,
> Nothing will be rejected of them;
> For Allah knoweth well those that do right.
> (Qur'an 3:113–15)

"Have you memorized the entire Qur'an by heart?" Stephen asked.

"Yes, I know every verse that was sent down to the holy Prophet."

"Well, those verses are very interesting," Stephen said to the emir. "Do you mean to tell me that all Muslims believe that the

Mormons are the People of the Book who will follow God's laws and believe in the last days?"

"Isn't the name of your religion The Church of Jesus Christ of Latter-day Saints? Don't you see that Muslims and Mormons follow the same reflective way of life? Don't you feel it in your heart, Al-Mormon?" Al-Ibrahim pressed Stephen for an affirmative answer.

"I am not sure," Stephen said. "However, I did have a strange experience when I first came to Saudi Arabia. The customs agent hugged me and called me his brother. For some reason, I had the sensation that he was telling me the truth. But you didn't answer my question. Do all Muslims believe that the Qur'an predicts the coming forth of the Mormon faith?"

"No, they don't. It is only the theory of the *ulema,* or religious scholar, who taught me in Cairo. It is also my hope. I have prayed for the day when Christians and Muslims will join together in the ranks of righteousness. I believe that the Mormons could be the bridge Allah has sent to bring the world's two greatest religions together."

The Bedouin prince and the Mormon cowboy spent the afternoon discussing the common threads of their religions. They realized there were many differences, but each was pleased to learn that there were also many things their religions had in common. This was especially true for the nomadic emir who had been waiting for years to sit with a Mormon and discuss with him his theory that the Latter-day Saints were the People of the Book that would believe in the last days.

Unfortunately, the hours passed too quickly, and the time came for the two men to depart for their camps. But Stephen had one last question for Al-Ibrahim.

"You must tell me, friend. Is the mountain of Musa, or Moses, found in your land?"

"I can talk with you about many things, Stephen, but of that I cannot. We forbid all foreigners from traveling in a certain part of our land, and that is all I am permitted to say."

"If Mount Sinai is in your land, then all righteous people should be able to visit it and worship Allah on its slopes."

"Of course, Al-Mormon, but as you know, most people are not righteous. They would abuse that which is sacred. I am sure you don't let everyone into the beautiful temples you talked about. That is all I can say about it."

"But your men said they would kill me if I entered your land. Is that true?"

"No, it is not. The beni Ibrahim will not kill you, but we have the responsibility to keep foreigners from wandering into our land."

"I would not abuse anything or anyone in your land. And besides, I have the permission of the emir of Tabuk to survey all of Midian."

"That you might, but I am the law here, and I have been charged by my forefathers and my king to honor our inherited responsibility. Besides, Al-Mormon, I am not keeping you out of my land because you might abuse a sacred site; I am keeping you out for your own protection. Where there is great righteousness, there also lurks great evil on its borders. Where there is good to be had, there also Satan waits to harm those who would seek Allah. Please do not enter my land without an escort. Soon I will invite you to my tent. I will send my warriors to guard you. They know the way, and they know our ways."

Notes

1. See Genesis 9:4; Leviticus 9:4; 3:17; 7:26–27; and Acts 15:20–29.
2. *The Interpreter's Dictionary of the Bible*, vol. 1, Buttrick, et al., eds. (Nashville: Abingdon Press, 1976), s.v. "Arabians." John Gray, *I and II Kings: A Commentary* (Philadelphia: The Westminister Press, 1963), 338–39. Quoted in Daniel Peterson, *Abraham Divided* (Salt Lake City: Aspen Books, 1995), 55.
3. Qur'an 3:113–15.

Chapter 21

A Muckraker's Nose

I came across the Mohican tribes near New York and asked
them, "Whose descendants are you?" They replied, "We are of
Israel."

Joseph Wolff, 1845

Jake Sorensen

Summer 1989
Requesting Microfilm from Texas
Week Six of Ten-week Internship

It was discouraging, but I knew I had to let Mac Pastore know the only information I found in the CALTOC files was a dead lead. To convey the bad news, I decided not to waste anymore of our company time. We arranged to have lunch together in the camp's dining hall, where I filled in the PAMMCO VP on every detail of Stephen Markham's file . . . basically nothing. Stephen Markham's was the only file from Tabuk, and its sole contents were a death certificate dated 1938, a one page description of his 1936 hiring and first assignment to Midian, and the memo indicating the CALTOC records were on microfilm in Houston. "So you see," I concluded my report, "Tabuk is a dead end. Where do you think I should look next for the White Bedouin?"

"Jake, I thought you wanted to be an investigative journalist," Mac said. "Unless you get a lot more tenacious, you're not going to succeed as a reporter."

"What do you mean by that?"

"You have to keep asking questions. For example, what do you know about Stephen Markham's death?"

"Nothing," I conceded.

"Back in his day," Mac continued, "it was crazy times up in the Midian area. He might have been the only foreigner in the entire region, and if there was anyone else, they were probably English or German spies. In 1938 everyone realized war was brewing and sent out recognizance spies to prepare maps. How did Markham die? What happened to his remains? If he is not the White Bedouin, you certainly have found another interesting story for the *Moon Crest* magazine. That man was one of the very first oil pioneers in Arabia and, probably, the first American to have ever lived in Midian. Follow up on him; he'll probably turn out to be a fascinating story."

"You're right, Mr. Pastore. If I am ever going to be a muckraking reporter, I'll need a nose transplant. I promise you, I'll try becoming a real story sniffer. If I'm on the trail of a story that loses its scent, I'll learn to recognize the whiff of another promising lead and take up the new trail."

"That's the way, Jake. Besides, if the White Bedouin is a ghost, you might find that both trails lead to the same man. Let's not write off Markham quite yet. I'll put in a call to Houston and have them send over copies of all the microfilmed records they have on Stephen Markham. The next week's PAMMCO service flight leaves Houston on Friday. I should have his records to you in about a week."

"Thank you, Mr. Pastore. That's very nice of you. And believe me; I'll pursue this investigation until we know Markham's real story."

I left lunch that day realizing that Mac was a lot more interested in the White Bedouin than he had let on. I was beginning to believe he was convinced that Hank and Willy had really experienced a demon in the deep desert and had been rescued by a saint. And if not a saint, then a ghost.

Chapter 22

The Poetry of the Nomads

All that is best in the Arabs has come to them from the desert: their deep religious instinct, which has found expression in Islam; their sense of fellowship, which binds them as members of one faith; their pride of race; their generosity and sense of hospitality; their dignity and the regard they have for the dignity of others as fellow human beings; their humor, their courage and patience, the language which they speak and their passionate love of poetry.

Wilfred Thesiger, *Arabian Sands*, 1959

Stephen Markham
March 1938
Camp of the beni Ibrahim

March is the best month of the year in Arabia, Stephen reflected as he sat at his camp table and enjoyed a corned beef sandwich and a tin of peaches. Though his German friends might consider Midian a barren land, to Stephen the scattered patches of winter grass and the small, delicate wild flowers reminded him of springtime in southern Utah. When he was a boy, his mother would smile at him when he presented her bouquets of the wild flowers that he had collected. *Where is Mom now?* he wondered. *If she were still alive, what advice would she give me now that I have only a few months left on my contract? What is there left for me to go home to in Utah? And how can I go home to Richfield? I'm bound to bump into Jan and her husband every now and then.*

He had already saved enough money for a secondhand car and a down payment on a house, but since Jan dropped him last year, getting back to Utah had lost most of its meaning and all of its feeling. He was no longer embarrassed when the monthly supply truck came and it carried no mail for him. To be truthful, the only letter he had received since Jan's Dear John was a Christmas card from his sister the first Christmas he was in Arabia. The card didn't arrived until February. He could have written an old missionary companion or two, but what would he say? There was simply no way they could relate to what he was experiencing in Arabia, and besides, who wanted to hear about his lonely life in some far-off desert?

Honestly, since his dreams were crushed by Jan's rejection, all Stephen wanted to do was be alone and let his wounded heart mend. The last thing he needed was a stream of letters trying to cheer him up. Being alone was somehow numbing. He even joked to himself that he wished he could join the French Foreign Legion, but it was too late, he was already stuck in a desert with camels for company.

Stephen was so lost in his thoughts he didn't notice a small band of Bedouin approaching his site. When he finally saw them, they were close enough to be recognizable to him. The riders were some of the beni Ibrahim warriors who had escorted him to the lunch with Al-Ibrahim. Stephen wasn't alarmed, knowing that Al-Ibrahim had already honored him as his personal guest. Once they arrived, Stephen learned that the tribesmen had come to invite him to a feast that was being held by Al-Ibrahim. The emir was holding his annual poetry recital, and Stephen was invited to be his guest. *A poetry recital by shepherds?* Stephen laughed to himself. *You've got to be kidding. I wouldn't miss this for the world.*

After a two-hour ride on camelback, Stephen and his escorts arrived at the mountain encampment of the Bedouin prince Al-Ibrahim. His camp consisted of a dozen or so large goat- and camel-hair tents and several large palm frond corrals for the clan's herds of sheep, goats, and camels. Stephen could see that the camp was alive with activity. Boys were carrying firewood into the camp to keep several campfires burning. He could smell bread baking and mutton roasting. There were at least a hundred camels already tied to acacia trees next to the camp, and more riders on camels were approaching the camp. On the edge of the camp was an even larger tent than those that made up what appeared to be the family camp. The larger tent was at least thirty feet long and fifteen feet deep. It had only three sides. The wall of the front side of the tent had been split apart at the center, and it extended out from the corners to form a protected courtyard in front of the tent. Colorful rugs were laid inside the open tent and on the ground in the courtyard. Dark red pillows with orange, black, and white knitted patterns were displayed on the rugs for the guests to lean on.

Stephen and his beni Ibrahim escorts dismounted their camels. The warriors led Stephen to the large tent that was set up for the recital. The pleasant fragrance of a small campfire burning in the courtyard wafted through the tent's open side. Long-spouted coffee pots rested on the coals of the fire. Stephen was directed to sit inside the tent next to several Bedouin sheiks, who had already assembled from the surrounding valleys for the recital. Stephen recognized some of them, including his friend, the father of his former translator, Ahmed. The sheiks rose and welcomed Stephen with a firm handshake, kisses on each cheek, and a rub of noses. Although Al-Ibrahim had not yet made his entrance, Stephen felt close to all these proud and friendly men. He sensed good feelings directed toward him by these desert elders, and he settled into the expectation that this would be a very pleasant and memorable evening.

From another tent, Stephen could hear women singing, but only the men were assembled at the recital tent. Every now and then a timid looking young man in his late teens would enter the tent and its rugged courtyard, take one of the large pots of coffee from the coals, and serve the assembled men. Stephen learned later that this boy was Saad, Al-Ibrahim's oldest son, and in the absence of his father, it was his responsibility to make sure his father's guests were made comfortable. Another young Bedouin lad offered the audience dates adorned with fennel seeds. After the second pass of the refreshments, Al-Ibrahim himself entered and asked everyone to please follow him. The men rose and waddled in their robes like penguins to another area that was walled off by tent sidings. Within these portable walls, well-worn Persian carpets were laid out as flooring. Sitting on the carpets were at least ten large metal trays piled high with rice. On top of the trays of rice were roasted goats, heads and all.

By now Stephen knew the basic rules of Bedu etiquette. Guests were to dig into the rice and the meat with only the right hand. Guests were only to take pieces of meat from the part of the goat directly in front of them. If someone found a choice piece of meat and wanted to share it with another guest, he could just toss it in front of the person. Being the only outsider, Stephen could hardly keep up with the pieces of meat that were being hurled his way.

Stephen was amazed how deliciously the kapsa had been prepared from tent kitchens and open fires. It was the best meal he had eaten since the Black Angus steaks he barbequed on the last Fourth of July with his grandfather. By the time Al-Ibrahim announced it was time to return to the recital tent, there was very little meat left on the bones. The emir announced, "Men, we are finished. Let's return to the tent and hear the poetry you have prepared to share with us tonight. We shall leave the rest of the food for the women and children."

Stephen looked back at the bones and wondered just what there was left for the others, besides a pile of greasy rice and a few internal organs. *Oh well,* he figured. *It's a different world—no "women and children first" in this ultimate macho culture.*

As the men walked back to the recital area, Al-Ibrahim took Stephen by the hand and asked him to sit beside him. "This evening you are my honored guest. Please sit with me."

While the men had been enjoying the goat grab, baskets of apples, apricots, figs, and dates had been placed on the rugs in the recital tent and courtyard. Regardless of where one sat, he could easily reach the fruit. Al-Ibrahim must have had his men ride to Tabuk to purchase the fruit. Al-Ibrahim led Stephen to the center pillows in the back of the tent and motioned for him to sit down. As they did, several young men entered the courtyard and began serving the guests yellow tea. One small boy brought a pot of mint tea and placed it before Stephen. "That's my Essa," Al-Ibrahim said with pride. "He's my tenth son."

Al-Ibrahim asked Stephen how his surveying was progressing and if he was an admirer of poetry and song. About poetry, the

Utahn answered in the affirmative and then tried to show his appreciation for the art by translating for the emir a few stanzas of a cowboy poem. Al-Ibrahim smiled, but Stephen realized that his on-the-spot translation just didn't fly. The emir's smile meant he was being polite.

As they talked, Stephen noticed that a young woman entered the area where the men sat. She was holding a large incense burner. She was tall and slender for an Arab girl. Stephen tried to make out the features of her face, but the darkness of the night and the smoke from the incense burner veiled her. One by one, she stood before each of the men seated on the rugs. She waited as they inhaled the fragrant incense before going to the next person.

"Al-Mormon, she's my eldest daughter, Norah. She is almost as beautiful as her mother. She is as pure as she is beautiful. To be honest, I love her more than I love any of my sons."

"But why is she unveiled among all these men?"

"These are not strangers; they are the fathers of the beni Ibrahim tribe and our brotherly tribes that live around us. Norah can marry within these families. She is a princess of the beni Ibrahim, and her marriage to a son of one of these clansmen will form a powerful alliance. You might say I am showing her off tonight. She is already eighteen years old, well beyond the age when most Bedouin girls marry. By this time next month, I will receive many offers for her hand in marriage."

Stephen looked again at the young woman who was working her way closer and closer to where he was sitting next to her father. Suddenly, she lifted her eyes and saw Stephen staring at her. She blushed and smiled at the handsome American. *My goodness,* Stephen thought. *She is beautiful. She looks exactly how I imagine the Virgin Mary.* She seemed so innocent yet fair in the warm light of the tent. Her facial features were soft and similar to the Lebanese women he had met back at the CALTOC camp. Her black hair was long and straight and glowed by the light of the campfire. She wore a long purple dress that came up high on her neck and extended to her ankles, and covered her arms to her wrists. The sleeves were tight enough that she could wear several gold bracelets over them. What a jewel. Stephen needed to know more about the fate of this young woman. "So you will decide who she will marry?" he asked Al-Ibrahim.

"She's my daughter and a princess of the beni Ibrahim. Of course I will decide whom she marries. In our tribe, it's not like the people in Cairo who say they marry for love. Marriages among our people are for two reasons: to strengthen one's tribe or to bond two tribes in an alliance. Once the couple is engaged, they will learn to love each other. Of course, I would prefer for her to marry one of her beni Ibrahim cousins, but because of her importance as a tribal princess, I have not committed her to any of my brothers' sons. Indeed, I might marry her to the emir of Tabuk. That would be the very best thing for the beni Ibrahim tribe."

"You would have your daughter marry that old man?" Stephen gasped at the thought.

"Why not? Norah might not favor such a husband, but it would be good for her and her children. The emir of Tabuk is kind and wealthy and is related to the king. Such alliances must be considered, regardless of age."

"But the emir of Tabuk must already have grandchildren and maybe even great-grandchildren."

"Certainly. The last I knew, he had twenty-three children, but only three wives. In Islam he is entitled to one more, and I have heard that he is aware of Norah's beauty and is seeking an opportunity to meet her. Being a fourth wife shouldn't cause a Mormon concern."

"Perhaps it's not good that you know so much about my religion. You seem to have an advantage over me. I guess having your daughter marry an important emir is a blessing. She will make any man happy."

"A father can dream, can't he? Anyway, I am in no hurry to marry her off. She is my joy, and if I could have it my way, she would never leave my camp. I am guilty of constantly indulging her, yet she is not spoiled. Allah has blessed me with an extraordinary child. Every father should have a child like Norah. Stephen, why don't you give up your job with CALTOC, become a Bedouin shepherd, submit yourself to Islam, and marry her? That way she would not have to leave me, and I would have a camp full of blue-eyed grandchildren."

"You're not serious, are you?" Stephen asked.

"Of course not. First, you're not a Muslim, and no offense meant, but our women are forbidden to marrying infidels. Second, Norah is a girl of the desert. Your materialistic world would only make her miserable. She may be a simple desert girl, but she is the perfection of Bedouin womanhood. She can milk a camel, watch the sheep, weave Bedouin rugs, harvest wild herbs to cure the sick, and cook our Arabian food. I don't think she would be of much value to you in Outah." Stephen had to smile at the emir's pronunciation of his home state. The *u* sound does not exist in Arabic.

As Norah worked her way closer to the back of the tent, where Stephen was sitting with the chiefs, her beauty became even more evident. Her skin was the color of a creamy coffee latte and appeared invitingly smooth. Her features were delicate but firm, showing the breeding of strong Bedouin stock. The pupils of her eyes, highlighted by black natural powder on her eyebrows and lower eyelids, were like black diamonds sparkling in the light of the campfire. They were innocent eyes, yet they tempted a man to his core.

"Come, my princess," Al-Ibrahim called to his daughter. "Come here and sit with us. This is Al-Mormon. You have my permission to sit by him, but be careful, child. He has blue eyes, and if you stare in them, they will steal your soul."

"What?" Stephen protested to Al-Ibrahim. "Blues eyes can steal a person's soul?"

"It's just one of our old tales. Since the dark days of the crusaders and the blue-eyed Nordic invaders, the Arab people have suffered many broken promises from the Europeans. Sometime along history's course, the Arabs finally reached the conclusion that people with blues eyes couldn't be trusted. To warn their children to be careful around the people with blue eyes, they taught them that people with blue eyes could look into their eyes and steal their innocent souls. But don't worry, Al-Mormon, I trust you. Otherwise, why would I allow you to sit next to my daughter? Just keep your blues eyes off her."

"That's impossible for any man. She's too beautiful."

"A veil might work with my other daughters, but I allow Norah to get away with whatever she wants. As I said, I try the best I can to spoil her."

Norah heard the exchange of words between her father and Stephen and laughed as she sat down beside the tall American.

"Do you really think I am that beautiful?" she abruptly asked Stephen.

"Well, perhaps I was mistaken," the cowboy replied. "If I could look at you, I could confirm my earlier assessment of your beauty. But I cannot now. Your father believes my blue eyes will steal your soul. If he were as good a father as he claims he is, he should have covered you up in a veil."

"He could try to make me wear a veil, but I could still see your blues eyes through it."

"Let me correct you, my friend," Al-Ibrahim interrupted. "The beni Ibrahim are Bedouin. We don't veil our women, and we don't understand why the city Arabs do. There is no mention of veiling women in the Holy Qur'an. Furthermore, we don't believe that nonsense that blue eyes can steal a person's soul. It's only an old myth. For all I care, you can steal her soul, but just don't steal her heart."

"If that's the case, why did you have your daughter sit next to me?"

"That, Al-Mormon, is what I am asking myself right now! The men here must think I have lost my mind, letting you talk to our princess. Perhaps my need to be hospitable has caused me to go mad. Anyway, I am the emir, and Norah is a princess. It is good for her to know how to speak with foreigners."

"But, Father," Norah asked, "how can I learn to talk with foreigners if I am afraid they will steal my soul? I want to see his peculiar blue eyes under that funny hat. I have never seen a person with blue eyes, only a few goats."

"Please, you are both teasing me in front of the chiefs," came Al-Ibrahim's plea. "Of course you can look at each other, but behave yourselves. I will tell the chiefs that the American is teaching my daughter that ugly-sounding language called English."

"Do you want to steal my soul?" Norah sweetly asked the young American.

"If I stole your soul, where would I put it?" Stephen replied, still not looking the girl in the eyes.

"Within your soul. That would make us one soul."

Stephen was taken back by what he perceived as very forward language. *These Bedouin girls waste no time*, he thought. Then he realized that she was probably just thinking her soul would be taken into his soul through his eyes. She couldn't have been referring to the Mormon notions of marital oneness.

"No, that's not where I'd put your soul. I think I would put your soul in an oil lamp, like a genie, and only let you out when I needed the fragrance of pleasant incense. I would take off the lid, and you would pop out in a cloud of frankincense smoke."

"You wouldn't!" Norah gently protested. "That would be mean. My father says that the American is a Mormon and a godly man and a kindhearted boy. You can't be Al-Mormon. If you were, you wouldn't want to put little Norah in a lamp."

"I didn't say I wanted to. But that's where I would have to keep you. If I took you home with me to America, I would have to hide you. If I showed the blue-eyed men of Utah my beautiful Arabian souvenir, they would all try to steal your soul. You are too beautiful, and they couldn't help themselves. Yes, I would need to hide you in a lamp for your own good," Stephen said, feeling more than a little guilty that he was flirting with Al-Ibrahim's daughter.

"But Master of the Lamp, I would be a very unhappy genie. I love the light. I follow the lambs all day under the strongest sun and never faint. I must be free to follow my sheep and watch the green birds soar in the wind. No, you would not put Norah in an oil lamp. If you did, I could not see the blue eyes that made me their servant." As she said this, she looked straight into Stephen's eyes, and he looked into hers. What they felt neither expected. At that moment, they were one, as though their souls had reconnected after a lifetime apart. Stephen was certain that her dark eyes had just stolen a piece of his soul. He could never be the same, and Norah discovered that instant what the people of Cairo call love.

"Let's start our recital," Al-Ibrahim said. The great figure of a man stood up before his friends and recited the first chapter of the Qur'an. It was the traditional way of starting a formal meeting among Muslims.

> In the name of Allah, Most Gracious, Most Merciful.
> Praise be to Allah
> The Cherisher and Sustainer of the Worlds;
> Master of the Day of Judgment.
> Thee do we worship,
> And Thine aid we seek.
> Show us the straight way,
> The way of those on whom
> Thou hast bestowed Thy Grace,
> Those whose (portion)
> Is not wrath,
> And who go not astray.

"Thank you for honoring me by coming to my tent this evening," Al-Ibrahim stated. "Who would like to be the first to bring us pleasure through the words of our forefathers?"

Stephen was still tongue-tied by what had happened when he locked eyes with Norah. He could only smile, look at her, smile again, and then look away. That night, a passionate fire burned in both their hearts.

Before Al-Ibrahim had sat down again, an old gentlemen sitting just outside the tent stood and began to recite a poem from memory. He used all the gestures of a seasoned Shakespearian actor.

A Desert Encampment
The abodes are a desolate, halting-place and encampment too,

at Miná: deserted lies Ghaul, deserted alike Rijám,
and the torrent-beds of Er-Raiyán—naked shows their trace,
rubbed smooth, like letterings long since scored on a stony slab;
blackened orts that, since the time their inhabitants tarried there,
many years have passed over, months unhallowed and sacrosanct.
The star-borne showers of Spring have fed them, the outpouring
of thundercloud, great deluge and gentle following rain,
the cloud that travels by night, the sombre pall of morn,
the outspread mantle of eve with muttering antiphon.
So I stood and questioned that site; yet how should we question
rocks set immovable,
whose speech is nothing significant?
All is naked now, where once the people were all foregathered;
Labid[1]

Like a testimony meeting on a warm Utah afternoon, one after
another the nomadic shepherds stood and recited from memory long
verses of elegant poetry. One man stood and looked at Stephen,
apparently he was touched by the way Stephen was looking at Norah.
He began singing without instrumental accompaniment.

In Praise of His Love
I went out with her; she walking, and drawing behind
us, over our footmarks, the skirts of an embroidered woolen
garment, to erase the footprints.

Then when we had crossed the enclosure of the tribe,
the middle of the open plain, with its sandy undulations and
sandhills, we sought.

In complexion she is like the first egg of the ostrich—
white, mixed with yellow. Pure water, unsullied by the descent
of many people in it, has nourished her.

She turns away, and shows her smooth cheek, forbidding
with a glancing eye, like that of a wild animal, with young, in
the desert of Wajrah.

And she shows a neck like the neck of a white deer.
It is neither disproportionate when she raises it, nor
unornamented.

And a perfect head of hair which, when loosened, adorns
her back, black, very dark-colored, thick like a date-cluster on
a heavily laden date-tree.

Her curls creep upward to the top of her head. And the plaits are lost in the twisted hair, and the hair falling loose.

Her form is like the stem of a palm-tree bending over from the weight of its fruit.

In the evening she brightens the darkness, as if she were the light-tower of a monk.

Toward one like her, the wise man gazes incessantly, lovingly. She is well proportioned in height between the wearer of a long dress and of a short frock.

The follies of men cease with youth, but my heart does not cease to love you. Many bitter counselors have warned me of the disaster of your love, but I turned away from them.

Many a night has let down its curtains around me amid deep grief. It has whelmed me as a wave of the sea to try me with sorrow.

Oh long night, dawn will come, but will be no brighter without my love.

Imr-Al-Quais[2]

As the evening passed, Stephen was fascinated by the young princess next to him and the well-seasoned love poems. To a foreigner, these simple desert dwellers had appeared to be no more than nomads with the culture of a singular religious focus and a void of the more sophisticated arts. These men had no formal education, yet they were well versed in complex theology and romantic poetry lore, the most erudite of the fine arts.

It was a magical evening. Stephen's emotions rushed through his heart and mind like a torrent. He hadn't realized his emotions had been so tightly locked away. Now the chains were suddenly broken. It was the first time since he had heard as a young teenager that his parents had been killed that he felt the natural joy of happiness, the very gift to man that reveals the ultimate purpose of God.

Stephen listened to the stanzas flowing eloquently from the lips of the long-bearded Bedouin. He glanced at the campfire and then looked again into the penetrating eyes of Norah. How could he have such overwhelming feelings for a young woman from another world? Why did his soul desire so much to be with her?

"I am tired of the prose of old goats," joked one elderly Bedouin. "Let us hear the song of a beautiful songbird. I have heard that the emir's daughter has a voice of a lark."

"I have heard that myself," said a younger Bedouin man. "I was thinking of offering the emir all my camels and sheep, just so my son could marry the princess with the golden voice. But it would be a great risk to offer my all without hearing her sing for myself."

Other voices followed, beckoning Al-Ibrahim to allow his daughter to please them with a song. The gracious host had little choice. The emir smiled at Norah and asked her to sing for them.

Norah rose to her feet and walked to an open area near the fire. *She is so beautiful*, Stephen thought as he admired the young maiden. Norah looked to her father for permission to start and then began to sing a Bedouin love song. Her voice was golden. As she sang, Stephen felt as if her lovely voice had hypnotized him. And the way she slowly and delicately painted the emotions of the song with gentle arm and hand gestures made Stephen desire her love more than anything he had ever experienced. As she sang, her hands softly danced like the mystical smoke of an enchanted fire. Seamlessly, the princess slowly turned in a circle so that everyone received a portion of her attention. Yet it was clear to all the men that young Norah stopped turning when she faced the handsome foreigner.

> From the desert I come to thee
> On a stallion shod with fire;
> And the winds are left behind
> In the speed of my desire.
> Under thy window I stand,
> And the midnight hears my cry:
> I love thee, I love but thee,
>
> With a love that shall not die,
> Till the sun grows cold,
> And the stars are old,
> And the leaves of the Judgment
> Book unfold!
>
> Look from thy window and see
> My passion and my pain.
> I lie on the sands below,
> And I faint in thy disdain.
> Let the night-winds touch thy brow
> With the heat of my burning sigh,
> And melt thee to hear the vow

Of a love that shall not die.
Till the sun grows cold,

And the stars are old,
And the leaves of the Judgment
Book unfold!

My steps are nightly driven,
By the fever of my breast,
To hear from thy lattice breathed
The word that shall give me rest.
Open the door of thy heart,
And open thy chamber door,
And my kisses shall teach thy lips
The love that shall fade no more

Till the sun grows cold,
And the stars are old,
And the leaves of the Judgment Book unfold! [3]

By the time Norah was halfway through the last stanza, she was locked eye to eye with Stephen. Everyone present realized it was a passionately-charged moment between an American cowboy and a young Bedouin girl. It was too much for Al-Ibrahim.

The patriarch rose to his feet and walked over to Norah. "Thank you, my precious star. We have all enjoyed your lovely song. Now it is time for you to share your poem with the women. Good night, my lovely child."

Without protest, Norah excused herself and left to join the women, but as she did, she cast one last glance back at Stephen with her shiny dark eyes. Al-Ibrahim realized he had made a horrendous mistake by asking his daughter to sit with the American, but it was too late. She had already stolen Al-Mormon's soul.

As Al-Ibrahim returned to where Stephen was sitting, he was intercepted by an angry Osama. "Uncle, how could you let our princess display herself like that to a filthy infidel? Such behavior dishonors our tribe!"

Al-Ibrahim knew his daughter's behavior had crossed the line, but so had Osama's challenge to his authority and motives. Al-Ibrahim simply looked Osama straight in the eyes and said, "Watch your words, my good nephew. Before judging a person's actions as wrong, the Prophet Mohammed told us to always find seventy-two reasons why the action could have been right. Do you have seventy-two things you'd like to say to me?"

With fire in his eyes, Osama spun around in a fit of anger and left the poetry recital.

"Pay no attention to him," Al-Ibrahim said as he sat beside Stephen.

"I am sorry if I caused you any trouble," Stephen replied. "Should I leave?"

"Of course not. If you left now, I would lose face with my tribesmen and friends. Besides, you are my guest, and no one tells my guests to leave. Norah should not have sung that song to you; it made Osama furious."

"He is jealous?" Stephen asked.

"Osama? Not him. If he loved my daughter, I would understand why he was upset and would comfort him. But not Osama. He's a good captain of my troops, but he's not jealous of you. He's jealous of me. He is already married to two women but desperately covets Norah because she is my oldest daughter. He wants to marry the princess, so once I have died, he can challenge my son Saad for the emirship of the tribe. His father has asked several times for permission for Osama to marry Norah. I told my brother, 'Never.' She will be no man's third wife. Unless, that is, it's the wife of the emir of Tabuk," Al-Ibrahim said with a hardy laugh. "Enjoy yourself, Stephen. Osama is an overly ambitious buffoon." '

Notes

1. Adapted from "Labid," the Mu'allaqat. The title has been translated as "Suspended Odes," "Golden Odes," and "Collected Odes."
2. Ibid. (Some stanzas were removed to shorten the song.)
3. Bayard Taylor, "Bedouin Song," *The Poetical Works of Bayard Taylor* (New York: Houghton Mifflin Co., 1907).

Chapter 23

A Father's Fatal Error

The rearing of the camel is in this environment the predestined life to which every man-child is born. He is her parasite: her milk provides almost all his food and drink, her wool his shelter and clothing. Life is the quest for green pastures, rain the gift of God, and lightning man's pillar of fire.

Bertran Thomas, *Arabia Felix*, 1932

Stephen Markham
The Morning After the Poetry Recital
Camp of the beni Ibrahim

Stephen was asleep on pillows in the recital tent. The poetry festival lasted hours, and when it finally ended, all of the guests simply found a place on the rugs and fell asleep—all, that is, except the young Utahn. Stephen spent most of the night staring at the stars. He didn't believe he would ever fall asleep. As much as he tried to convince his mind to turn itself off and go to sleep, his heart forced his mind to relive, again and again, every moment he had spent in the presence of Norah. He tried to remember every feature of her striking beauty, her penetrating dark eyes, her pleasing voice, the sweetness and cleverness of her words, and on and on. He rehearsed over and over in his mind the brief moments they spent together. Just as the sky started lightening with the dawn, he nodded off.

"Wake up, Blue Eyes." It was the melodic voice of Norah. As if he was still dreaming of the Bedouin maiden, he didn't want to lift his head. "Wake up, you thief of young ladies' souls." Still he didn't move. "It is morning, my Ameriki friend, and everyone is awake but you," Norah pleaded and then followed up with a soft kick to Stephen's back.

Finally, a response came from dreamland. "Who's attacking me? It couldn't be the emir's spoiled daughter. I was told Norah is a well mannered lady."

"Please get up. I want to show your blue eyes a surprise." Norah continued beckoning her new friend. "Wake up. You might be big and strong, but you are a lazy man."

"Give me rest, you little pest."

"I know you didn't sleep well, but I have something good to show you."

"And how do you know I didn't sleep all night? Don't tell me you were spying."

"Princesses don't spy," Norah complained. "I know you didn't sleep well because I didn't sleep either."

That got Stephen's attention. He finally leaned his head up and smiled at Norah. "So, why didn't you sleep last night?"

"You know why, you untrustworthy Ameriki. You stole my soul. Now I am your genie slave. Come master, your genie has a miracle to show you."

"Okay, but I thought the genie was the slave. You sound more like the master. I see what your father meant by you getting whatever you want. Let me put my boots on."

"What kind of shoes are those anyway?"

"Cowboy boots, straight from the American West."

"Couw-bouy boots?" She tried to pronounce the English word using the sounds of her native Arabic. "Why do you call them couw-bouy boots?"

"Cowboys are men who look after cows."

"So the boots are they made from bouy couws?"

"No, they are made from cowhide and are worn by cowboys."

"I am confused," Norah confessed. "I think I will call my master the blue-eyed boy cow."

"Call me whatever you want in Arabic, but here's the first English word I will teach my genie: *cowboy*. Repeat after me, my genie: cowboy."

"Couw-boy."

"Good. That's close enough. Just don't call me a boy cow, just say cowboy. I'm Stephen Markham the cowboy."

"What is a Steben and what is a Markham?"

Stephen smiled again at the difficulties English poses for Arabic speakers.

"It's my name. My parents called me Stephen and my tribe is the family of Markham."

"I thought your name was Al-Mormon. That's what Father calls you. Follow me. There's something special for you to see, Couwbouy Steben."

Whatever she called him and wherever she wanted to take him, Stephen was happy to follow Norah. However, as a man, he wasn't about to let on how overjoyed he was to see her. Besides, this wonder of a young woman was used to getting whatever she wanted from her father. She needed to be shown from the very beginning who was boss. Like breaking a horse or training a dog, if Stephen didn't show Norah who was dominant from the get-go, it would be too late to ever reverse the pattern, and he would end up being the one inside the oil lamp.

Once Stephen's boots were on, Norah led him toward the animal corrals. At one of the smaller palm fond pens, several family members had already gathered, including Al-Ibrahim. The emir was not pleased to see that Norah had summoned Stephen without getting his permission, but what could he do? He had never disciplined his favorite daughter. Besides, he had never had any serious reason to do so.

"Good morning, Al-Mormon," the emir welcomed the American. "I see my curious daughter has made you her pet. That makes two of us she controls."

"Good morning to you, Al-Ibrahim. I enjoyed the food and the poetry last night. Thank you for inviting me. You are a generous host."

"That was last night," Norah said. "Today Allah has blessed us with a little gift. Look in the corral, cowboy. We have a new baby she-camel. Look how beautiful the little one is."

Norah went over and hugged the baby camel around the neck and then carefully petted the baby camel's back. "The birth of every camel is treated as a special event to a Bedouin family," Norah explained. "The all gracious and all merciful Allah has given us these wonderful animals. They can go for days without water. Without them, we would die in the desert. Just look, Steben. Isn't this baby so beautiful?"

What could Stephen say? He had never quite thought of she-camels as beauty queens. *The newborn is a miniature model of its ugly mother,* Stephen thought to himself. *Still, it is a newborn, and any infant, regardless of its species, is special.* It felt good being around a newborn animal again. The little camel reminded Stephen of his happier days as a boy when he and his parents would visit his grandfather's ranch. "Never seen a prettier camel," Stephen finally admitted.

"I am glad you like her," Al-Ibrahim said. "Because you find favor with my camel, as a good Bedouin I must give her to you. When she is ready to leave her mother, she will be your camel."

Stephen was caught completely by surprise. "A camel! Thank you, but what will I do with a camel?"

"Ride her, my couwbouy master," Norah said. "A genie whose master doesn't ride a camel is not even a second-rate genie. She would be less than a genie and would stay hidden in her lamp. Now that you have a camel, shall I call my master a camelbouy?"

"Well, thank you for the baby camel, but please, Norah, I am a cowboy."

"Until my master trains his own camel and rides her for the first time, I will not call him couwbouy or camelbouy. I will just call you bouy."

So much for trying to establish dominance with this girl, Stephen thought. *She's already in charge.*

"How do I train a camel?" Stephen asked.

"Father," Norah said in a pleading voice, "can I show Stephen how to take care of his camel and teach him how to train her?"

Al-Ibrahim was clearly unhappy with Norah's request. As a good Muslim, he wanted to be a gracious host. As a Bedouin chief, he wanted to uphold the tribe's legacy of limitless hospitality. However, as a Muslim father, he was upset that the Christian and his daughter were clearly bonding in front of his own eyes. How could he stop their flirtations without making his favorite child unhappy? And how could he show hostility to a foreigner who, by the standards of his American culture and religion, had done nothing wrong?

"My dear father, please, please let me help Al-Mormon with his camel. You said yourself that I know more about camels than my brothers. I will do all my chores, and you know I will not disappoint you. Please, my loving abu."

Al-Ibrahim was proud that he had never had to say no to Norah's requests. But this was very different from anything he had ever faced before. Bedouin girls don't flirt with boys, and clearly his daughter was openingly admiring the American. Then there was the American; what would he think if Al-Ibrahim declined his daughter's request in front of him? How did the emir get himself into this mess?

"Okay, my daughter. You may work one afternoon each week with Al-Mormon and his camel. But there is one condition. No more playing master and genie. A Bedouin has no master. We are a free people. We are Bedouin."

"Shukran, my noble father. Thank you."

Al-Ibrahim was pleased to see Norah's face light up with his approval. However, as her countenance grew in joy over the prospect of being able to see Stephen once a week, he realized that his compromised solution had only accentuated his string of fateful mistakes. Eventually, he would have to step in and forcefully say no. He knew that the longer he waited, the more it would hurt Norah.

"Remember, my daughter, Allah likes those who do a job perfectly when they decide to do it. I don't want this cowboy falling off his camel." Not wanting to make yet another mistake, Al-Ibrahim retired to his tent. The others followed, leaving Norah and Stephen to care for his baby camel.

Still trying to play the macho cowboy by showing as little excitement as possible, Stephen started the conversation. "Well, Norah, what is the first lesson I must learn about being the papa of this little critter?"

"First, you must learn how to get your baby camel away from its mother."

"That sounds like a good starting point, but first I want to know something."

"And what is that?"

"Do you really believe I stole your soul last night?"

Norah was no fool. She knew how to win this bout. She stared Stephen in the eyes, smiled at him until she knew his emotions were rushing like a sandstorm, and then said, "Mother camels are very protective and they are very smart. They can hold a grudge for years. If she knows you took her baby, one day, maybe years later, she might bite you or kick you to death with her strong legs. One of our camels realized that my uncle Najib stole her calf. A day doesn't pass without that she-camel trying to bite him. He never returns back to his tent at night without camel spit on him. The poor man. His camel hates him, but he won't part with his best breeding she-camel. That's why, Al-Mormon, when you find a girl to marry you, you must be sure she loves you."

"I thought you were here to show me how to train a camel, not a husband."

"Oh, it is easy to train a husband," she replied. "Teaching a camel takes real skill."

Stephen realized he stepped into that one, so he went on the offensive. "What do you Bedouin women know about love? I thought your parents wed you off to the highest bidder."

"You seem to know less about Bedouin women than you do about camels. Of course we want to please our parents, but a Muslim woman does not have to marry anyone she does not want to. My father has already introduced me to three very handsome and rich young men. I have refused to marry each of them. It's my right. I know the kind of man that I can love, and when I find that man, I will train him by loving him with all my heart and soul."

"And how will you know when you find that man?"

"When I look in his eyes, my soul will burn with fire, and through our hearts, we will share each other's fire."

"Do you think that technique would work for the man?"

"I don't know about all men, but I know it will be a sign to the man I marry. I will sense the fire he has for me burning within my own heart."

"I see, kind of like the fire I feel for my baby camel?" Stephen sweetly mocked.

"You are impossible to train, couwbouy," Norah said with a touch of frustration. "I had better stick to training camels. Couwbouys are clueless. If you are so smart, couwbouy, tell me how you will know the woman you will marry."

Stephen looked into Norah's eyes and smiled. "That's easy. When she kisses me, her lips will tell me of 'the love that shall no more fade.' " He mockingly quoted her song from the night before.

"Oh, couwbouy, you are mean and lazy. My donkey knows more about love than you. That was only a song. You don't really think I was singing it to you, do you?"

"Well, sister, I was hoping you might have been thinking a little bit about me while you sang that love song, but since you weren't, I guess we better get back to your lessons. Now, how can I get my baby camel away from its mother without her knowing about it?"

"Listen carefully, Al-Mormon. If you do this correctly, the mother camel will remain your good friend. If she bites you, you will have deserved it because you were staring at me and not listening."

"I am listening."

"Good. Ideally, as soon as the baby is born, you would hide the little one from its mother's nose. As soon as she smells her baby, she is bonded to it. The mother camel does not recognize her own calf until she smells it. For example, if a mother camel, called an *um*, is ready to breed again, and another she-camel gives birth to a dead fetus, we can bring the calf from the um camel and present it to the she-camel with the dead fetus. As long as the she-camel hasn't smelled the fetus, she will bond with the substitute calf. But it's already too late for your little baby. Your camel has already been with its um."

"But wouldn't the she-camel realize that the calf is much older than a newborn?"

"It won't matter to her. She will automatically adopt the calf and continue to give milk. In the meantime, one can milk the um camel and have her breed again."

"But, Norah . . . didn't you say it was too late for my little camel?"

"Yes, you won't be able to take your baby away from her um. You'll just need more lessons. Besides, Um camel and I will take care of your baby while you're out in the desert looking for oil."

Norah's gentle words about ums, babies, and love were working magic on Stephen's heart. He was falling in love with Norah, and she knew it. The young woman was so connected to the world God created, her natural environment without watches, cars, electric appliances, radios, or any other technologies that detach man from nature. *Love,* he thought, *should be simple and wholesome.* He could see that the same principle applied to Norah's connection with God. It was complete yet without pretense. Her faith in Allah was simple and without reservation.

The new friends spent three hours together. Stephen learned many interesting things about raising camels, none of which he would be able to remember the next day. Norah was surprised to know how much the oilman knew about horses and cattle; though, at that moment, she really didn't care. Time passed quickly, and soon it was midafternoon. Stephen had to return to his camp, so his escorts could return before dark.

"When is my next lesson, my faithful trainer?" Stephen asked.

"I thought you wanted me to stick to training camels, not couwbouys," Norah sweetly replied. "Aren't you first going to give your little daughter a name?"

"I'll give her a Spanish name, Camelita," the American replied.

"I know what that means," Norah laughed. "*Camel* is *jameel* in Arabic and *ita* is for something small. As you know, Al-Mormon, many Spanish words come from Arabic. Little camel. I like the name."

"So when is my next lesson?" Stephen asked again.

"Like father said, only one afternoon a week. Come again next Thursday. I will finish all of my chores in the morning."

"Good, so what shall I bring for Camelita?"

"Nothing. Her mother and I will take care of her until her papa comes back. But there is one thing you must bring with you."

"And what is that, Norah?"

"My soul. Like your shadow, you must never travel without it," Norah said with a smile. Then she dashed away to her tent.

Stephen knew when it was time to hold on to a golden moment and not risk spoiling it by overindulging in its sweetness. He asked for an escort back to his camp. Al-Ibrahim thanked Stephen for coming to the poetry recital. Stephen returned the gesture by thanking the emir for the baby camel. After a short hug, the emir turned and ordered the same riders who had brought Stephen to the festival to return with him to his camp.

When they were a short distance from camp, Osama rode up to them on his black camel. There was no traditional greeting between the men, just a stern looking Arab and an American cowboy who was looking too happy to not be falling in love.

"I told you to stay out of our lands. I warn you, infidel, my order still stands. I don't want to see you here again."

Stephen was so awestruck and captivated by Norah that he really didn't care what this Osama character thought. "I remember you telling me that only your uncle could order someone to stay out of his lands. Why don't you go tell him what you just told me? Are you afraid of what he will say?"

"Listen, Ameriki, this has nothing to do with my uncle or our lands. It is between you and me. Norah will be my wife, and any man who tries to get in my way will die."

"Look, Osama, I have no fight with you. Let's be friends. I am an American Christian, so I am not going to marry your cousin. But, partner, you had better remember one thing. If you threaten to kill an American, you have better put up or shut up."

"Put up what?" Osama asked.

"Forget it. Just shut up."

"What do you mean by shut up?"

"Let's go," Stephen ordered the others. "This clown is wasting my time."

"What do you mean by clown?"

Stephen rode south.

Chapter 24

Water from the Rock

Man is not the creature of circumstances. Circumstances
are the creatures of men.

Benjamin Disraeli

Stephen Markham
March 1938
Midian, Saudi Arabia

It was good to be back in the first-class company of Klaus and Gerhard. They were not just Stephen's loyal friends; the Germans remained his only links to a world with which he was quickly losing touch. It had been seventeen months since Stephen left the CALTOC camp and twenty-one months since he last saw the red sandstone cliffs of southern Utah or sat in a sacrament meeting on a beautiful spring afternoon, yet here in Arabia he felt closer to the Lord than at any other time in his life.

Today the threesome planned to venture north from the village of Al-Bada' in search of another Exodus campsite, the place where Moses struck a rock and water came forth. The exploring comrades figured they already knew the location of the first three campsites of the Exodus on the east side of the Red Sea. They had to be Marah at Maqna, where the twelve springs flowed to this day; Elim and its twelve wells at the Valley of Lemuel; and Wadi Musa (Moses) just north of Al-Bada'. It was there that Jethro visited Moses and helped him organize the children of Israel. There was only one more camp where the children of Israel stayed before approaching Mount Sinai. The last camp was where Moses brought forth water from solid rock.

From the primitive maps they had constructed, Klaus and Gerhard figured the miracle took place somewhere to the north. Moses had to lead the masses to the back or eastern side of the mountains as described in Exodus 3:1. The Germans calculated that the closest way to reach the sacred side of the holy mountain was to follow Wadi I'fal north until it reached a river canyon. They could see on the map that the canyon led toward the east or backside of the Jebel Al-Lawz Mountains. Once past the mountains, the children of Israel would have turned south until they reached Mount Sinai.

It was evident that there was no way the children of Israel could have climbed over the steep granite mountains. They had to loop around the northern end of the range. The Jebel Al-Lawz Mountains were one continuous wall of rocky cliffs and impassable summits. The mountains had to have been circumvented by the children of Israel, and the northern route was shorter than going south.

The explorers reasoned that the rock where Moses drew water would be approximately halfway between Wadi Musa and the midway point down the east side of the Jebel Al-Lawz Mountains. That would place the fourth campsite of the children of Israel somewhere along the northernmost part of their trek. As confident as they were with their calculations, the threesome still felt their chances of actually finding the campsite were slim at best.

Crammed into the cab of Stephen's Ford pickup, they were able to follow a rough and rocky road up Wadi I'fal. However, at the end of the wadi, they needed to turn east and find a way up a dry riverbed canyon without the aid of a road. The going was slow. Most of the way they simply followed the riverbed, which only knew the taste of flowing water when there was a prolonged downpour. Stephen drove as Klaus scanned the rocks to the left and Gerhard the rocks on their right. They weren't quite sure what they were looking for. They agreed to stop and evaluate any signs that water had flowed out of a rock. Just what that meant, they could only conjecture. Perhaps they would find water stains partway up a boulder. Maybe they would find a dry streambed starting at the base of a solid rock face. "Besides," they surmised, "no one alive in 1938 really knows what happened three thousand years ago when Moses' rod smote the rock."

Whether they found the campsite or not, Stephen thoroughly enjoyed feasting on the intellectual dexterity of his German friends. They seemed to know an awful lot about any subject Stephen could think of, and they never seemed to take offense at whatever offbeat question he threw their way. This morning Stephen wanted to discuss a subject that had been weighing on his mind since the first day he arrived in Arabia.

"I'll tell you what's been bothering me. It's my theory that the mother tribes of Ephraim and Manasseh are living today among the Muslim nations. I was always led to believe that when the tribe of Ephraim fled Assyria, they wandered north until they eventually reached Europe and, in particular, England. That's why so many Mormons with European ancestors believe they are from the actual bloodlines of Joseph. That would include our Prophet Joseph Smith. The Book of Mormon states that he was a direct descendant of Joseph of Egypt."

"Northern Europe?" Klaus laughed. "And why not Germany! At least that's what Adolph Hitler the Great believes. That idiot is about to start a bloody war and get us all killed because of his sick racist mind. Take my advice, Stephen, and don't worry about who is chosen and who is not. God loves all his children, and until the religions of the world teach that, we are doomed."

Gerhard was amused by Klaus's disrespectful description of their leader, and for once he became a bit humorous himself. "Stephen," Gerhard said, "that is not the full picture. There are those who believe, like you do, that the lost tribes blended in with the Caucasian races of Europe. There are some archaeological hints that in the seventh century BC the mysteriously appearing tribes known as the Cimbri, Ghumri, Cimbrians, Cymbry, Gimmerori, Gilmirrai, Cimmeri, and Sigambrians, and perhaps even the Celts, might have included elements of the ten lost tribes of Israel.[1] These tribes subsequently invaded Europe. From Buckingham Palace to Berlin's gang of nazi crazies, every European leader tries to justify his right to reign by claiming some vague connection to Israel through those tribes. Even the Swedes believe that they are the frozen-chosen. If you visit Sweden in the winter, it is hard to believe that they think their country is the Garden of Eden."

Klaus cut back in. "I'll tell you an even more humorous lost tribes fable. There is a Burmese tribe that believes that they are descendants of the lost tribes of Israel. Can you imagine how confused the first Christian missionaries must have been after they cut their way through the jungles of northern Burma just to discover the Karen people practicing Jewish-like customs. No Hindi temples, no white elephants, just a bunch of natives dressed up like Jews. To top it off, the Karen people even call their god Ywa, quite reminiscent of the Hebrew YHWH. They believe that their Lord Ywa had his younger 'white brother' build a ship so he could take a book of gold and travel cross the ocean. After that, they believe their Ywa ascended into heaven. To this day, the Karen believe their God will come again, but first their white brother will return with his book of gold that contains the true gospel."[2]

Stephen nearly crashed the Ford into a boulder. What had he just heard? Didn't the Lord say to the Nephites that he had yet other sheep that he would visit?[3] *Did Christ*, he wondered, *visit the Karen in Burma and tell them about the Nephite golden record? Did he instruct them to look for the coming forth of the Book of Mormon through the hands of a fair-skinned latter-day prophet?*

"Better watch where you're driving," Gerhard said. "If the Swedes and the mountain people of Burma think they are the lost tribes, then anything is possible. Besides, there is a straightforward explanation as to how your British ancestors might have gotten injected with the blood of Ephraim. Do you remember how we talked about the blood of the Arabs mixing with the people of southern Spain?"

"Yes, you said they ruled Andalusia in Spain for seven hundred years, and most of the Spanish sailors who migrated to the New

World had Arab blood in their veins. You also mentioned that the same blood mixing would have taken place in the Philippines," Stephen replied.

"Ser gut! The Arab sailors and merchants of southern Spain frequented the ports of Southampton, Liverpool, Amsterdam, and the ports along the Rhine. As the saying goes, a sailor has a girl in every port and as many children to prove it. Just take a good look at Klaus. I think his grandmother was from Frankfurt am Rhine."

"That would make me your Semitic cousin," Klaus broke in. "I love you, Gerhard, but I'll disown you if you try to stop me from eating pork. But Gerhard is right; there is still another way Arab bloodlines mixed with those in the British Isles. There were hundreds, perhaps even thousands, of Spanish sailors who involuntarily immigrated to Scotland."

"Scotland?" Stephen was surprised. "I'm one quarter Scottish myself. My great grandparents were some of the first Mormon converts in Scotland."

"Well, I didn't say Strasburg!" Klaus laughed. "Philip, the king of Spain, sent the Spanish Armada against Elizabeth of England in 1588. Philip was a staunch Catholic, while Elizabeth was an unyielding Protestant. To complicate matters, the Scots were angry with Elizabeth for beheading her cousin Mary Queen of Scots in 1587. The excuse Elizabeth gave for checkmating Mary was her refusal to disavow Catholicism. From what I gather, most of you Americans believe that the English navy defeated the Spanish Armada. That's just another example of English bull! Do you Americans realize that the English wrote your version of European history?"

"Unfortunately for the armada, the Spanish warships sailed into two severe storms. The first was in the English Channel. It blew them against the French shoreline and forced them to forgo a direct battle with the English fleet. They encountered a second storm when they tried to circle around the British Isles to sail out into the Atlantic Ocean and back to Spain. A navigation error put them far too close to the Scottish and Irish coasts. When strong gales hit the armada, most of its 130 ships were crushed upon the rocky shores of the northern isles. There were nineteen thousand Spanish sailors aboard the ships. In Protestant Northern Ireland, most of the Spanish were hunted down and killed. However, in Scotland, hundreds, or perhaps even thousands, of Spanish sailors were welcomed into the Scottish communities as heroes for having taken up arms against the English. So you see, Stephen, if you believe the Arabs have the blood of Ephraim in their veins, it is quite likely that a good deal of that blood made its way to the British Isles by way of the Arab-blooded sailors of the Spanish Armada."

"How many Spanish ships actually wrecked against the Scottish shores?" Stephen asked.

"No one really knows what happened to which ships. But undoubtedly, many Spanish sailors were integrated into the Scottish community. A common joke in Ireland is that in the debris that washed up on the Irish shores from the Spanish Armada was a bouzoukis, and Irish music has never been the same."

With such interesting discussions, the day passed quickly. It was already two o'clock when they bumped into a group of mounted Bedouin. Stephen was wondering if this would be another nauseating meeting with Osama and his boys. For sure, he didn't have time for another invitation from the beni Ibrahim to leave their lands or else. They still had another twenty miles to go in what they considered their search zone, and there were only four hours of sunlight remaining. They also needed to find their way back to the road in Wadi I'fal before it got dark. Stephen stopped the truck, and the three men got out to greet the five Bedouin on camelback.

The Bedouin commanded their camels to kneel, and they dismounted. "Salaam Alekium," the Arabs said in greeting the westerners.

"Wa alekium salaam," came the standard reply.

"What brings you to this beautiful land that Allah, praised be his name, has created? Isn't his land magnificent?"

"Yes, Allah is great," Stephen replied. He had been so busy steering the truck up the boulder-laden riverbed that he hadn't taken the time to notice the beauty of the mountains and cliffs that formed the canyon. "Oh, yes, his creations are wonderful. We're surveying this land for oil."

"You mean the oil we burn in our lamps?"

"Yes, oil for your lamps and gasoline to run trucks like this one."

"We have no need for trucks. Allah has given the Arabs the camel. The camel is Allah's special gift to the Bedouin, and we will never give up our camels for a machine that needs to drink gasoline. Perhaps Allah's gift to you infidels is your trucks. We welcome you to our land, but we need to warn you that you can't continue past this canyon. That would put you in the lands of the beni Ibrahim."

"Are you beni Ibrahim?" Stephen asked. Having the best Arabic skills of the three, Stephen was the natural choice to be their spokesman.

"No. We are beni Jabr. Do you know the beni Ibrahim?"

"I was a guest at Al-Ibrahim's feast last week. He's a good man. So why can't we continue up this valley?"

"Our chief attended his poetry recital. If you know Al-Ibrahim, then you know that his tribe will not allow you to cross their land. They will kill you if you try."

"I doubt they would kill me, but why do the beni Ibrahim keep people out of their land?"

"They didn't tell you? They are the protectors of Allah's Mountain of Moses."

"Do you mean Mount Sinai?" Stephen asked.

"We don't know if it is Mount Sinai or not. Our fathers call it the Mountain of Musa. After Mecca, Medinah, and Jerusalem, the tribes around here believe the mountain is the next holiest place on earth. The beni Ibrahim believe that infidels should not visit the shrine, and the king has authorized them to enforce their belief. But for us, the mountain is only a pile of rocks. Give us one hundred riyals of silver, and we will take you there."

"Thanks for the offer. Someday we might take you up on it. However, you might be of help to us today. We are looking for the place where Moses struck the rock and water came out."

One of the younger Bedouin couldn't hold it in. "I know where that is. I can take you there." The older Bedouin who had been speaking for the group looked disturbed by the hasty disclosure. Clearly, the young man's disclosures had cost him bargaining power. He would be putting the younger member of their party in his place that evening.

"Alhamdellah," Stephen declared. "Our prayers have been answered. You can show us the way. Now we will see where one of Allah's great miracles took place."

"Just a moment," the Bedouin said. "You are welcome in our land, but we didn't agree to show you the sacred rock."

"How much would it cost us to have the beni Jabr show us the place of Allah's great miracle?" Stephen had the tribesmen trapped, and he knew it. He had invoked the name of their tribe, and, at the same time, questioned the measure of their generosity.

"Some other tribes would charge you a high price, but the beni Jabr will never take a stranger's money. Follow us, and we will show you the place."

The three westerners couldn't believe their luck. They got back in the truck and started following the Bedouin directly to the place the people of Midian believed to be the location where Moses struck the rock to quench Israel's thirst.

They followed the Bedouin and their camels another four miles up the canyon. As slow as the camels walked, it was still hard for Stephen to keep up with them. At this point, the tribesmen turned north into a canyon. Gentle rolling mounds of sand formed the canyon's floor. Not having to avoid rocks, Stephen found the driving much easier. However, in the sand he had to gear down and keep the revs high.

Stephen admired the sandstone cliffs on both sides of the canyon. The scenery reminded him of Zion's Canyon in Utah. His German friends were surprised to learn that Stephen's Utah looked much like this red sandstone canyon. War or no war, Klaus and Gerhard both promised the Mormon that they would someday visit him in America.

After about two miles, Gerhard pointed out that there were several large fig trees growing on the west side of the valley. The trees had sprung up from a ledge about fifty feet above the base of the sandstone cliffs. "What an odd sight," Gerhard said. "Fig trees growing wild in the desert so far from the nearest village." Their excitement grew as they noticed that the Bedouin had directed their camels toward the trees.

As they approached the small grove, they saw that the trees stood beside two pools of clear water. "This must be the place," Klaus concluded. "The water is still here! The miracle is still alive. Christ taught that the fig tree is a symbol of the tribes of Israel and the kingdom of God. Since the waters are still flowing, it's another sign that the twelve tribes are alive to this day."

They drank from the pools and found that the water was cool and sweet. The pools were shaded beneath a shallow overhang in the cliff. The water did not flow from a desert spring, but constantly dripped into the pools from the ceiling of the sandstone overhang instead.

"Here is the place where Moses struck the rock," the young Bedouin proudly said. "Water has been showering from the rock ever since. Bedouin come here from far away to drink from these pools."

"The water and the red figs are gifts from God. They can heal you of many illnesses," the Bedouin leader claimed.

Stephen remembered seeing a similar natural phenomenon in Zion's Canyon in Utah. Did the Lord start the water flowing from this rock at the touch of a staff? Stephen could only speculate. What he did know was what his eyes were seeing and his ears were hearing. He was standing in a harsh desert, but at his feet he saw pools of water that flowed from what appeared to be solid rock. As he stood there, Midianite Bedouin, the sons of Jethro, were confirming to him that Mount Sinai was in the land of the beni Ibrahim.

Notes

1. Dale Nelson, *The Migrations, Alliances, and Power of Israel in Western Europe and Central Asia: A Latter-day Saint Perspective of the Lost Tribes* (Orem, UT: Sharpspear Press, 2001).
2. Tudor Parfitt, *The Lost Tribes of Israel: The History of a Myth* (London: Phoenix, 2004), 127.
3. 3 Nephi 16:1–3.

Chapter 25

The Man Who Didn't Know How to Wear Shoes

Our life is what our thoughts make it.

Marcus Aurelius Antoninus

Stephen Markham
March 1938
Camp of Al-Ibrahim

It took Stephen a frustrating four hours to drive from his surveying camp to Al-Ibrahim's tent. With even the coarsest road, it would only have been a drive of an hour or less. But this would be the first motorized vehicle to ever reach the emir's tents, and Stephen was doing the job of the pathfinder. Several times he had to turn back to scout another way through the rocks. Each time, he almost went into a panic, thinking he might not be able to reach the camp. He did not want to risk missing his weekly visit with Norah. All week, the only thing he could think about was seeing the Bedouin princess. It had been seven long days since he last saw the beautiful young woman, and he didn't fancy the idea of having to wait another seven days.

Finally, he pulled into the emir's camp. The camels bellowed, the saluki dogs attacked, and chickens flew in every direction. Even the women and children screamed. Apparently, only the men who traveled to the cities and patroled their lands had seen motorized vehicles. When the dust settled, Stephen got out of the mechanical monster and settled down the dogs by throwing pieces of jerky their way. Looking away from the slim greyhound-like dogs, Stephen searched for Norah. She had already left the women's tent and was standing beside its door. He then noticed that Al-Ibrahim exited his tent as well and seemed in a hurry to greet him.

The two men traditionally embraced and kissed cheeks. After almost two years, Stephen had learned to appreciate Arabian greeting gestures. Besides, he had read in the Bible how Christians were to greet each other with a kiss, although Stephen didn't think that applied to kissing the bishop's wife. Norah stood patiently near the door of her tent while Al-Ibrahim asked Stephen to sit on a rug and update him on the news from the outside world. Mint tea was served while Stephen tried his best to recall the last week's events that had been broadcast over the BBC radio station.

Europe continued its march toward war, but there was nothing reported that week on the land of Arabia or the far side of the Atlantic. Al-Ibrahim appreciated the news but was annoyed by Stephen's frequent glances in the direction of the women's tent. Still, what could the emir do but try to monitor his daughter's relationship with the American and keep it as tame as possible? *Inshallah*, he thought. *God's will the flame that they have for each other will soon die out.*

"So, you are here to take care of your camel. Norah tells me you named it Camelita. Do Americans give names to all of their animals?"

"Only the ones they consider their pets, usually dogs and cats. I once raised two turkeys on my grandfather's ranch. Grandpa named one Thanksgiving and the other Christmas. My grandfather was a tough old cowboy. He never expressed much love for people, but he had a name for every horse on his range."

"Now a horse," Al-Ibrahim stated, "there is an animal worthy of a name. The Arabs will ride into battle on she-camels. They are faster and easier to maneuver than a bull camel, so we fight on them. However, an emir will always have a fast stallion with him. If he sees that he is losing the battle, he will jump on his Arabian stallion and ride off to safety."

"So, friend, where is your stallion?" Stephen joked.

"The beni Ibrahim don't need stallions." Stephen got the message. "Not all tribes use their Arabian horses for running from a fight," the sheikh continued. "Some tribes, if they see that they are losing a battle, will take a young virgin, dress her in white, put her on a horse, and have her enter the battlefield. The warriors of her tribe will take courage from her bravery and rally to protect her honor and that of the tribe. Our history tells us that many Bedouin wars have been won due to the inspiration of a brave young woman on horseback. You can see how important it is to the Bedouin to protect their young women. That's especially true for the girls' fathers. Please, Al-Mormon, I trust you with my daughter because she is not your kind of people, and I am sure that you understand that."

"I will not touch her in any way," Stephen emphatically promised.

"Because you are a Mormon, I have faith that you will keep your word. But you can break a young girl's heart without touching her. She is not the same girl she was a week ago. A father knows when his daughter's thoughts are somewhere else. You're like a prince from another world, a world and a life to which she could never adapt. Please, Al-Mormon, let Norah show you how to care for a camel, and let me see that you know how to treat a father's daughter."

"Yes, sir," Stephen said, half doubting he could keep his word.

"Go now and learn how to take care of your Camelita. If Norah stands there any longer, she will melt in the sun."

Stephen left for the women's tent, but before he reached it Norah ran to join him. Side by side, they walked together to see the week-old camel. Sensing her father's warning, Norah did not looked Stephen in the eye nor smile until they were beyond Al-Ibrahim's view. "So, how's my baby?" Stephen said with a lover's friendly smirk.

"As best as can be expected when her father has been absent for an entire week. Actually, your little camel is not so little. She has grown quite a lot while you were away. I know she would like to see her father a lot more often."

"I would like that too, but I don't think her Grandpapa Al-Ibrahim would approve."

"Oh, Abu Al-Ibrahim is a nice father. I am sure I can get him to like the idea. I see you are still wearing your cowboy boots."

"Like I told you, I wear them everywhere I go. I even wear them to church."

"And what, may I ask, is a church?"

"A church is a building Christians use as their mosque."

"But the Bedouin don't have buildings. For a mosque, we mark off an area of land with stones. We shape out a small space for the imam to lead the prayer, and there beneath the sun we pray. However, we do not wear boots, shoes, or even sandals into the mosque."

"Why's that?"

"When we pray to Allah, we want to believe we are in his presence. Do you know the story of Prophet Moses on Mount Sinai?"

"Of course. I've known it since I was a little boy."

"Then you know that when Moses saw the burning bush, Allah commanded him to take off his shoes. He was on holy ground. To us, even if a humble mosque is made from only a few rows of stones lying in the sand, it is a holy place. That's why we remove our shoes."

"Good to know. If I ever enter a mosque, I will remove my boots."

"I still don't understand why you always wear those big boots. Aren't they heavy and hot in the desert? Perhaps you don't know how to wear regular shoes."

"Of course I know how to wear shoes. I'm not a caveman."

"Then perhaps you have made a sacred promise to never wear regular shoes?"

"Now why would I do such a thing?"

"Well, Al-Tanbori did, and he was at least as smart as you are."

"I've never heard of Al-Tanbori. Who is he? One of your admirers your father says wants to marry you?"

"No, you jealous cowboy. Al-Tanbori lived a long time ago in Baghdad. His full name was Abu Al-Kasim Al-Tanbori. He wore very old shoes that he liked so much that he did not want to change them. The older his shoes got, the more comfortable they were for his elderly feet. So for many years he wore the same shoes, until the people started to refer to him as the one with the old shoes. Each time a new hole would appear in his shoes, he patched it with whatever cloth or leather he could find. Because he had plenty of money, his friends and everyone who knew Al-Tanbori advised him to buy a new pair."

Stephen realized his boots had gotten him into one of those long but intriguing Arabian tales that had probably been told around campfires for a thousand years. "I like this guy. He's kind of like me and my cowboy boots," Stephen intervened.

Norah gave Stephen a "you'll see, smarty pants" smile and continued. "Over time, Al-Tanbori's shoes became very heavy from the leather patches and pieces of cloth that were added to them. Al-Tanbori made a good living by selling bottles of rose water. One day he decided to buy some fine glass bottles of the highest quality and use them for the rose water he sold. He knew of a glassmaker in Syria, and so he imported his most expensive bottles from Aleppo.

"Just before the Eid holidays began, he placed the bottles of rose water in the entrance to his house where people could see them. He knew that the more people who saw the beautiful bottles when they came to visit him, the higher the price he could command for them. Al-Tanbori used most of his money to buy the fine bottles from Aleppo.

"One day Al-Tanbori went to a Turkish bath. When he finished and was leaving the bath, he came to the place where everyone had left their shoes before entering the building. There he found a beautiful pair of new shoes next to his old shoes. He thought to himself that he could take the new shoes and no one would see him. So he did."

"Well, that wasn't very nice of him," Stephen noted. "I'd never trade my cowboy boots for the best shoes in Paris."

"Don't let Satan hear that, Stephen. He might think you're tempting him. Besides, if you do the wrong thing, you might end up like Al-Tanbori. You see, the shoes he stole belonged to a judge. It was not hard to discover who had taken the judge's shoes because the only shoes that were unclaimed at the bath that day were the famous, ugly old shoes of Al-Tanbori. So the authorities went to Al-Tanbori's house and found the judge's shoes. As punishment, the judge ordered that Al-Tanbori be given several lashes with a whip, beaten, made to pay a fine, and after all of that, he was placed in jail for his crime.

"Of course, Al-Tanbori was very mad because of what had happened to him. When he got out of jail, he went to the river to get rid of his ugly shoes. When he got there, he tied the shoes together and threw them as far out into the river as he could.

"After a few days, a fisherman caught the old shoes in his net and immediately recognized them to be Al-Tanbori's. The fisherman said to himself, 'Al-Tanbori loved these old shoes. I must take them back to him.' He took the old shoes and went to Al-Tanbori's house. The fisherman knocked on the gate, but there was no answer, so he threw the shoes over the fence into the courtyard of Al-Tanbori's house.

"The shoe's landed on the expensive perfume bottles that Al-Tanbori had purchased from far-away Aleppo. Most of the bottles were broken beyond repair. There went all of Al-Tanbori's savings."

Stephen couldn't take his eyes off Norah. Like the first time he saw her reciting the Bedouin love song, her expressions and gestures matched perfectly the story she was portraying. *How wonderful*, he thought, *it would be to have a wife who could tell children's bedtime stories with such animation and passion.*

"When Al-Tanbori came back to his house later that evening, he saw his fortune gone, and the old shoes on top of the broken bottles. Now he hated the old shoes even more. He decided to dig a hole in his yard and bury the shoes in the ground so he would never see them again. The neighbors heard the digging in the middle of the night and went for the authorities. Because he was digging next to the wall of the neighbors' house, the authorities assumed that he was breaking in. They arrested him, beat him, jailed him, and fined him once again.

"After he got out of jail, Al-Tanbori thought of how he could get rid of his old shoes without causing any more problems. He decided to throw them in the sewer, where they would not be found by anyone. Within a few days, the sewer was blocked, and water started rising into the streets, causing everything to smell very bad. The workers went down to clean the sewer line and found the shoes, which they all knew very well. They reported the shoes to the police. Again the authorities arrested Al-Tanbori, gave him lashes, fined him, and jailed him for sabotaging the public sewer.

"Al-Tanbori decided that since he could not get rid of the old shoes, he would keep them. He washed them and put them on the flat rooftop to dry. A dog that was running along the rooftops found the shoes and started to play with them. As the dog jumped from one roof to the next, it dropped the shoes on the head of a pregnant woman. The woman miscarried and lost her baby. Once again, the police found the cause to be Al-Tanbori's shoes, so it happened again. Al-Tanbori was punished and jailed.

"By this time, poor Al-Tanbori had lost all of his money, all of his respect, and all of his dignity because of his old rotten shoes. In desperation, he went to the judge of the judges (the highest ranking judge) and asked to have written a declaration that he had no further relationship to those old shoes, that he should be exempt from any problems the shoes may cause in the future, and that the city municipality should receive his shoes from him. Al-Tanbori then swore to God that he would never wear shoes or anything else on his feet again so long as he lived.

"Al-Tanbori lived to be very old and became rich once more. People who did not know him wondered why a rich man didn't wear shoes. They finally decided that Al-Tanbori didn't wear shoes because he didn't know how to. So, my friend, Mr. Stephen, if you wear those cowboy boots everywhere, people will assume that you don't know how to wear regular shoes."

Stephen chuckled. "So the whole moral of the story is to make sure you don't wear the same shoes every day?"

"Of course not," Norah said. "It is to teach our children that they should never take something that is not theirs, even a pair of shoes, especially when they think no one will see them do it."

"Our children?" Stephen questioned.

Norah looked in Stephen's eyes till he was ready to burst. Then she said, "Yes, today you need to teach our little Camelita not to steal. She's been wandering away from her mother and sucking on the teats of other um camels."

Chapter 26

Strength in Beauty

Behold, I stand here by the well of water; and the daughters of the men of the city come out to draw water . . . I shall say, Let down thy pitcher, I pray thee, that I may drink; and she shall say, Drink, and I will give thy camels drink also; let the same be she that thou hast appointed for thy servant Isaac.

Genesis 24:13–14

Stephen Markham
March 1938
Camp of Al-Ibrahim

Since Stephen had forged a trail the week before, he found it much faster to find his way back to Al-Ibrahim's camp the following week, yet to him it seemed to take even longer. He checked his watch and was surprised to find that it took him a full hour and a half less to reach the Bedouin camp this time. Time is relative, he realized, to how much you miss being with someone.

After greeting Al-Ibrahim and filling him in on the week's BBC news, Stephen searched the camp for Norah. What he found confused him. She was at the tribe's well, drawing water for a small herd of camels. *That's a man's job,* he thought. *Don't these Arabs have any respect for their women?* Then he remembered how Moses exploited such an opportunity to impress the daughters of Jethro.

"Good morning, young lady. I see you could use some help."

Norah smiled to see the handsome American. Rather than answer him, she continued drawing the heavy bucket of water until it reached the surface. She then took the bucket and slowly poured it into a small trough where the first camel in line was drinking.

"That's a man job. Please let me help you," Stephen requested.

Norah dropped the bucket into the well. "A man's job?" she inquired.

Stephen noticed how the camels seemed to patiently wait in a single line for their turn for water. "Okay, maybe a woman can draw water, but if you let me draw the water, I can do it a lot faster. That way we can spend more time training Camelita."

"You think you can draw water faster than a woman?" Norah smiled.

The cowboy realized that the petite beauty was challenging his manhood. It was time to show off the biceps he was so proud of. He rolled up his sleeves. "Give me that rope, little girl."

"If you are so strong, I'd better let you," Norah said with a giggle. Then she backed away from the well.

Stephen took the rope and started lifting the bucket. "How is my little camel?"

While the cowboy lifted bucket after bucket of water, Norah gave a daily report of Camelita's activities. After four buckets, Stephen realized that the first camel was still drinking the water as quickly as he could lift it. "How much water can this creature drink?"

"Don't speak so unkindly to the camel," Norah protested. "She is Camelita's aunt, and she is a wonderful animal. Camels can vary their body temperature depending on the season. No other mammal can do that. They store heat during the day and release it at night. By doing this, they perspire much less than any other animal and can go days without water. When they finally drink, they can swallow huge quantities of water. If you're going to raise Camelita, you're going to have to learn to appreciate the talents of your little daughter."

Stephen was starting to realize what he had gotten himself into. By the time the fourth camel walked away from the trough, his arms were aching. Like the story of the turtle and the hare, he had lifted the water with fast spurts of energy. His hard muscles were quickly tiring. He could not lose face as he tried to impress Norah. He gritted his teeth, smiled, and continued lifting the buckets at a more even-handed pace. "Tell me what else you do besides draw water for the animals."

Norah volunteered a long list of the duties required of a young Bedouin lady. Being a princess did not free her from the hard work of desert life. Surviving in a barren landscape required the full strength of every member of the family, beautiful daughters included. But Stephen was only catching some of Norah's words. After the tenth camel, his biceps were cramping in pain.

Stephen set the bucket beside the well and started talking about what girls do in Utah.

"Are you tired?" Norah asked.

Stephen knew his short break was over. He smiled, dropped the bucket into the well, and painfully drew water for the last five camels. There was no way he would let on to Norah just how tired he was or how glad he was that the laborious task was finally completed.

The pain was worth it. The rest of the afternoon was spent playing with the small camel and talking of the things they enjoyed doing. Norah talked of how much she loved the month of Ramadan, the season when Muslim families fast during the daylight hours and then give gifts and feast with relatives during the night. Stephen spoke of his fond boyhood memories of Christmas.

Before leaving Al-Ibrahim's camp, Stephen returned to the emir's tent to bid farewell. He passed an angry-looking Osama. The warrior's face telegraphed how envious he was of the time Al-Ibrahim was allowing his daughter to spend with the infidel.

By the time Stephen reached the sheik's tent he had already forgotten Osama's evil eye. "How is your little camel?" Al-Ibrahim asked.

"Growing like a weed, but she still does not seem to recognize her master."

"Master?" Al-Ibrahim laughed. "Don't you know by now that you'll never master a camel? They have a will that is much stronger than a man's. We are our camels' slaves. Didn't I see you drawing water for them earlier this afternoon?"

"Yes, I drew the water. I can't believe how strong Norah must be. Please don't tell Norah, but it took all my strength to draw the water. I thought those camels would never stop drinking."

Ibrahim smiled at the cowboy with the deflated ego. "Young man, our Bedouin women are renowned for their beauty. However, they are also famous for their strength. Our women are even stronger than they are beautiful. True beauty does not come at the sacrifice of strength."

Chapter 27

Beyond the Lamp Light

I respect the dog for the sake of the owner.

Arabian proverb

Stephen Markham
Thursday Night, March 1938
Stephen's Surveying Camp

Stephen was a changed man. Before sitting down to start his evening scripture studies, he washed his dishes, swept off the table, and put everything back in its proper place. Perhaps he was hoping that sometime he might receive a surprise visit from Al-Ibrahim, and just maybe he would bring along his daughter. *What would Norah think if she saw my camp the way things are usually stacked up?* he worried.

While he was hanging up the towels on the clothesline on the edge of camp, he noticed something odd. It was dead quiet. *That's strange*, he thought. *I haven't heard a wild dog bark or a night owl screech for a half hour. Oh well.*

The cowboy smiled at the thought of how the beautiful Norah could lift endless buckets of water for the camels. *Now that's a girl my grumpy grandpa would like*, Stephen daydreamed. *He always told me that looking for a woman to marry was like buying a horse. Check her teeth and the width of her hips. You want a healthy woman who can bare you a dozen kids.*

Stephen walked to the camp table to turn up the oil lamp. As the light brightened to the point where he could read from it, he thought he heard a camel some distance from camp. That too was odd, for the Bedouin corral their animals at night. Perhaps the animal was lost.

A cold breeze bit at his arms, so he decided to retrieve his coat before opening his Book of Mormon. He walked away from the light and entered the darkness that encompassed the tent and all that surrounded his small campsite. He was reaching for the door of the tent when a feeling impressed him to look away from the camp and into the darkness past the campsite.

He heard quick footsteps. Suddenly, as if from nowhere, the figure of a man leaped at him with a knife that looked to be the size of the moon. Stephen lunged back, and the man's body flew passed him. The assassin was dressed in black. As he hit the ground, he tumbled expertly, immediately leaping to his feet to face Stephen. The attacker's face was hidden under a black head wrap. The attacker waved the curved knife back and forth in a figure eight and then ran at Stephen.

Stephen looked for something in the darkness to defend himself with, but he could not see anything useful to reach for. Just as the assassin came within striking distance, he tripped on a tent rope and crashed face down in front of the American.

"Fourth down and time to punt, you pig snot." The big cowboy stepped forward then kicked the black assassin as hard a he could. The man flew through the air, landing three feet away. On hitting the ground, the knife fell from his hand. Gasping for air, the attacker held his ribs where Stephen's boot had made contact.

"Off-sides. Darn it! I'll have to repeat the down." This time Stephen took a running start before punting the villain's body into the air.

"That should pretty well do it," Stephen said. He pulled up a camp chair and waited for the man to come around. After a long minute, the attacker struggled to his feet. Stephen just sat their admiring the man's resolve. "How do you like my cowboy boots? A little more useful in a fight than your sandals."

The man slowly staggered over and reached down for his knife. Stephen figured he'd had enough of this fellow. He stood up, grabbed the man, and ripped off his head wrap. It was Osama. "Here's what I meant by 'put up,' " the American said. Stephen clinched his fist and belted Osama right between the eyes. The warrior flew back and crashed flat on his back. He was out like a brick.

Stephen tied the visitor's hands and feet. Then he threw a bucket of water on him. That brought Osama somewhat back to his senses.

"So what have I done to earn a visit from Al-Ibrahim's nephew?" Osama said nothing.

"You're making my boots awful mad. They're itching to get to meet you again. Let's make it easy. Why are you trying to kill me?"

"I told you to stay away from Norah. Everyone is talking about how she loves you. She will be my wife, you infidel pig!"

"Now, that seems downright unfair to me," the American replied. "You already have two wives, and now you want to get your hands on another one. Just look at poor me. I live all alone in the desert. Instead of feeling sorry for me, you want to kill me."

"You'd better kill me, Al-Mormon. If you let me go, I will cut your throat."

"Not without your jumbia." Stephen picked up Osama's knife and rammed its blade into the wooden camp table. "I think I'll keep your knife as a token of our friendship."

"Kill me, or you'll never be able to sleep another night."

"Well, you'll probably force me to get a dog. Even though you go around trying to kill people, you probably claim to be a Muslim. An unclean dog should keep you away."

Osama spit on Stephen's jeans. "You Ameriki coward. You don't even have the guts to kill me."

"As I told you before, I have no reason to harm you or any other man. Al-Ibrahim already told your father he would never allow you to marry Norah. Besides, she would rather marry a pig than you."

"You die! You die, you infidel dog!"

Stephen jammed the point of his boot into Osama's left nostril. Osama's eyes nearly popped out of their sockets. "I am going to let you go, but, partner, it's my turn to warn you. I don't like people who try to kill me. I wish I was a better Christian, but the next time you draw a knife on me, you're going to find my boots four inches farther up your nose. Just try me."

Chapter 28

Dealing with the Devil

Those who stand for nothing may fall for anything.

Alexander Hamilton

Osama
March 1983
Mount Sinai

Bruised and humiliated, the frustrated Osama rode his camel north from where he received the beating of his life from the younger American. Rebellious from birth, he couldn't bear the fact that he would have to live his entire life under the leadership of another man. For years he had schemed ways to marry Norah, get rid of his uncle Al-Ibrahim, and then wrestle the emirship from timid Saad, the emir's oldest son. He had dreamed that once he became the emir, the people would come to him for advice and favors, and he would be invited to royal events in Tabuk and, perhaps, even Riyadh. With talk of oil riches in the air, he imagined himself receiving a prince's share and becoming an oil sheik, of buying fancy cars, traveling the world, and buying the favors of women whenever it pleased him. These were the vanities his uncle despised. Left to live under his uncle's rule, Osama would never be more than a poor beni Ibrahim warrior, riding around on a camel all day, protecting a stupid mountain. Even now, in the darkness of a moonless night, he was headed for that very mountain.

As if baiting a vampire, for hours Osama patrolled the base of Mount Sinai holding a stick with a black sash tied to it. It was just after midnight, and he was just about ready to give up his search. It was then that he heard a deep voice. "Why do you beckon me?"

"I've come to make a deal with you," Osama answered in the darkness.

"Stay where you are. Why does Osama, head of beni Ibrahim warriors and the nephew of my enemy, seek to please me?"

It was so dark Osama could not see anyone, only the black outline of the great mountain. He felt a deathly cold in the air. He had never been so afraid nor so determined. He couldn't bear the thought of living without power, riches, and the praise of men. "Your enemy is my enemy. I want to destroy Al-Ibrahim and his American friend."

"If you want my help, you know my price." The voice sounded from somewhere in the surrounding mountains. "Your uncle is a truthful man, and he tells no lie about those who follow me. Are you willing to pay the price?"

"I will pay any price, so long as I become the emir of the beni Ibrahim. When I rule my people, I will be your subject."

"And what do you want from me?"

"I need to you to kill the American, have Al-Ibrahim's oldest daughter marry me, and then kill my uncle. I can do the rest."

"Why the American? He is of no harm to you and means little to me."

"He is looking for oil. Certainly you don't want the Americans to discover oil in Arabia. It would make the Saudis and their American friend allies against your kingdoms. It would open Arabia to the world. It would give King Abdulaziz and his religious colleagues the resources they need to become the most powerful of all Islamic nations. With oil money, they could reenergize the faith of a billion Muslims."

"Don't tell me what I already know. I am trying to delay the discovery of oil, but it is something that the Father promised the seed of Joseph, so it will be. The last thing I want is the Americans to be the ones who discover it. They pledge their allegiance to the Father and defeat my armies. For this reason I will raise up armies of assassins and secret orders of crazed religious fanatics to attack them. I will drive a wedge through the house of Joseph. I will do all that is in my power to break the covenants the Americans enter into with the Arabs. But why kill this insignificant American? He has learned he is wasting away his time and his life. He will never find oil in this part of Arabia. The black gold he is looking for lies far to the east. What did he do to you, take the jumbia from between your legs?" the voice laughed.

"Why laugh at me?" Osama cried out. "I said I would be loyal to you, even to the point of betraying my own people."

"I respect the young American, for he practices his religion and has power therein."

"The Christian is an infidel pig. His lies are winning the heart of our princess, Norah, the woman I need to marry if I am to rule over my people."

"Now that is news. The Mormon is pursuing a Muslim woman. He is weakening faster than I supposed. I will kill him if that's part of our contract. Killing Al-Ibrahim will take more effort, but I can arrange that also. But his daughter, I cannot force this Norah to marry you. You can buy her, kidnap her, rape her, put a gun to her head and tell her to marry you. I can offer her fruit from the Garden of Eden, but even the great Al-Dajja cannot force her to say yes to you. Our Father gave women agency. Al-Ibrahim's daughter is your problem."

"So you agree to help me?" Osama cried out in the darkness of the night.

"Nephew of my enemy, you are but desert scum. You have now covenanted with the darkness. I have a use for you. Are you ready for your first command?"

Chapter 29

The Black Sabbath

Where do consequences lead? Depends on the escort.

Stanislaw Lem

Stephen Markham
Black Sabbath, March 1938
Midian

A full week had passed since Gerhard, Klaus, and Stephen had followed the Bedouin to the place his people claim Moses struck the rock over three thousand year ago and water sprang forth to quench the thirst. Stephen tried to spend every Friday morning, the Muslim Sabbath, studying his scriptures and recording in his journal the wonderful experiences he was having in Arabia. This Friday morning he tried to put in words the feelings he felt for Norah and to note the thoughts he had about the place the Bedouin showed them with the water flowing from solid rock. He also recorded how grateful he was to be able to live in Midian and to witness firsthand the great challenges Moses had faced when he took a multitude of freed slaves into this barren land. The prophet of the Exodus had called it a desert land of scorpions, serpents, and drought. In his seventeen months in Midian, Stephen had seen a lot of all three. Fortunately, he had avoided being bitten or stung. He knocked on the wood of his camp table.

He added to his journal the deepening appreciation he had for the companionship of Gerhard and Klaus. He was content to be working alone and felt at home with the Arab tribes. Still, the two Germans provided Stephen with something that Moses's desert could not—discussions based on western logic and humor. Stephen noted in his journal that it would be a true loss if war broke out in Europe or the Germans were ordered back to Berlin before his CALTOC contract was up.

Stephen had nearly finished updating his journal when he heard camels approaching. There were two men riding from the north. They were undoubtedly the tribesmen of his friend Al-Ibrahim. Visits from the beni Ibrahim were becoming a regular practice. As usual, the tribesmen had brought along a spare camel. He could see that he was being beckoned again to the tent of the emir. The American went into his small supply tent for a tin of orange juice and some cups for his approaching guests. However, he was surprised that the beni Ibrahim men did not dismount their camels.

"Mr. Stephen, you must come with us. Al-Ibrahim is asking for your assistance."

"Of course, if your sheikh needs me I will come. But what is the problem?"

"Come, we will tell you on the way. We must hurry, Al-Mormon."

Stephen put back the juice cans, grabbed a light jacket in case he didn't return until evening, and mounted his four-legged transport. To be honest, he welcomed the opportunity for an unscheduled visit with Al-Ibrahim's beautiful daughter.

The three riders headed north at an accelerated pace. "So what is the problem that calls for my help? I can find oil, brand cattle, and shoot a rifle, but that's about it."

"We found the body of an American in our land this morning. He had been murdered. We think he is an oilman. We need someone to tell us what we must report to Riyadh about him, and we need you to show us how to bury a Christian."

"When did you find the body?"

"At dawn this morning, while our patrols were near the sacred mountain."

"Why are you in such a hurry to bury him?"

"We must. It is our way. Muslims should bury the dead the same day they die. Don't they do this in your land?"

"No," Stephen replied. "We usually wait two or three days to allow the family to convene."

"How is that, Mr. Stephen? How can you stand the stench of a dead body after such a long period?"

"We put the body on a block of ice so it will not decay."

"Ice? There is no ice in Arabia, and if there were ice, why would we have our dead kin put on ice? That is disrespectful."

Stephen realized he was making no sense to the men who lived in a land where the temperature sometimes reaches 130 degrees in the summer. Obviously, if someone died, the body had to be in the ground within a few hours. This was their reality, not his. This poor fellow, whoever he was, died within the world of the Bedouin. They needed to find out who he was and get him in the ground. Yet with all the concern over a dead man, it was not lost on Stephen that the beni Ibrahim warriors openly mentioned a sacred mountain. The beni Ibrahim must, he assumed, be guarding Mount Sinai.

When they reached the camp of Al-Ibrahim, Stephen noticed that at least a dozen beni Ibrahim camels were saddled and readied to ride. He also noticed that all the men in the camp were toting rifles. The warriors instructed Stephen to dismount his camel so they could exchange the tired camels for fresh ones. As they did, Al-Ibrahim appeared from his tent with several of his men. They all greeted Stephen in turn.

"Thank you for coming, Al-Mormon," Al-Ibrahim said. "I need your advice. An American has been killed on our land, and we need you to help us document this tragedy for our government and your government. We will also need to know how to bury him according to your Christian ways."

"Did you bring the body here?" Stephen asked, while looking from the corner of his eyes for Norah.

"No, we don't want an infidel's body buried near our camp. We left the body were we found it, so we can determine how he died. Two of my men are guarding the body, so the hyenas and wolves won't attack it."

"I will do what I can. Do you have his papers and personal items?"

"No, a Muslim would not remove another man's possessions, even a man who is dead. Unless we killed him in a fair battle, we would not have the right to his spoils."

"We'll need something to dig a grave with. Do you have shovels?" Stephen said as he looked around the camp, pretending to be looking for a shovel but actually trying to spot Norah. His pretense was completely transparent.

"Yes, Al-Mormon, we have shovels. Can't you see they are already tied on the camels? To save your neck from getting sore, my daughter is not here. She is watching the sheep with her younger brother."

"Please tell her I missed seeing her."

"Of course, Al-Mormon, but I will not tell her she has cast a spell on the American oilman. She might get some crazy notion in her head that she could marry someone outside her faith. Come, my friend, we must bury this man before sunset."

As Stephen expected, Osama was nowhere to be seen. Stephen was sure the prideful warrior had two black eyes to conceal and broken ribs to mend. The burial party consisted of a dozen beni Ibrahim tribesmen and Al-Mormon. They rode west through a long wadi framed by rocky foothills on both sides. Stephen was aware that the American had been killed near the sacred mountain. *Which peak was it?* He wondered. *If I get permission to go there, how will I find my way back here?*

After about an hour, the party turned north and headed up another long valley. This wadi was wider, and there were tall mountains on its western side. Stephen thought, *These have to be the eastern side of the Jebel Al-Lawz Mountains, the very area Gerhard and Klaus had concluded Mount Sinai's archaeological monuments would be found.*

They had not gone far before Stephen noticed that in the distance two men were standing near what looked like the remains of a body. The corpse was on the ground about three hundred yards farther up the valley. The camels of the men that guarded the body were resting under the shade of an acacia tree, for it was high noon, but the body rested under the direct sun. Stephen wished he didn't have to look upon death, but his camel steadily shrugged forward at its relentless pace. Whatever was up there couldn't be pleasant. Stephen wanted to pass the time in conversation, but it was no time for small talk. They had their own morbid work to carry out. Only when that was finished could they return to camp and discuss the day's events. Rather than look ahead, Stephen tried to distract himself by watching hawks soaring overhead.

Finally, the camels came to a halt and lowered themselves to their knees. Stephen knew it was time to get off the camel and approach the body of the unfortunate man. He prepared himself and then stepped forward. His kneels nearly buckled because of what he saw. It was not a fully formed body, but the facedown stump of a human. The man had been quartered! Hopefully not alive, Stephen silently prayed. What kind of human would do such a thing?

Stephen looked around and saw that the man's arms and legs had been stacked some thirty feet away; presumably they had been found and placed there for burial by the two beni Ibrahim guards. The bloody torso made Stephen's stomach turn. How could he reach through all the blood to retrieve the man's wallet for identification? "Please turn the body over," Stephen asked the two men whose job it had been to watch the corpse. As they did, Stephen's heart seemed to stop. It was Gerhard!

"It's my friend. It's Gerhard!" Stephen shouted. He turned and walked away. Suddenly, he spun around and looked at Al-Ibrahim. "You killed him! Your men killed him over a stupid mountain!" he yelled. "He was a good man! He was my friend!"

As Stephen stepped aggressively toward Al-Ibrahim, the beni Ibrahim warriors instantly pounced on him, dropped him to the ground, and held him there. This didn't stop Stephen. "What kind of people are you? You killed a man in your so-called service to God!"

"Let him go," Al-Ibrahim said to his men. "He is mad, mad over the death of a friend. If I saw one of my people butchered like this, I would be mad as well. Let him up, I say."

Stephen got back to his feet and looked Al-Ibrahim straight in the eyes.

"I told you, Stephen, I would not kill you if you tried to visit the mountain of Moses. So why do you think my men would kill your friend? We are not butchers. We protect a mountain; we do not kill innocent people. We are Muslims. We are a people of peace. It is our duty to stop people from entering our land, not to kill them. Believe me; none of my people harmed this man. Why don't you believe me?"

"Maybe you didn't kill him with you own hands, but tell that to that crazy nephew of yours. Last night Osama tried to kill me in my camp."

"I warn you, Al-Mormon. It is a serious matter to accuse one of my family members of trying to kill you. I will find Osama and confirm what he did to you. If he attacked you, he will be whipped. As the captain of my militia, I gave him strict orders to harm no one. But as a man, he is furious that you are spending time with Norah. Maybe his anger at you is beyond his ability to control it. However, that would not give him reason to kill your friend. I am sure Osama had never even met the man."

"I am telling you, Al-Ibrahim, your nephew is dangerous. Not just to me, but you'd better watch your own backside."

"Look at your friend's body, Stephen. This is not the work of Osama or any other man, even a madman. No Muslim would desecrate a body that way. Where there is great holiness, there is great evil at its gates. My people know how to avoid this evil. But why do your people come to Arabia? I'll tell you: it's for money, and money is the root of all evil. Even you, Al-Mormon, you did not come here to help our people, did you? You did not come here to serve Allah, did you? You came here for money!"

"Gerhard wasn't here for money! He was not an oilman, nor even an American. He was a German."

"Then it is Allah's will that he is dead. If he was in Arabia, then he was here to spy for the Germans and Turks! I spit on them both. The brutal Turks ruled over us for four hundred years, and the Germans are their allies. My father died in the fight to drive the Turks out of our land. They took from us whatever they wanted. They raped our mothers and sisters. From what I hear about this Hitler, you had better use more care in selecting your friends. Someone was paying the German to be here, and it wasn't his Christian church."

Stephen knew Al-Ibrahim was right. Gerhard was on Hitler's payroll, and if Stephen had been more responsible, he would have warned the emir of Hitler's intention to bring his army to Mount Sinai. Man, had he been wrong, and his shamefulness was starting to cool down his emotions. "You and your holy mountain. The Germans were my friends."

"You are so young, Al-Mormon, and so naive. You have much to learn about the devil and how he uses his evil empires. When something is truly evil, it will not spare good men. If you are to survive, young man, you need to learn a lot more about the nature of evil and how it conceals its motives. We might be shepherds, but we know the nature of the wolf and what happens to you when you start to believe that the wolf has changed its nature. You said, 'The Germans.' Are there any more Hitlerites in my land?"

"Yes, Gerhard never went anywhere without Klaus. He is also from Germany, and they are both archaeologists."

"I don't know what *archaeologist* means, but I assure you they were making maps of our lands and taking notes about our fortifications. So where do you think we can find the spy you call Klaus?"

Just then Stephen remembered seeing birds flying high above them as they approached Gerhard's remains. He looked again. Sure enough, they were not hawks; Arabian vultures with lowered talons were circling a hilltop less than a hundred yards to the west. Stephen felt even worse with the sickening thought that the fun-loving Klaus was dead, and his body was now carrion.

Al-Ibrahim had followed Stephen's eyes. "Come, Al-Mormon, let's see if your other friend is there. Come with me. I will help you, my friend."

Stephen did not know what to do. He was lost in his emotions and had no alternative but to follow Al-Ibrahim as the emir started toward the hill where the raptors were landing. As they climbed the hill, Stephen's anger subsided into a state of emotional numbness. His mind was fully alert, but his feelings were suspended. He climbed the hill as if taking footsteps through a dream.

Even before reaching the top of the hill, Stephen knew they would find the remains of Klaus. It was now his duty to recover what was left of him and give him a decent Christian burial. Although he thought he was prepared, when his eyes finally rested on the dead body, he nearly passed out. Klaus's head had been cut off and thrown on a pile of rocks. His eyes had been removed and a black sash had been shoved in his mouth. A yard or so of the sash remained outside of his mouth and flickered back and forth in the wind.

Al-Ibrahim and his men reverently brought the remains of Klaus down to the wadi floor where they had found Gerhard. Under the shade of the acacia tree, the tribesmen dug an Islamic style grave, a deep ditch with two grooves cut out of each side. They placed the men's bodies in the grooves with their heads facing Mecca. To Stephen, the form of the grave and where it pointed were of no consequence. What did matter was that they were dead. Hitler's evil motives had killed two dedicated Bible scholars.

Stones were placed between the two remains to keep them apart, and the men slowly refilled the graves. While they shoveled, Stephen found two branches and formed a simple cross to place on the grave.

He knew that Klaus was a Lutheran, so he assumed he would have liked a cross marking his resting place. To designate the grave, the Bedouin placed stones on top of the loose dirt.

The final chapter in the Germans' time on earth was a Christian prayer said over their Arabian grave by a cowboy from Utah. Perhaps they should have abandoned their duty to their fatherland, but they were Stephen's good friends.

Night had fallen as the riders approached the camp of Al-Ibrahim. Stephen had remained silent since leaving the resting place of his friends. "Al-Mormon," Al-Ibrahim said in a comforting voice, "please stay in my camp tonight. You must rest. And I want to show you something tomorrow. Please stay in the protection of the beni Ibrahim this night."

"Thank you. I don't feel well," Stephen replied. "Al-Ibrahim, will you ever forgive me for the terrible words I said about you and your people?"

"Allah is most gracious and most merciful. What limited mercy a man like I can give, I will. I would have reacted the same way had I found a beni Ibrahim tribesmen killed in that manner. Of course you are forgiven."

"I am sorry. A Christian should never behave the way I did. I am ashamed."

"You are young and as strong as a bull camel, Al-Mormon. It took six of my men to hold you down. You have the strong body of a Bedouin warrior but the soft heart of an Arab um. You are a good man, Al-Mormon. You are my friend."

"Thank you, Al-Ibrahim. You are my friend as well. I am not afraid, but I know the great evil that stalks your lands. I know who killed my friends."

"So do I, Al-Mormon. I see you have already met Al-Dajja, the anti-Christ. He is our enemy. He is the evil one," Al-Ibrahim said slowly. "He thinks he can claim God's holy mountain, the ruins of ancient temples, and other holy sites. But Christ will come again, and cast him out of all of them, hunt him down, and kill him."

"Is Al-Dajja the one in black?"

"Yes. His evil has no limits. He is my enemy. He kills, rapes, and plunders at will. But what I fear most for my people is that his powers are growing. If the Americans discover oil, it will bring much good to our people. However, Al-Dajja will try to twist our people's minds so that the wealth will destroy the Bedouin and end our perfect way of life. With such wealth, he could have the Arabs turn the world upside-down."

"Should I stop looking for oil?"

"I don't know, Stephen. The British found oil on the island sheikdom of Bahrain two years ago. CALTOC believes it is close to discovering oil along the Persian Gulf,[1] the fountain of the Euphrates River. If oil is discovered in Iraq, Kuwait, Iran, and the basin of the Euphrates River, then I am afraid that the prophecy of Mohammed, peace and prayers be with him, will be fulfilled, and the last day will be upon us."

"What prophecy is that?"

"The Prophet said the last day will not occur till a mountain of gold rises in the Euphrates River. He said a treasure of gold will be found, but those who are there should not take it. Men will fight over the treasure until ninety-nine out of one hundred people are killed, and the people will say, 'May I be the one to be spared?' Believe me, the anti-Christ knows how to use greed. Killing people in such numbers is his dark joy."[2]

"Can the anti-Christ be stopped?" Stephen asked.

"Al-Dajja is either Satan himself or one of his chief generals. The Qur'an tells of a meeting in heaven that took place before Adam came to earth. Allah, praise be his name, commanded Satan to bow before father Adam, who represented all of mankind. Satan refused, saying that he was made of light and fire while Adam would go to earth and be made of mud."

"So Muslims believe that Satan is made of only light?" Stephen commented. "Mormons believe that the devil who tempted Adam was called Lucifer, which means 'bringer of light.' What this means is that this Al-Dajja is a spirit with no body. He is an evil spirit."

"That's right, Al-Mormon. Al-Dajja is not a man made from mud and blood; he is an evil genie. When Satan refused to bow before Adam, God became angry and cast Satan out forever, saying that those who follow him would not go to heaven. So Al-Dajja is here on earth gathering as many people as he can to follow his evil plan."[3]

"That's why we call him Perdition," Stephen commented. "Perdition means 'lost forever' or 'cast out forever.' You would think people would be smart enough to recognize Al-Dajja's motive. His only intent is to destroy people. It's so obvious, so why don't people get it? Why did Klaus and Gerhard have to die?"

"Most of the time it's because Satan blinds people with pride. Your friends probably knew Hitler was evil, but secretly they wanted to become famous for discovering the sacred mountain, so they continued spying even though they knew what they were doing was wrong. Satan knows that if people become materialistic and greedy, they will focus on only the gods of their own creation. Once he embeds pride in their hearts, people forget to thank Allah, the one who provides all lasting prosperity. It's a sad cycle. Humble people remember Allah. He blesses them with prosperity, but the taste of wealth makes men greedy, and their souls rot like overripe fruit. They become consumed in greed. What I fear in the core of my heart is that the oil the Americans find will make my people wealthy. It will then be only a matter of time before they forsake both their God and their tribe. If that happens, then nothing will stop Al-Dajja from destroying my people, unless the Messiah comes and kills him."

"The Messiah? Who is the Islamic Messiah?" Stephen asked.

"You know who the Messiah is. You are a Christian. Mohammed taught us that the Messiah is Jesus Christ.[4] Like I said before, Christ, the Messiah, will come a second time, and when he does, he will kill Al-Dajja.[5] But tell me, Stephen. Have you met the anti-Christ before? How did you survive? Mohammed taught that if a non-believer receives his smell, he will die."[6]

"As long as I walk with Jesus Christ," Stephen said, "and keep my covenants with him, I fear no devil. The name of the Messiah puts fear in the heart of this Al-Dajja monster. And from what Mohammed taught, I see why."

"Then perhaps the Mormons are among the righteous Muslims of the world who are immune to Al-Dajja's powers. Mohammed said that after Christ kills the evil one, Jesus will go to the people Allah has kept immune from the anti-Christ. He will then wipe off their faces and let them know their rewards in paradise. At this time, Hazrat Isa (Christ) will receive a message from Allah, the Most High, stating, 'I have brought out some servants of mine with whom nobody has power to fight. As such you take my servants in safety of Mount Sinai' (Qur'an 7:11–18)."

Notes

1. The British named this body of water the Persian Gulf, but the Arabs prefer to call it the Arabian Gulf.
2. Imam Abu Zakariya Yahya Bin Sharaf an-Nawawi, comp., *Riyadh-Us-Saleheen*, vol. 2, S.M. Madni Abbasi, trans. (Riyadh: International Printing House, no date), 881.
3. Qur'an 7:11–18.
4. Imam Abu Zakariya Yahya Bin Sharaf an-Nawawi, comp., *Riyadh-Us-Saleheen*, vol. 2, S.M. Madni Abbasi, trans. (Riyadh: International Printing House, no date), 873.
5. Ibid.
6. Ibid.

Chapter 30

Mormon on Mount Sinai

Draw not nigh hither: put off thy shoes from off thy feet, for the place whereon thou standest is holy ground.

Exodus 3:5

Stephen Markham
March 1938
The Mountain of Moses—Mormon on Sinai

As they mounted their camels the next morning, Stephen was still deeply upset. He hadn't slept that night. He didn't know where Al-Ibrahim was taking him, but ten rifle-bearing warriors escorted the emir and his guest. As they left camp, they headed back in the direction of the fresh grave that held the bodies of his two friends.

All night the American replayed over and over again how Klaus and Gerhard must have died. During the course of the night, his grief and disgust slowly evolved into unbearable anger. Anti-Christ or not, the Al-Dajja monster had made an eternal enemy, and his name was Stephen Markham. If they met again, Stephen pledged he would avenge the death of his friends.

"I am sure you didn't sleep well," Al-Ibrahim said to his America friend. "I didn't sleep either, but not because of your German friends. I was worrying about you. I do not want your hate for Al-Dajja to darken your own goodness. You are a good man. Don't let the evil one change you. He only has power over you if you allow his evil deeds to cause you to hate. If you do, Al-Dajja will turn your hate for him into a hatred of your fellowman and finally into a hatred of yourself. The opposite force is Allah, who is pure love. Remember, love and hate cannot exist in the same heart."

"That's good advice, Al-Ibrahim," Stephen replied, "but even you said you would have gotten angry if it had been two of your tribesmen and not the Germans."

"Yes, but if two members of my own family had been killed, I would put their bodies to rest at sunset prayer and say, 'Inshalah. The will of Allah is manifest.'"

"Inshalah?" Stephen complained. "How could it be God's will that my friends were tortured to death?"

"Please, Stephen, don't question Allah. He knows all things, and he gives each man just enough time in this life as he needs. Besides, this Al-Dajja, who thinks he is so mighty, is nothing more than a pawn in God's almighty hand."

"Good, then I will be an instrument in God's avenging hand."

"No one can kill Al-Dajja except Jesus Christ. That is Allah's will. Remember, Stephen, God is love. What might appear to us as injustice might not be so. Was not your own Prophet Joseph Smith murdered in cold blood?"

"Yes, Joseph and his brother Hyrum were murdered by a mob with painted faces."

"Then he is a martyr, and he will be in paradise with Allah. Inshalah. Forever his followers will thank him for sealing his message with his own blood."

"Yes, we dearly love our Prophet Joseph."

"Protect your heart, Stephen. You must keep it pure, for Allah will judge you by both your actions and the desires of your heart. To lift your spirits, I have decided to do something I probably should not. I am taking you to Mount Sinai."

"Are you sure it's okay to do it? You won't get in trouble, will you?" Stephen asked.

"Trouble? With whom? The poetry of my tribe tells of Jethro asking my forefathers to protect the holy mountain and only to allow the pure in heart to visit it. Is your heart pure this morning?"

"I think so. I will try to keep the Spirit of God in my heart and try to drive away the hatred I am feeling."

"Good, now let's ride to his holy mountain. It is what your friends would have wanted you to see."

As they rode west toward the tall mountains, Stephen tried to remember all the archaeological attributes Klaus and Gerhard had told him should characterize the real Mount Sinai. As he did, he also remembered the special moments of discovery he'd experienced with them, the Christmas they'd spent together in Jethro's town, and all the laughs they'd shared. The more he thought of them, the more gratitude he felt to God for these two wonderful friends who had taught him to appreciate the religious antiquities of Midian.

Just as they had the day before, they turned north when they reached the east side of the Jebel Al-Lawz Mountains. They continued riding and passed the grave of Klaus and Gerhard. Passing the resting place of his friends, Stephen tipped his cowboy hat in respect and admiration. Beyond the grave, they rode for another ten minutes before Al-Ibrahim stopped the party and said to Stephen, "There she is, the mountain of Moses." The emir was looking straight ahead to a tall mountain shaped like an inverted *V*. Toward the summit, the color of the granite was black, as if it had been burned. The shape of the mountain was familiar. Stephen had remembered seeing the west side of the mountain from the town of Al-Bada', Jethro's town. It was the same peak he had spotted the first time he drove into beni Ibrahim land and was stopped by Osama and his warriors. It was a magnificent mountain and worthy of its status as a wilderness temple and the home of the law of Moses.

"Before we go to the altar, I need to show you what belongs to Al-Dajja, and where he stays when he is near the mountain," Al-Ibrahim stated. "As you know, the first of the Ten Commandments given to Moses was to worship no other Gods but Allah. Thus the greatest of all sins is to turn one's back on God, who has given us everything, and to worship a deaf and dumb idol of metal or stone. Yet that is the very thing Al-Dajja wants man to do—to worship stones, trees, large houses, and other material things, and whatever else will distract us from Allah's glory. To destroy a man, all Al-Dajja needs him to do is turn away from God. He is the one who convinced the children of Israel to worship a golden calf. That over there is Al-Dajja's altar."

Al-Ibrahim pointed to a natural formation made up of giant boulders. Some of the great rocks were twenty feet in height. The emir and his men refused to go near the evil place, but Stephen had no hesitation. He rode over and dismounted his camel. The boulders formed a circular monument roughly thirty feet high with a diameter of about fifty feet. As the American walked around the monument, he saw large petroglyph drawings of Egyptian-style calves on all sides. There were at least a dozen large carvings of calves, yet no other animals were pictured. He climbed up the boulders to reach the top of the altar. There it was. Atop the monument was a high altar carved into the stone. It was an idolatrous altar, like those that had been used by the heathen nations of the Nabataeans of Petra. There was no doubt in Stephen's mind that this was the altar of the golden calf. Oh, if only Klaus and Gerhard could have seen it!

Stephen was convinced that this monument belonged to Al-Dajja. It had been a long ride that morning. Stephen unzipped his khaki pants and urinated on the altar. As he did, he yelled out, "That's for you, Al-Dajja. It's partial payback for my friends."

After soaking the idolatrous altar, Stephen got back on his camel and rejoined the beni Ibrahim party. "I saw what you did," Al-Ibrahim said. "I told you to keep Al-Dajja from your heart. The last thing you want to do is provoke him. It is not wise to dare evil's powers to come upon you."

"You're probably right, but it sure felt good. It's the cowboy way of sending Al-Dajja a message. I think my heart just started to heal for the loss of my friends," Stephen said with a smile.

"Honestly, Al-Mormon, you must be careful. Al-Dajja is powerful and pure evil. He is no one to play with, and you certainly don't want him coming after you. My friend, you're either very brave or very foolish."

The party continued another two hundred yards until it came to the small elevated valley at the base of the mountain. They stopped next to a seasonal stream still flowing with a trickle of what was left of the winter's runoff. Al-Ibrahim pointed to a sizable cave on the mountain about five hundred feet above the valley floor. From the cave's position on the mountain, Elijah could have seen the monuments below and anyone approaching the sacred mountain.

The men dismounted their camels and immediately removed their sandals. From here on out, they would be walking on what the beni Ibrahim men considered holy ground. Stephen took off his boots and wondered how he would fare walking barefoot across rocks and hot sand. Al-Ibrahim led the men up the streambed. The Bedouin seemed undaunted by the fact that they were barefoot, but Stephen had to muster up all the self-hypnosis skills he had to ward off the pain and keep up with the group. *Besides,* he consoled himself, *this is a pilgrim's saga.*

No one spoke a word as Al-Ibrahim led the men up the streambed. After what seemed like about 150 yards, the emir climbed up the right bank of the streambed onto the valley floor. There, no more than twenty feet from the stream, was an odd L-shaped structure made up of three side-by-side rows of stones piled not more than a foot high. Together the three rows formed two walkways. The entire length of the edifice was approximately seventy-five feet. Al-Ibrahim explained in a soft, reverent voice that the Levite priest would enter at the foot of the *L* and follow the right passageway up the *L* until he reached the top of the structure, where there were large unhewn stones. The large stones, he explained, formed Moses's altar. It was at that very place that the children of Israel entered covenants to worship only the One True God. Once they completed the covenant, the newly submitted faithful left the *L* using the left passageway.

For a moment, Stephen thought of Adolph Hitler standing at the altar and a million Nazi soldiers waiting in line for their turn to enter the altar of Moses. What a nightmare. Perhaps it was God's will that his friends had died after all. Klaus and Gerhard no longer had to face the dilemma of betraying their fatherland, delaying a bloody war, or saving their families. Germany's war machinery was already in motion. Now that Klaus and Gerhard were missing, it would be too late for Hitler to send another team of archaeologists to Arabia. The mad Fuhrer would have to start his war of purification without the powers of Mount Sinai.

The Mormon decided he must clear his mind and think only of the sacred purposes of this holy place. He needed to contemplate the fact that Moses and Aaron had stood before this altar. He wondered if Mohammed was right that someday the Lord Jesus Christ would bring millions of faithful followers here from the surrounding Muslim nations. If he did, it would probably be to have them fulfill the old covenant of sacrifice and to introduce them to the new and everlasting covenant of the New Testament. Stephen sat on a rock and closed his eyes. It was time for a silent prayer of gratitude.

After the prayer, he looked around and saw a dozen or so large pieces of a broken white marble column that had once stood by the altar. Al-Ibrahim explained that representatives of the twelve tribes of Israel used to come to Mount Sinai each year to perform sacrifices. The pilgrimages from Palestine only ended when Solomon built the great temple of Jerusalem.

After meditating for half an hour, Stephen decided to climb out of the valley and onto the mountain itself. He took a visual bearing on Elijah's cave and ascended the mountain. Within forty-five minutes, he was at the cave's entrance. It was a shallow cave, perhaps only twenty feet deep. Its height and width were about equal, roughly twelve feet. Having spent many rainy nights in the mountains of southern Utah, Stephen realized that the cave would have been a good place to weather the winds and tempests that Elijah reported. It would also have been a good place to look out upon the valley below and feel the same still small voice that revealed to Elijah the presence of God. At that moment, Stephen couldn't help but feel close to the same diety.

Stephen looked out upon the valley and tried to picture what it must have looked like when two million Hebrews camped below this mountain. There was plenty of room for all their tents, a seasonal stream for water, manna from the sky, and many square miles of good fodder for their animals.

From the cave's entrance, Stephen could see eleven large piles of stones with holes in the middle sitting on the valley floor. He figured that the holes must have once held timbers on which the tribes flew their banners. He counted eleven campsites, and, even more important, the piles, or *cairns*, were lined up within twenty feet of the mountain. The monuments ran alongside the mountain, situated approximately two hundred yards apart. Stephen remembered how God had commanded Moses to build markers to keep the children of Israel from coming to the holy mountain. There they were, eleven banners marking the camps and forming a clear boundary, beyond which the Israelites were not to cross. Stephen first thought he must have miscounted, for there were twelve tribes. Then he remembered that the tribe of Levi had no land. They were the priests who lived among and administered to the other eleven tribes.

Standing alone at the entrance to Elijah's cave, Stephen knew that this was the real Mount Sinai. The physical evidence was undeniable. Here in this desert wilderness, the monuments were still preserved, unspoiled by the hands of archaeologists and tourists. For all he knew, the mountain was still a dedicated temple, and he was grateful that he had kept himself worthy to stand on holy ground. Stephen walked to the back of the cave and knelt to offer yet another prayer. Perhaps he was kneeling in the very place where Elijah knelt each evening to plead with the Lord that his people would repent and recommit themselves to the covenants they had entered into at the altar in the valley below through their ancestors.

Chapter 31

Shifting Dead Men's Bones

Courage is being scared to death—and saddling up anyway.

John Wayne

Jake Sorensen
Summer 1989
Mac Pastore's Office, PAMMCO Headquarters
Week Seven of Ten-week Internship

A week turned into ten days, but finally I received the call I was waiting for—Mac Pastore had on his desk the printouts of the microfilmed CALTOC records of Stephen Markham. Mac was calling for me to come over to his office to discuss them.

On my way to his office, my mind was dealing with still another reporter's dilemma. I respected this Markham character for being an oilfield pioneer, and I wanted to share his story in print, but perhaps I should let the dead rest. I was not digging up his remains, but looking into his confidential files seemed almost as disrespectful. *Oh well,* I told myself. *If I am going to be a Jack Anderson–style muckraker, I'll have to learn to be a lot more indiscrete. Besides, why would a dead man care about his personnel records?*

When I finally had a copy of the printouts in my hands, I was surprised by how scant they were. Mac figured that the lack of detail was due to the fact that CALTOC probably had no need for a full-fledged administration office in Arabia in 1938. Since the company was just starting to find oil, what we call human resources today meant getting as many geologists and wildcat drillers into Arabia as quickly as possible back then. Nobody else was needed. For my part, I figured the corporate world of that day had never heard of lawsuits being filed by employees. Wrongful dismissals, discrimination suits, and unfair labor practices were not in the cards at that time, so why keep detailed records? From what I had read about the Great Depression of the thirties, there was no thought of how employees were treated. Most people were just grateful to have a job to put food on the table. Taking care of the basic necessities was paramount.

Markham's records totaled just six pages. The first page was a copy of his brief résumé, nothing much since his only professional experiences after leaving college were a few short stints with oil companies in Texas. From the printout, it appeared that the next page had been stapled to Markham's résumé. It was a one-page standard form filled out at the time he was interviewed for the job. "Nothing we didn't expect on this page," Mac commented. "They wrote down Christian/Mormon as his religion. We already figured he was LDS. The Saudi government would have required that he be a Christian or a Muslim."

"Did you see the comment under experience?" I said. "The interviewer noted: 'Experienced desert ranch hand. Might fare well in remote desert assignments.' "

"Interesting. Let's go to the next page," Mac suggested.

"Wait just a moment," I requested. "Isn't it interesting that they have as his next of kin a sister in Oakland, California? We know from his résumé that he was single and twenty-five years old. Why not notify parents in Utah or even grandparents?"

"What's your point?" Mac asked.

"Well, maybe he was alone. Perhaps Markham was someone who had lost his family—a young man with no real ties back home, someone who could disappear without breaking a mother's heart."

"Why, Jake, I think you're growing an investigative reporter's nose. Good insight. Anything else?"

"Only that the Depression was still on, so there weren't many job opportunities in America. He might have thought that the future economy in America offered no real future for him to go home to. At that time there would also have been rumors of war in Europe. Arabia would have been alive with speculation of what Hitler was up to and how England and France would respond. I can picture Markham sitting in his camp at night listening on the radio. The airwaves must have been full of war rhetoric. If CALTOC didn't ship a body back to the USA, perhaps Markham faked his death. It wouldn't have taken a genius to know that if Europe went to war, the United States would be dragged into it as well. Markham was single and twenty-five years old. He would have been prime meat for America's war machine. Perhaps he was a draft dodger, like the dentist thought."

"I'm impressed, Jake Sorensen, but what proof do you have? Seems to me that you have a very weak case. You Mormons might seem a little nutty to the rest of us Christians, but we know one thing about Mormons—they aren't draft dodgers. I've been in Salt Lake City on the Fourth of July, and there's no doubt how your people feel about the U.S. of A."

"You have a good point. It's far-fetched to think that a Mormon from Richfield, Utah, would fake his death to dodge a war that hadn't even started."

"Let's go on," Mac suggested, "but let's not rule out your idea that he faked his own death. A good reporter leaves all avenues open."

The third page in the report was a medical report showing that Markham was in good health. "I wish there had been a section on the form for mental health," I said to Mac.

"Good point," Mac agreed. "Over the years, a lot of Americans have lost it over here. The cultural and religious differences between America and Arabia are so extreme that we have had more than our share of suicides and nervous breakdowns. One of my past assistants flipped out one day, and they sent him home in a straightjacket. When I escorted him to the airport, he had taken on the personality of a four-year-old."

"Do you think it's possible, since Markham was working alone in the desert, that he went mad? Perhaps he wandered into the wilderness to die or perhaps he was found, cared for, and adopted by a Bedouin tribe."

"Possibly. At least that's more likely to have happened than a Mormon becoming a draft dodger. Let's keep this theory on the table. Something made him go mad. But what was it? The heat, the culture, the loneliness, or an enchanting genie?"

The next two pages of the personnel file consisted of a log for assignments and evaluations. The oilman's only performance review was a simple evaluation of his first year's survey reports. His work received an overall evaluation of outstanding. The final page was a request for a Saudi Arabian exit visa from Arabia for the end of his contract. The visa was requested on March 3, 1938, but was never used.

Chapter 32

A Scholar's Confession

These . . . giants . . . the Arabian sons of God . . . can carry
a whole camel on one shoulder . . . It is well known that their
religion is the Jewish religion.

Obadiah ben Abraham of Bertinoro, 1450–1510

Stephen Markham

March 1938
Apartment of the Deceased, Village of Al-Bada'

As Stephen placed the Germans' personal items into their separate trunks, he pondered which course he should take. Should he inform Hitler's Third Reich that their countrymen had been murdered (indeed, tortured to death) trying to help Hitler play out his fantasy of standing his army before Mount Sinai to make them invincible? On the other hand, perhaps he should delay as long as possible Berlin's knowledge of their tragic deaths. Once Hitler knew Klaus and Gerhard were dead, perhaps he would send another team of Biblical scholars to Midian in the secret employment of the Fuhrer. Then again, the mad dictator just might see their demise as an omen that his efforts to find Sinai would be fruitless and start his war to conquer Europe.

Stephen's cowboy senses told him to pack up his friends' possessions and store them with their landlord. He would then instruct the apartment owner to do nothing with the trunks until someone from Germany inquired about the scholars.

As Stephen cleared the papers from Gerhard's makeshift desk, he found an envelope addressed to himself—Stephen Markham. *How odd,* he thought. *If Gerhard had something to tell me, why didn't he just say it?*

Stephen sat on Gerhard's chair, opened the envelope, and started reading the sealed letter.

Dear Stephen, mein Amerikanish freund,

I truly enjoyed discussing your peculiar theories about the lost tribes of Israel, the Book of Mormon, and your Prophet Joseph Smith.

As I am a Biblical scholar of some regard in Europe, you will understand why I need to write this letter without my comrade Klaus's knowledge. I wouldn't want him to overhear a converstaion and conclude that I profess such unscholarly conjectures as I'm about to reveal to you. I know you'll understand, so please do not share the contents of this letter with him.

As Christian and Jewish missionaries discovered remote peoples, they often had the dubious practice of attributing a group's religious practices, cultural traditions, and even facial features to those of Jews. This practice certainly got the congregations back home excited, and the money started pouring into the missions to convert the newly found lost tribes.

As a result, from the Tutsi[1] in Africa to the Samurai[2] of Japan, there are scores of imagined claims of Israeli linage. For this reason, I am certain that Klaus does not take seriously your claim that the tribes of Ephraim and Manasseh are in Arabia. Initially, I was also skeptical of your ideas. I saw them as just another imagined relationship between a particular subset of people and the traditional Jewish stereotype. However, there is something in your stories of Joseph Smith and the lost tribes of Arabia that resonates truth. Please let me explain what I mean.

As a rabbinical and biblical scholar, I can firmly state that the rabbis have always believed that the lost tribes would be found residing on both sides of the Red Sea.[3] This would include the Falashas Jews of Ethiopia and, of course, any other Israeli tribes dwelling among the Arabs on the east side of the Red Sea. There is even the Zimbabwe tribe of the Lemba who claim they are Jews. Another common belief among Jews is that the ten tribes are among the Pathan tribes of Afghanistan.[4] It is not surprising then that if you study the claims of the Falashas and the Lemba, you will find that both these tribes have Arabian origins.[5] Even the Afghani Pathan Jews have ties to Arabia, having been converted to Islam when their emissaries were invited to Islam by the Prophet Mohammed.[6]

You said that your Prophet Joseph Smith was born in the state of New York in 1805 and that he was given the keys by Moses to gather the tribes of Israel. Furthermore, you believe that Joseph's prophetic calling came in 1820 in what you referred to as "the First Vision."

It was roughly at that same time that the Jews experienced a period of great interest in the coming of the Messiah and the gathering of Israel. There was a real fervor in Judaism that the Messiah would soon come and that the lost tribes needed to be located and gathered again in Palestine.

I am starting to wonder if the prophetic calling of Joseph Smith Jr. triggered the desire to gather Israel, including the remnant of Joseph that is mentioned in Isaiah 11:11 and the gathering of Judah in the following verse. I remember how you told me that the sign that the gathering of the remnant would begin was the coming forth of the Book of Mormon, that when it was published it would show to the world that the Father's work to gather Israel had already started.[7] If my assumptions are correct, it would mean that the gathering of the tribes would have started shortly before the year 1830.

In this regard, I developed a timeline based on the notes I took during our discussions as well as my knowledge of the ongoing fervor the Jews are experiencing for the gathering.

1820 Joseph Smith was called to be a prophet.

1823 Joseph Smith was visited by an angel you call Moroni. During this revelation, the angel recited to Smith Isaiah chapter eleven, which describes the gathering of the remnant and the Jews.[8]

1824 Rabbi David Dee viet Hillel set off from Palestine to Syria, Kurdistan, Iraq, Persia, and India to try to locate the lost tribes. Although he believed the lost tribes to be in Ethiopia and Arabia, he located people in Syria and Kurdistan who claimed to be members of the ten tribes.[9]

1829 An emissary was sent from Palestine to southern Arabia. The emissary reported that he met a member of the tribe of Dan in southern Arabia who told him of an independent Jewish kingdom in the eastern part of Yemen. The emissary disappeared abruptly thereafter.

1830 The Book of Mormon was published, establishing the divine sign that the Father's gathering of Israel had already begun.

1831 Rabbi Yisrael of Shklov sent another emissary, R. Barukh ben R. Shmuel of Pinsk, to southern Arabia. The emissary carried a letter from the rabbi addressed to "our holy and pure brethren, the sons of Moses . . . who dwell beyond the shabatyon . . . and the ten Tribes."[10] The letter was signed by Rabbi Yisrael and other Palestinian rabbis.[11] The emissary was told that the tribe of Dan was living in the eastern reaches of Yemen.[12]

1846 Another Palestinian rabbi, Omram, was sent off to find the lost tribes in Arabia.[13] Unfortunately, Omram was robbed by Bedouin and forsook his effort. In the following years, several other Jewish emissaries were sent to southern Arabia to seek the help of the lost tribes.[14]

1874–79 A Jewish merchant visited Yemen and claimed the "warrior Jews" made up one-third of Arabia's population and that they had good relationships with the Arab nomads.[15]

Although this timeline appears to confirm the prophetic calling of Joseph Smith, the question still remains: Do the lost tribes in Arabia include the tribes of Ephraim and Manasseh? In other words, is part of the remnant spoken of by Isaiah still found in Arabia?

The earliest record we have claiming that the lost tribes were in Arabia came from the famous ninth-century Jew Edlad ha-Dani. The explorer made some extravagant claims. Among these is his declaration that Ephraim and one half of the tribe of Manasseh lived near Mecca in Arabia.[16] Perhaps the greatest early Jewish explorer was Rabbi Benjamin ben Jonah of Tudela. In 1160 the rabbi embarked on a thirteen-year expedition that took him to far-off China. He returned by way of southern Arabia, where he declared that he had found one half of the tribe of Manasseh.[17]

As you see, Stephen, some of the most famous Jewish rabbis and explorers died believing, as you do, that Ephraim and Manasseh are found in Arabia. I hope you find this letter informative.

With fondest regards,

Dein Bruder,

Gerhard Goldman

The cowboy stood up, folded Gerhard's letter, and placed it in his back pocket. He closed his eyes and thanked God for having known the two Germans. *What good men,* he thought. *What true brothers I will know in the hereafter.*

Notes

1. Tudor Parfitt, *The Lost Tribes of Israel: The History of a Myth* (London: Phoenix, 2004), 207–12.
2. Ibid., 182–84.
3. Ibid., 229.
4. Ibid., 141–44.
5. Ibid., 10, 224.
6. Ibid., 138–39.
7. 3 Nephi 21: 1–3, 6–7. The remnant is specified in verse 2.
8. Joseph Smith—History 1:20
9. Tudor Parfitt, *The Lost Tribes of Israel: The History of a Myth* (London: Phoenix, 2004), 235.
10. Ibid., 236.
11. Ibid.
12. Ibid., 235.
13. Ibid., 237.
14. Ibid., 237–38.
15. Ibid., 238.
16. Ibid., 9.
17. Ibid., 12.

Chapter 33

The Apostle of the Restoration

The want of foresight is an anomalous part of the Bedouin's character, for it does not result either from recklessness or stupidity.

A. W. Kinglake, *Eothen*, 1844

Stephen Markham
Thursday, Late March 1938
Al-Ibrahim's Camp

Camelita was growing bigger by the day. So was Stephen's desire to be with Norah. Each week, the seven days between their visits seemed to take longer to pass. He wondered if his wristwatch was breaking, or if it was his heart. Even the thought that his CALTOC contract would be over in three months was now something he was starting to regret. Leaving Arabia meant he would not only long for Norah, but he would miss the friendship of her father. In the emir, Stephen had found a father figure that filled the void left by the loss his own father. He no longer needed to question his feelings. The American knew in his heart that the Midian desert and the beni Ibrahim tribe had become his home and had taken over his life.

As tribal honors demanded, before he could start his Thursday afternoon camel training charades, he had to be welcomed to the camp by the emir. This required at least a full hour, four cups of wild mint tea, and filling Al-Ibrahim in on the world affairs from the BBC. This week the two men discussed how Stephen would return to America at the end of his contract in June. Would it be by way of Europe and the Atlantic? Or would he need to find passage through the Indian and Pacific Oceans? If Britain and Germany engaged in war, Stephen thought he would need to take the longer route to the east. However, Al-Ibrahim was convinced that he could still fly from Cairo to Morocco and then on to Lisbon, where ocean freighters could provide passage to New York. Finding a way home through Morocco sounded romantic to the American, but in reality he just wanted to find a way home without being caught up in someone else's war.

Besides the latest news, the two men discussed religion. Both were interested in knowing why their religions seemed to have so many peculiar similarities. Stephen had shared with Al-Ibrahim his theories about the remnant of Israel being the tribes of Joseph and how they might be found living among the Muslim people. During his scripture studies the previous Friday, Stephen had read a passage in the Islamic Qur'an that seemed to support his ideas. He looked forward to asking his friend what he thought of it.

"I am puzzled by a passage in the Holy Qur'an," Stephen said to the emir. "It appears to be talking about the tribe of the remnant, a Christian apostasy, and a Christian restoration. As you remember, *remnant* is a code word for the two tribes of the sons of

Joseph of Egypt. His brothers brought the remnant of Joseph's coat of many colors to his father and pronounced that he had been killed by wild animals. Here, let's take a look at the verses."

Of the wrongdoers the last
Remnant was cut off
Praise be to Allah,
The Cherisher of the Worlds
Say: "Think ye, if Allah
Took away your hearing
And your sight, and sealed up
Your hearts, who—a god
Other than Allah—could
Restore them to you?
(Qur'an 6:45–46)

"Mormons," Stephen continued, "believe that after Christ's death and resurrection, there was a complete apostasy and that men's hearts and minds were blinded. Without the light of new revelation, the Christian world degenerated into the Dark Ages, and many truths were taken from the Bible by evil-minded men. Eventually, the heavens were opened again, and the gospel was restored to the Prophet Joseph Smith. I believe this could be what this verse in the Qur'an is talking about."

Al-Ibrahim hesitated to reply. Finally, he said, "The Qur'an talks about a great gathering before the Day of Judgment, but it says nothing about a new prophet. You should read on, for in the same chapter of the Qur'an, Allah tells us that we must submit ourselves to the Lord of the worlds—to establish regular prayers and to fear Allah—for it is to him that we shall be gathered together.[1] I don't think that the Holy Qur'an is referring to a restoration. Perhaps it is only a reminder for the Muslims to obey what they have been commanded in the Qur'an. If there is to be some kind of restoration before the last days, I believe it already happened through the teacher Imam Mohammed Al-Wahabbi. His teachings are certainly helping the Muslims prepare for the great gathering when they will be restored to Allah. His followers are the fundamentalists called the Wahabbis. You have probably never heard of the Wahabbis, but it is a powerful movement that will someday affect the whole world. Even so, Mohammed Al-Wahabbi only professed to be a teacher, not a prophet. Besides, the verses you are referring to are discussing the restoration of the remnant, which you believe are part of the lost tribes of Israel. Why would you think that an American would be the prophet of the restoration of the lost tribes?"

Stephen answered without hesitation. "Because our Book of Mormon foretold that Joseph Smith would be the prophet of the last dispensation and that he would be a pure member of the house of Joseph. The Prophet was a direct descendant of Joseph of Egypt through the tribe of Ephraim. A New Testament apostle, James, foresaw the last days and sent out a specific invitation to the scattered tribes of Israel in our day. James invited the tribes to return to God in the last days and be perfected.[2] He then provided the very key that would open the heavens again. James wrote to the descendants of the scattered tribes: 'If any of you lack wisdom, let him ask of God, that giveth to all men liberally, and upbraith not; and it shall be given him' (James 1:5).

"When Joseph Smith, a direct descendant of Joseph of Egypt, read that verse, he wrote, 'Never did any passage of scripture come with more power to the heart of man than this did at this time to mine. It seemed to enter with greater force into every feeling of my heart.'[3] As I see it, it's very possible that the restoration of the remnant to Allah was fulfilled through the calling of the Prophet Joseph Smith."

"That is impossible," Al-Ibrahim interrupted. "Mohammed was the last of all the prophets to be called."

"I have read the entire Qur'an," Stephen replied, "and the book doesn't say anywhere that Mohammed would be the last prophet."

"You are wrong, Al-Mormon. The Qur'an states that Mohammed was the seal on the prophets. If he is the seal, then he has to be the last chapter of the book before it is closed."

"Even the Muslims believe that God sealed the heavens between the time of Christ and Mohammed, and the verses I read in the Qur'an talk about the taking away of the hearing and sight and then how it will be restored and the sealing of their hearts will be opened. If I am right, then the Qur'an itself teaches that a sealing by Allah is not permanent. God can undo a sealing whenever it pleases him. As I read it, it's straightforward: the Holy Qur'an implies that the sight, hearing, and hearts of the remnant of Joseph will be reopened by Allah."

"As I stated before, any restoration was probably only a new teacher, like Al-Wahabbi. A teacher only reminds us of what Allah has already given us, his complete word, the Holy Qur'an."

"Well, perhaps Allah will not send another prophet to the Muslims, but the Qur'an states that he will restore his word to the remnant. I remember that the Qur'an tells us that prophets were sent to every people.[4] My nation didn't even exist when the Qur'an was revealed. I also remember reading in the Qur'an that 'if the ocean were ink (wherewith to write it out), the word of my Lord, sooner would the ocean be exhausted than would the words of my Lord, even if we added another ocean like it' (Qur'an 18:109). Certainly not all the words of Allah are in the Qur'an and certainly Allah continues to speak and to send prophets to all nations."

"I see you are trying to become a student of the Qur'an. You have a good heart, Stephen, but as a student you are confused. The Qur'an is the last testament, and the heavens were sealed with the Prophet Mohammed."

"But isn't that the same excuse the Christian gave to Mohammed when he declared he was a new prophet and that the heavens had talked to him through the Prophet Gabriel? The Christians said they had a Bible and that they didn't need a Mohammed. Now the Muslim clerics use that same argument to reject any new prophets that Allah sends to the world."

"Perhaps Allah will cause a restoration among your people," returned Al-Ibrahim, "but the Muslims already have the complete gospel of God in its pure form. The ulema I studied under in Egypt, the one who told me about the Mormons, also wondered about a restoration of the children of Israel in the last days. However, he believed that if there were to be a restoration, it would be led by a new apostle, not a prophet. He quoted the second chapter of the Qur'an:

O children of Israel! Call to mind
The special favour which I bestowed
Upon you, and that I preferred you
To all others (for my Message).
Then guard yourselves against a Day
When one soul shall not avail another.
Remember We made the House
A place of assembly for men . . .

And remember, Abraham said:
'My Lord, make this a city of Peace,
and feed its People with fruits—
such of them as believe in Allah and the Last Day.'

And show us our places for
The celebration of rites;
And turn into us (in Mercy)

For thou art the Oft-Returning
Most Merciful.
Our Lord! Send amongst them
An Apostle of their own
Who shall rehearse Thy Signs
To them and instruct them
In Scripture and Wisdom,
And sanctify them.
(Qur'an 2:122–29)

"As you can see, Al-Mormon, this restoration you speak of would not be for the Muslims. The Qur'an prophesies that an apostle will come from his own people in the last days to instruct the people. He will teach them to make the signs of God. He will show them places for celebrating these rites and instruct them by way of scriptures and wisdom. We Muslims already have all the scriptures we need in the Holy Qur'an."

"I understand your position," Stephen was finally able to intervene. "What the ulema does not acknowledge is one very important historical fact. Joseph Smith was more than a prophet. He was called by revelation from God to be the first apostle of the restoration of the house of Israel in the last days.[5] Not only did Joseph Smith come from his own people, a direct descendant of Joseph of Egypt and the house of Israel, but as a sign, he was even named after Joseph of Egypt. He also restored temple work in the house of God,[6] where men are commanded to assemble.[7] The Prophet was the source of more new scriptures coming forth than any prophet in history, including the Word of Wisdom, a health code similar to the one revealed to Mohammed. Finally, the Qur'an states that the apostle that Allah sends to the people of the world will sanctify them. The Mormons have been commanded, by revelation through the Prophet Joseph Smith, to be sanctified."[8]

"I don't understand why there are so many parallels with our religions," Al-Ibrahim said with an air of pleased frustration. "Perhaps Joseph Smith read the Holy Qur'an and used some of its prophecies to make these accurate predictions."

"Well, Joseph Smith has been accused of copying early Christian scholars, the Kabbalah, Jewish rabbis, and Protestant preachers, so why not Islam? The truth is no one will ever be able to explain how an uneducated farm boy from the backwoods of New York could have revealed the astonishing body of religious knowledge that he did. To the unbelievers, it's a puzzle. They can try to mock their way free of it and its implications; however, as diligent as their arguments are, they cannot explain away or fault a single verse of the divine genius found in the scriptures restored through Joseph Smith. To the believer, it is obvious he was a true prophet who communed with God in the same fashion as Moses, Mohammed, and all the other great prophets."

"To be honest with you, Al-Mormon, I don't understand why our religions are so similar, yet so different. We don't believe in the divinity of Christ, and you've told me you worship Jesus as the son of God. Believe what you may, but for Muslims, Mohammed is the last prophet until Jesus Christ comes for a second time and brings our people here to Mount Sinai. Until that day, it is the beni Ibrahim's calling to keep the holy mountain sanctified."

"But tell me, my friend," Stephen asked, "do you believe both our religions have the same source, the One Supreme God, our Heavenly Father? Both faiths began through prophets, but one operates under the covenant of Sinai while the other promises salvation through Jesus Christ."

"How can we know such mysterious things? We are not prophets. While I was in Egypt, I learned to appreciate an old saying. It applies to the question you just asked me. 'Perhaps it is not. Perhaps it is so. To be exactly correct, I do not know.' "

"Good answer. I am as baffled as you are," Stephen said. "I believe there must be some relationship between our faiths. Yet, I know that it was impossible for Joseph Smith to have had an English translation of the Qur'an available to him. What I would like to do is meet the Egyptian ulema who told you about the Mormons and see if he can answer my questions. Do you think it would it be possible to meet him?"

"I am sure he would enjoy meeting a Mormon in the flesh, but he's in Cairo."

"That's no problem. I have vacation time coming out my ears and a salary I have no place to spend. If I pay for our way to Cairo, will you introduce me to the ulema?"

"His name is Ulema Abdulkarem, and it would be good to see my old teacher again. Yes, I will introduce you to the ulema. When shall we go?"

"How about next week?" Stephen replied.

"Insahalah," the emir replied. "We shall start for Cairo next Thursday."

"That's wonderful. Would it be possible to take Norah with us?" Stephen suddenly found himself begging permission from a reluctant father.

"My friend, you are severely testing me," Al-Ibrahim said. Then suddenly he smiled and after a moment of hesitation said, "Yes, I think it would be good if Norah came with us."

If Stephen were truly honest with himself, he would have recognized that the excitement he felt was not so much over the possibility of discussing religion but the chance to show Norah the sights and sounds of a great city. He spent the afternoon filling her head with all the wonderful things they would be seeing in Cairo. Norah too was excited, not so much with the expectation of seeing the pyramids as by the thought of being escorted there by a tall American cowboy.

As it was growing dark, Stephen said good-bye and started to leave.

"Aren't you going to say good night to your little daughter?" she asked.

"Camelita?"

"And who else? Are you responsible for her or not?"

"What should I do, tell her a bedtime story?"

"What is a bedtime story?" Norah asked.

"In America, to help put their children to sleep, parents tell their children a fairy tale," the cowboy replied.

"What is a fairy tale?"

"They are made up stories that are only believable by young children. My favorites stories were about cowboys like Pecos Bill, who could rope a rain cloud. Girls usually like fairy tales about falling in love with a handsome prince."

"Don't you believe that a cowboy can grow up to marry a princess?"

That stopped Stephen in his tracks. "They're only fairy tales that help young children to have good dreams. Tonight, before I go to sleep, I will tell myself the story of the cowboy who married an unbelievably beautiful princess and took her down the Nile River."

"I like that story," Norah softly said.

"Shall I tell that story to Camelita?"

"No, you can tell it to me in Cairo. When Muslims put their children to bed, they read them the last three Surahs of the Qur'an. It calms our children and protects them from nightmares. My mother recited them to me every night. When you learn them, you can recite them to Camelita. This is one of them:

I seek refuge with the Lord of the Dawn
From the mischief of created things,

From the mischief of Darkness as it overspreads,
From the mischief of those who practice Secret Arts;
And from the mischief of the envious one as he practices envy.
(Qur'an 113)

As Stephen drove back to his camp that night, he marveled at a culture in which parents recite scriptures to their children each night before they fall asleep. But was it only a cowboy's fairy tale that one day the Muslim Norah would be reading verses to his children from the book of 3 Nephi?

Notes

1. Qur'an 6:71–72.
2. James 1:1–4.
3. Joseph Smith—History 1:12.
5. Qur'an 16:36.
6. Doctrine and Covenants 20:1–2.
7. Doctrine and Covenants 125:40.
8. Refer to the solemn assemblies discussed in Doctrine and Covenants 109:6.
9. Doctrine and Covenants 43:11.

Chapter 34

Mercy or Justice?

The highest standards of behavior were the standards of the desert.

Wilfred Theisger, *Arabian Sands*, 1959

Stephen Markham

Friday, March 25, 1938
The Camp of Al-Ibrahim

He thought he wouldn't be seeing the emir until they started for Cairo the next Thursday, but the very next day, the emir summoned Stephen to his camp. The warriors who paged Stephen told him that it was about a very important tribal matter, and it was absolutely necessary for Stephen to come.

Every time Stephen visited the emir's camp, he seemed to experience something he never thought he would experience in his entire life, and this day was no exception. A large crowd had assembled next to the tribe's outdoor mosque, the sacred structure that Norah had described as being made only of a stone outline. Noon prayers on Friday included a sermon by Al-Ibrahim, and it was the custom for the entire tribe to congregate to his mosque that day each week.

When the Christian arrived at the mosque, he discovered another purpose for Friday prayers. Just outside the simple mosque was Osama. He was on his knees, and his hands were tied behind his back. Just behind him was a large muscular man leaning on a long executioner's sword.

It was as if the entire crowd had been waiting for Stephen's arrival; everyone seemed relieved to see him.

"Thank you for coming, Al-Mormon," Al-Ibrahim welcomed Stephen. "We couldn't continue without you."

"Continue what? Why is Osama tied up?"

"He is preparing to meet Allah and receive punishment from his creator."

"Are you going to kill him?" Stephen asked.

"Only if that is your choice."

"What?" Stephen protested.

"Yes, it is up to you. I met with the sheiks of the tribe, and we have decided that you must represent the families of the two Germans."

"Families? Gerhard and Klaus weren't married and didn't have any children."

"It doesn't matter. We would normally have to consult with their fathers or elder brothers, but that's not possible. You were their friends, so you will decide the fate of Osama."

"What fate? Why are you prepared to kill him?"

"Osama betrayed our tribe, he betrayed me, and, most important, he betrayed the Islamic faith. I trusted Osama, made him the captain of my warriors. I even taught him the secret of how to be immune to Al-Dajja's evil powers, by invoking Allah's names and reciting the Qur'an. Now I find out that he confessed to his brothers that he was asked by Al-Dajja to bring the two Germans to him. The evil one saw the Germans from far off. He saw your friends hiking in the darkness of the night toward Mount Sinai and asked Osama to meet them and offer to show them the holy mountain. Osama knew what Al-Dajja would do to them, yet he willingly led the Germans into the jaws of death. He has been a willing partner with Al-Dajja in the death of two men, and justice requires that his life be taken."

"Isn't that your decision? What in heaven's name does it have to do with me?"

"As the representative of the Germans' families, you must decide Osama's final judgment. You can exercise the law of justice and have him killed. The law of Moses has already condemned him to that fate. Or you can show mercy on him, forgive him, and let him go free. You may also require compensation from his family and take blood money in exchange for his life."

"Blood money? I've never heard of that."

"The concept is found in your Bible,[1] and it is God's way of taking care of the victims of crimes."

"It sounds a lot better than what happens in the United States," Stephen interrupted. "Someone can be robbed, beaten, and raped, and no one does anything to help the victim. The criminal might get a light sentence, but the poor victims, what happens to them? Who compensates them for what has been taken? Who pays for the victims' medical bills? Who tries to repair the life of the rape victim? Who takes care of the wife and children of the father who has been murdered? In America it's not the criminal. In my country, no one takes care of the victim. If you ask me, the victim suffers the crime twice."

"In Islam, the Holy Prophet taught us that the criminal or his family must compensate the victims, and that is the only way that the criminal can truly repent. So it is your responsibility to state what compensation Osama's family needs to pay the German families. They can give the money to you so you can arrange to send the money to Germany."

"That makes sense to me, but why behead Osama? He didn't kill my friends with his own hands. Aren't there prisons in Arabia?"

"We have prisons, but they are not for confessed murderers. Allah requires an eye for an eye and a life for a life, and Osama helped take the lives of two men."

Stephen was uncomfortable with the predicament in which he had been placed. Al-Ibrahim had him squarely in the chasm between the law of justice and the law of mercy. It was the eternal gap that can only be reconciled through the Atonement of Jesus Christ. Stephen was being forced to understand just how real the dilemma between the laws was. "Look, Osama didn't kill me. Why not give him another chance? Why not let him go?" Stephen asked.

"That's a question, not an answer, Al-Mormon. The executioner is ready to do his job. He will be paid whether or not he swings his sword. But before you set Osama free, you had better think about the consequences of your decision. You said he tried to kill you. He led the Germans to a certain death. Have you thought of whom he will kill next? Have you thought of what will happen to the family of his next victim? How can Osama repent for taking the lives of two people, unless he foregoes his own life? In Arabia we respect the law of Moses. We do not negate its blessings by applying the law of mercy without a price."

"That's interesting," Stephen said. "In my country, we seem to have forgotten the law of Moses. Our judges seem to believe they can apply mercy without balancing it with justice."

"In Arabia our laws are based on the laws of Moses. They require justice, unless there is someone who can pay the price for the crimes that have been committed against the victim."

"The law of justice was established by the Lord for all eternity. Justice is eternal, just as God is," Stephen added. "The law does not change, nor does God. Because American judges have ignored the law of justice, our citizens are now plagued with violent crime. A woman cannot walk in a park at night without the fear of being raped. And if she is, the rapist might spend a year or two in prison before being released to hunt down another victim."

"In Arabia, we cut off the hand of the robber to remind him and those who might be tempted to rob. We stone to death the rapist to remind all that there is a serious consequence to this most grievous crime. And the murderers, Allah requires they be slain by the sword. As a result, crimes seldom happen in Arabia. Because our judges use the Qur'an to decide the punishment, our people seldom become the victims of the wicked. For thirty-five years, I have been imam and emir of my tribe, and Osama is the first person I have had to try. Taking Osama's life for what he has done is not the beni Ibrahim's way; it is Allah's way. So what is your decision, Al-Mormon? The justice of the executioner's sword or mercy and freedom? Remember, my friend, if he kills again, you must live with the consequences of your decision."

What would the Lord do? Stephen thought. He was trying to appeal for help from the only one who could reconcile the two timeless laws. Finally, Stephen looked into Osama's eyes as if trying to predict his motives. The cowboy then walked over to him and bent down to ask his foe in a soft voice. "When you led the Germans to Al-Dajja, did you know he would kill them?"

Osama said nothing.

"Is it your intention to kill my friend and your emir, Al-Ibrahim?"

Osama said nothing.

Stephen stood up and looked at the executioner. "Kill the poor soul."

Notes
1. Genesis 34:11.

Chapter 35

The Missing Radio

The eyes see only what the mind is prepared to comprehend.
Robertson Davis

Jake Sorensen
Summer 1989
PAMMCO Headquarters
Al-Khobar, Saudi Arabia
Week Eight of Ten-week Internship

My phone rang. "Jake, this is Mac Pastore. Can you come to my office?"

"Sure," I replied. "Anything new?"

"Yeah, it dawned on me that we didn't check the CALTOC Midian Surveying Reports for 1936 through 1938. I ordered them from Houston. I think you'll find them interesting."

I rushed over to Mr. Pastore's office, wondering what possible mysteries from the past might be revealed in oil survey reports. I had barely entered his office when Mac began speaking.

"Our white Bedouin went to Midian with a translator named Ahmed bin Al-Hajri."

"Who's he?"

"Who's he? He was a PAMMCO vice president, that's who. He retired about five years ago. He started working for CALTOC as a translator about the same time Markham arrived in the kingdom. It appears that Markham is part linguist. He learned Arabic so well that Ahmed was transferred back to CALTOC headquarters in December of 1937."

"Perhaps he knows what happened to Markham," I replied.

"Maybe, but probably not. From these reports, everything seemed to have been going smoothly for the Midian survey until the supply truck arrived on May 1, 1938."

"What happened then?"

"The supply truck driver reported that when he got to Markham's camp, the truck was there, but there was no sign of the geologist. The driver waited two days, and still there was no sign of him. He finally left the supplies and returned to Khobar."

"That's strange."

"Yeah, and listen to this: the driver reported that everything in Markham's camp was neatly packed away and in its place except for the company rifle, a short wave radio, a generator, and two barrels of gasoline. On the camp table he found an envelope containing 175 U.S. dollars and a handwritten invoice for one rifle, one radio, one generator, and the two missing barrels of gasoline. The invoice was signed by Stephen Markham. The supply truck returned in June and found that the camp had not been touched."

"For me, that's pretty strong evidence that Markham is not dead. He's a war deserter," I said.

"Perhaps," came Mac's reply. "But there's another note in the Tabuk files. When Markham failed to turn up the second month, CALTOC sent a team up to investigate what had happened to him and to close down his camp. They reported that the local Bedouin said that they had found his body and buried it. The Bedouin told the team that Markham had been shot."

"That's not very promising," I said. "I have another theory. The note and the money indicate that he planned his disappearance, sort of a clueless suicide note showing he was in control of what he did. Perhaps he had a girl back home, and he was gone so long that she left him. Heartbroken and lonely, he had no reason to go home at the end of his contract. Instead of using his visa, he gave a few CALTOC items to some Bedouin, walked out into the desert, and shot himself. However he died, it appears our Stephen Markham is, once again, a dead lead."

"Remember, a reporter never gives up. Let me see if I can set up a meeting for you with Ahmed bin Al-Hajri."

Chapter 36

Dreams of the Desert

He is crazed with the spell of far Arabia. They have stolen his wits away.

Walter de la Mare, "Arabia"

Stephen Markham
Early April 1938
The Voyage to Egypt

Stephen drove the Ford pickup as far as Duba, a Red Sea harbor town one hundred miles south of Midian. The ride was uneventful, but not something Stephen would have wanted to repeat in Utah. He drove, Norah rode shotgun, and sitting between the two lovers was the emir. *What are friends for?* the cowboy thought. Besides, the one thing that needed to be done that day was to get to Duba in time to book passage on the ferry to Egypt. The plan was to make time, get there, and get out of the town before dark. Stephen remembered the Germans complaining about the lodging in Duba. They said something about its only hotel being a centuries-old inn that was frequented by large herds of man-eating cockroaches. Of course the Germans had embellished the horrors of the Duba hotel, but Stephen did not want to take a chance. Duba sounded like no place to introduce Norah to the wonders of city living.

Seated three across in the cab, Papa Ibrahim was a formidable wall between the cowboy and the beautiful princess. Stephen had grand plans for showing the sheltered Bedouin girl the wonders of the modern world. For now, he would have to pass the time by talking with the emir.

"Do you remember what you said about the problems great wealth would bring to your people?" Stephen asked Al-Ibrahim.

"How could I forget? I worry day and night about the fate of my people. What will become of them? What kind of children could Norah raise if they were swimming in material riches?" the emir replied.

"I admire the way your people live. If I discover oil in Midian, will I be helping to bring to pass their demise?"

"Young man," Al-Ibrahim said, "you must answer that question for yourself, and one day you will face Allah's judgment. I might be a simple Bedouin, but I know that you can't turn back time. If it had not been you, the Americans would have sent someone else."

"You're probably right. The forces of change are beyond our control. When I think about what I am doing here, I have the feeling that God wants the Arab people to become incredibly rich."

"Allah blesses those who worship him, but it is difficult to remain focused on God when one is rich. Doesn't your Bible say that it is more difficult for a rich man to enter heaven than for a camel to pass through the eye of a needle? So why would God want the Arabs to be wealthy?"

"I have been trying to figure that out myself. Mormons believe that in the last days God will raise up a mighty nation of Gentiles in America. The true gospel will be restored to them, and then the light of the gospel will be recognized by kings.[1] The only place on earth that still has kings with real power is Arabia and the other Islamic nations."

Al-Ibrahim seemed annoyed by the theory. "Do you mean to tell me that you believe that the Americans will restore the true gospel, and then they will send it to the Muslim kings? If you tell that to King Abdulaziz, you had better stand beyond the reach of his sword."

"I am not sure, but that's what the Prophet Isaiah seems to have believed. He wrote of the great gathering[2] and how the forces of the Gentiles will come to the lands of the kings. The Gentiles will convert the riches from the sea for them.[3] Another CALTOC geologist told me that they expect to find the largest oil fields in Arabia beneath the waters of the Persian Gulf."

"Interesting," the emir said. "But I find it hard to believe that infidels from America would teach our noble Islamic kings."

"But don't you see? It is American-Gentile technology that is about to make your people wildly rich. Your own King Abdulaziz surprised everyone by selecting the Americans over the British and French to extract your nation's riches."

"Why are you so sure Isaiah was talking about our kings?"

"That's what I found so amazing about his prophecy. He identified the lands of the rich latter-day kings as Midian and Sheba.[4] These are Arabian lands, and Midian would include you, one of its emirs."

"Again, that is interesting, but why would Allah curse me with great wealth?"

"Perhaps you'll need the wealth in order to finance the great gathering of the Muslim people to Mount Sinai. Furthermore, once at the holy mountain, you'll need to make a great offering in righteousness to the Lord."

"I should not let Norah listen to your nonsense about riches. The next thing you know, she will want me to buy her a golden palace."

"Please, Abu," Norah interrupted, "just one little golden palace for your favorite daughter."

They all laughed. "Have I ever denied you anything, my dear?" Al-Ibrahim asked. "I will buy you a little one in Cairo, the kind they sell to foreign tourists to take back with them to their homelands."

They laughed again, and Stephen changed the subject. It was obvious to him that Al-Ibrahim had no interest in becoming wealthy and even less interest in hearing that Americans would be his spiritual mentors.

The time passed quickly, and before they knew it, the three travelers reached Duba. The good news they received was that there was still time to board the afternoon ferry to Egypt. The bad news was that Norah took one look at the Red Sea and became nervous. She had never seen a lake, let alone a large body of water that she could not see across. She asked to return home, but Al-Ibrahim would have none of it. Stephen was somewhat surprised by the insensitive manner in which Al-Ibrahim dealt with his daughter's fear.

The situation grew critical when the ferry appeared on the horizon and closed in on the Duba pier. The largest machine Norah had ever seen was Stephen's truck, and to her the rusting ship was a mechanical sea monster. Stephen could only guess what was going on in her mind. Her anxious gestures evolved into tears and panic.

"Why don't we return to Midian?" Stephen asked Al-Ibrahim. "We can take Norah back to your camp and leave for Cairo next Thursday."

"No, it is good for Norah to see the world outside the desert," Al-Ibrahim replied. "The world of machines is closing in on my people, and I must prepare my children for a new kind of humanity, one where people will be dependent on machines to live their lives."

Stephen tried to comfort Norah by talking about the nature of machines and all the sights they would be seeing in Cairo. By the time the ferry docked, he had just about convinced her that the giant ship was safe to board. But as the gangplank was lowered and the first passengers disembarked, Norah started screaming. "They are naked! They are naked!"

At first the Mormon thought Norah's fear had caused her to hallucinate. "What's wrong?" he asked the princess.

"The ladies, they are naked!" Norah replied pointing to the women coming down the gangplank.

The response from the Egyptian ladies was mocking laughter. They chuckled to each other and pointed to the silly young Bedouin woman. They must have thought that the Bedouin girl was some kind of human dinosaur.

"Why do you think they are naked? They are wearing beautiful dresses," Stephen said to try to calm Norah.

"Look at those filthy women," Norah said loud enough to be heard by everyone leaving the ferry. "Look, they do not cover their arms. They show off their ankles and legs. They even expose their knees. They unveil their hair and wear makeup in public. Don't they have any respect for their bodies? What must Allah think?"

It suddenly dawned on Stephen that Norah had never seen a woman dressed in western-style fashions. "This is the way all women dress in Egypt and America," he tried to assure Norah.

Al-Ibrahim just stood there observing Al-Mormon's ineffective attempts to calm his daughter. The emir watched in silence.

"Do you mean to tell me, Stephen, that American mothers and daughters walk around in public showing their bodies off to strange men? We have a name for women who try to attract men by using their bodies," Norah said with a renewed sense of righteousness.

"Well, to be truthful, that is the way my own sister dresses."

"You allow your sister to expose herself like that to men? Look at those things you call dresses. They are so tight, you can see just how pointed are their breasts and how big are their butts!" Norah said, this time without the least degree of nobility and in a voice that carried to the Egyptian ladies who were now hysterical with laughter.

The baffled cowboy was beside himself, not knowing what more he could say to the girl he loved. *Why can't she just relax and accept the world as it is?* he thought. *What's the big fuss about?* Then he realized that if his own Mormon pioneer great-grandmother were to be resurrected today, she would react the same way to seeing how modern Mormon women dressed. *Norah is right,* he realized. *What on earth has happened to the standards of western society? Our women have become little more than enticing billboards for strange men's eyes.*

The old ferry would dock for three hours before trudging off again for Egypt. It took Stephen all hundred and eighty minutes to calm Norah for a second time. For the Mormon man who loved the Muslim girl, it was frustrating. Yet he didn't blame her. Clearly, Norah was pure and innocent and understood, without compromise, the way a righteous woman should dress. However, he was becoming more and more upset at the way her father seemed to show no concern at all for his daughter's distress.

Once on board, the three arranged to meet for supper in the dining hall, and Al-Ibrahim escorted his daughter to her cabin. However, Norah didn't appear for dinner. Al-Ibrahim claimed that the motion of the ship had made her ill.

"Are you sure Norah is all right?" Stephen questioned. "Perhaps there's a ship's doctor who can give her something. I really wanted her to enjoy the voyage. I thought she would be excited to see life outside of Arabia."

"I am sure she will be fine," Al-Ibrahim replied. "She just needs some rest and some time to adjust. She also needs to acquire what you Americans call sea legs."

"Call it what you may, but I think legs are part of the problem. She had a frenzy when she saw the tight-fitting, high-hemmed dresses the Egyptian women were wearing."

"Why does that shock you, Al-Mormon?" the emir asked. "How would your mother have reacted if you took her to a place where the women went topless, showing everything from the waist up?"

"My mother? First, she would have killed me for taking her to such a place, and if she failed to kill me, she would lecture me for a week on how filthy my mind was."

"Well, that is exactly what my daughter is thinking. Why would her father take her to a place where women play up their bodies for men? By her standards, these women are as corrupt as the western women who show their breasts. Norah is in her room, and she will not come out until we reach Egypt."

"I understand how she feels. She's a good person. But I regret the fact that she will miss seeing the Red Sea at sunrise."

"I will take her some food, and if she feels better, she can eat. But believe me, Al-Mormon, it is better for both of us that she stays in her cabin. What do you think she would say if she went out on the deck in the morning and saw women sunning in French swimsuits?"

Stephen got the point.

That evening, Stephen had difficulty sleeping. After several attempts to fall asleep, he decided he must finally face the issue that was weighing on his heart. He dressed and walked to the port side deck. It was a beautiful night. He thought of Norah and wished they could watch together the moonlight dancing across the face of the Red Sea.

He looked westward into the dark empty sky. Tomorrow the ship would land in Egypt, the motherland of both Ephraim and Ishmael. Perhaps the river kingdom would reveal to him a clue as to why the Mormons and Muslims seemed to have common sentiments. Unlike the other tribes, Ephraim and Manasseh enjoyed an elevated status in Egypt. The Mormon remembered that when Solomon sought the life of the Ephraimite king Jeroboam, the Egyptian king Shishak gave Jeroboam refuge.[5]

But wherever Stephen's mind wandered, it quickly returned to beautiful Norah. Two questions kept recurring in his mind. Should he ask Al-Ibrahim for Norah's hand in marriage? And, could he?

He tried to put aside these burning, ominous questions. He looked again at the moonlight on the sea. He wondered what connection the prophet Lehi had to Egypt. Lehi was of Manasseh, and his native language was Egyptian.[6] However, as Stephen began contemplating the question, he found himself thinking of Norah and the questions that troubled his heart.

How could he make sense of what had happened to him since the night he met her at the Bedouin poetry recital? How could he ever live without her? He passionately loved her. But was he mad or just madly in love? Perhaps he was suffering from a severe case of the noble savage illusion. Stephen remembered hearing rumors of ex-missionaries returning to the poverty-stricken Polynesian Islands to marry grass-skirted dollies and settle down to lives in beach huts. Were his feelings puppy love or an eternal attraction? Were they superficial, temporary, and the mere illusion of love? If he now denied the desire of his heart, would he live forever regretting what he had lost? Maybe he'd been gone from Utah too long and just needed a long vacation to figure out what was real. Certainly he had to regain his Mormon perspective. He was living an isolated existence in an exotic land where it was easy to lose one's way. Had he become the genie inside the oil lamp—living inside a small world where he had become enchanted by the beauty of a Bedouin princess? Despite all the questions, he had not a single answer. However, he did know one thing: Norah's fire burned hot in his soul.

The next morning Stephen met Al-Ibrahim for breakfast. "How is Norah?"

"She excuses herself. The sea and her stomach are waging war. As soon as she got to her cabin yesterday, she laid down on her bed, and from then on, she has been dizzy. When she tries to stand up, she says her cabin turns in circles around her. I think the last thing she wants to smell is food."

"Oh, I'm so sorry for her."

"I am sure she misses having breakfast with us."

The waiter took the men's orders and left for the kitchen.

"Al-Ibrahim, last night I stayed up nearly the entire night."

"Are you also sick?"

"In a way, but it was not from the rocking of the ferry. My good friend, I am in love with your daughter. So much so that I do not think I could live happily without her. What should I do?"

"If you were a good Muslim, you could promise me a large dowry and ask for her hand in marriage. If you were a Bedouin, you could introduce me to your father and we could talk for hours about the living arrangements for my daughter. But, Al-Mormon, you are neither. I know you will never give up your religion, and there is no way you can properly care for Norah in your western world. She is a delicate desert flower. Take her from the only life she knows, and she will die a thousand deaths."

"But I am sure she would come with me if I asked her to."

"Of course she would. But are you blind?"

"What?" Stephen reacted.

"You must be in love, for you can't see your nose in front of you. Norah loves you. But she needs her nomadic life even more than she needs a husband. We are free in the desert. We rely upon our God and hard work to meet our needs in a land where most people would die within days. We have our simple ways, our noble stories, and our poetry of faith. Our only possessions are our tribe, our animals, our tents, our barren land, and God. It is all we need, and we are content.

"Let me tell you a true story. Once there was an emir who ruled the island of Taruk on the Persian Gulf coast of Arabia. He saw a beautiful Bedouin girl and fell deeply in love. He arranged with her brother to take her to wife. He paid a handsome dowry for the girl and brought his new wife to his glorious palace by the sea. But he soon discovered that his Bedouin woman could not live in houses with rooms where she could not see the desert horizon. She preferred tents made of goat hair and the aroma of the desert.

"This was the fate of Sheikh Abdul Al-Fayani, one of the richest and most powerful people in the Persian Gulf. He married the beautiful Bedouin girl Khaznah bin Hazam Al-Hethlain Al-Aimi and placed her in his palace on Darien Island of Taruk, near Al-Khobar. The Sheikh loved his Bedouin bride very much. He gave her everything, but she was still unhappy. When ships arrived at the harbor of Taruk, the sheikh Abdul decreed that his wife would be the first to go to the ship and purchase whatever she wanted of the imported silks from China, perfumes from India, carpets from Iran, and whatever other precious items she desired. However, she remained sad. One day the sheikh overheard his wife reciting a poem she had written.

> Oh my brother, no one but you
> Who have dumped me in a place
> Where no one of you has ever lived.
>
> I do not need 'Darin' or 'Qatif'
> And I do not need its people.
>
> I wish I had a camel with a harness
> Rather than having those ships
> With all the ropes that tie them up.

I am dreaming that I see the desert of 'Raseif'
In the spring time and I would like to see
The 'Harmalyyah' mountain even if it's mad at me.

I would love to wander and pick the truffles
From the green fields after the rain
And smell the aroma of the desert plants and grass.

"When the sheikh overheard his wife reciting the poem, he was heartbroken. However, because he loved her so much, he agreed to send her back to her tribe in the desert. Al-Mormon, you might love my daughter with all your heart, but if you really love her, you will not take her away from her desert life. Please understand, Stephen. You are from another world, one in which my daughter could never survive. Look at her. She hides in her cabin because she is frightened and embarrassed. She is not so much seasick as she is sick of what she sees. From our point of view, the West is a world where people don't really care to live the commandments of God, while for us it is natural to obey. I wanted you to see this for yourself, Al-Mormon. This is the very reason I allowed Norah to come with us to Egypt. You are a good man, but you could never make her happy. If you married her, Norah's unhappiness would eat away at your heart. Believe me, Al-Mormon, I would love to call you my son, but I can't allow you to marry Norah. She is a woman from a different time, a different land, and a different religion."

Notes

1. 1 Nephi 13:12–25; Isaiah 60:1–3.
2. Isaiah 60:4.
3. Isaiah 60:5.
4. Isaiah 60:6.
5. 1 Kings 11:40.
6. 1 Nephi 1:2.

Chapter 37

A Lesson in Morals

Never believe that a few caring people can't change the world.
For indeed, that's all who ever have.

Margret Mead

Stephen Markham
April 1938
Cairo, Egypt

What American child has not dreamed of seeing the great pyramids of Giza, Cleopatra's Nile, spooky mummies, and the exotic markets and cafés of old Cairo? Stephen had dreamed of all those images, yet on visiting the fabled Egyptian monuments, he felt an impending emptiness and a mounting sadness. While Al-Ibrahim was making contact with Ulema Abdulkarem and setting up a time when they could meet, Stephen set out on foot to see the wonders of Egypt. Before that day, he had only seen sketches of Egypt's antiquities. Now he was seeing them with his own eyes but sharing the experience with no one. Norah refused to leave the small hotel in the colorful old district of Cairo.

Within the walls of the old district, Saladin the Great had built his citadel. The majority of the women who walked along the old district's narrow streets wore traditional clothes. However, like Cleopatra, the Egyptian women wore heavy makeup and didn't cover their hair when in public. Not only was Norah having difficulty accepting the way even the women of the old district dressed, she was also overwhelmed by the number of people who walked Cairo's streets. The young Saudi girl had never seen so many people at one time. The narrow streets and alleyways were packed with more people than she thought lived in the entire world. She felt she could hardly breathe among the street merchants, students rushing to school, donkey carts, loud shopkeepers trying to lure people into their small establishments, robed clerics murmuring verses of the Qur'an as they hurried on their way to Mosque, whistling policeman trying hopelessly to direct Cairo's traffic, stray dogs and cats, and the odors of a thousand eateries and countless piles of uncollected garbage. The only two-lane avenue that passed through the old district was gridlocked with buses and taxis. The huge buses were like struggling landlocked whales. They constantly sounded their horns and packed as many people as they could inside their bellies. Before Cairo, Norah's entire world had been the sheltered wilderness of Midian. She was afraid to venture out into Cairo's dynamic metropolitan mass of over one million people living and working inside a few square miles. To a Bedouin girl, it might as well have been Dante's inferno.

But those were not the only reasons keeping Norah in her room. Ever since they landed in Egypt, Stephen had behaved toward her with an odd coolness. She desperately needed to know what was wrong with her cowboy. What had happened to his constant smile and the spark in his eye that testified of his love for her? Had her father said something to him? All Norah knew was that Stephen had suddenly changed. He was keeping an emotional distance from her, and it was tying her heart into a painful knot. Oh, how she wished she had never come on the trip. All she wanted now was to be back at her family's camp with Stephen, pretending they were training the little she-camel.

The first two days they were in Cairo, Stephen was left alone to walk the streets. Originally settled as a Roman fort, the beautiful Cairo was once the largest and perhaps most important city in the world. After the sacking of Baghdad in 1258, it became the cultural and political center of Sunni Islam and remained in that state of importance until the rise of the Turks. The city was eventually captured by the Ottman Empire under Selim II in 1517. Through its more recent architecture, Stephen could see the influences of the French and British occupations. On the second day, he walked through the Coptic Christian neighborhood and remembered how baby Jesus had lived in Egypt. Despite the thrilling mosaic of history that Stephen was experiencing, he couldn't muster the slightest smile. The sole thought that pounded on his mind was that of innocent Norah and the vastly different worlds that separated them.

Stephen could not take it any longer. After they had retired to their rooms that evening, he walked down the hall and knocked on the door to Norah's hotel room.

"Stephen, what are you doing here? My father must not see you at my door."

"I understand. Can you please meet me in the lobby in five minutes?"

"I will be there. Now go quickly."

Stephen waited patiently, however it was twenty minutes before Norah appeared in the lobby. Stephen rose and pulled out a chair for Norah so she could sit across a small lobby table from him. "Thank you for coming."

Norah wore a long, flowing crimson gown. She needed no makeup. Her carmel colored skin was as smooth as silk. Her lips were inviting. She had combed her black hair so it sparkled like the moonlight on the Red Sea. As always, her black eyes were hypnotic. Stephen had never touched the princess, but now found himself fighting the temptation to take her hand and lead her into a tender kiss.

"Why did you asked me to meet you?" Norah asked.

"I want to take you shopping. Please agree to join your father and me tomorrow. I will buy you whatever dress you want."

"I am sorry, Stephen, but I do not wear the kind of dresses they sell in Cairo."

"I don't understand. On the one hand, Bedouin women don't cover their hair and bodies with black abiyas like the Saudi women in the cities. On the other hand, you go crazy when you see the dresses Egyptian women wear. Aren't all Muslims alike?"

"They might be Muslims, but they are not like me. In the first place, I do not wear an abiya or cover my hair because that is not the teachings of the Qur'an. It is only a tradition Arab men use to control their women. The Prophet Mohammed taught us how to dress in a manner that would please Allah. The Holy Prophet told our men that they should wear white thaub robes, for it was the manner of dress that God had chosen for them."

"Did the Prophet teach women how they should dress?" Stephen asked.

"Alhamdalla. Thanks to God he had great respect for women and told them they should protect their bodies from the immoral thoughts of men. Before the Prophet, some Arab women exposed their breasts like African women. This was a sin. When the Qur'an was revealed, it expressly instructed our woman to never show their bosoms in public. You see, Stephen, the natural beauty of a woman's body is the sacred handiwork of Allah. It can tempt a weak man beyond his ability to control himself. For this reason, the Prophet taught Muslim women not to openly portray the form of their bodies. The only exception is for their husbands. If we were married Stephen, would you want other men thinking about my body?"

"Of course not."

"Would you want other men looking at me in a tight dress and wondering what it would be like to sleep with me?"

"Never."

"Good. But the women here in Cairo wear dresses that cling to their bodies. They willfully invite men to fondle their bodies with their eyes. It's a free invitation to have more."

"But what can you do about it? In Utah the men are taught not to stare at women and to keep their thoughts pure."

"Pure! Do you think men have pure thoughts when they see a woman in a tight fitting dress that exposes her shoulders, arms, and legs?"

"Sure, it's hard not to think of a woman's body when you see her in a swimming suit or a tight dress. However, real men have the strength to control their thoughts."

"Well, my father taught me that there are very few such men who can control their thoughts. Are you telling me that women in America wear clothes that intentionally highlight their bodies?"

"Well, not as much as they used to. About ten years ago, in what we called the roaring twenties, some women wore dresses that exposes their ankles, knees, and a lot more. But since hard times have come to America, the women tend to choose dresses that at least cover their knees."

"Tell me, Stephen. Were you offering to buy me a dress that was tight around the waist and exposed my legs below the knee?"

"Only if that is what you wanted."

Norah teared up. "Excuse me, Stephen." Norah stood up and started walking back to her room. After a few steps she turned and looked back at Stephen. "How could you ever think I would want such an evil garment? The beauty of my body is sacred, and its image and touch are for only one person, my husband. How could you marry a woman who would want other men to desire her body? Good night."

As if leaving him alone at the altar, the woman he loved walked away. Like a final knockout punch, Stephen felt his dreams fading away and was helpless to bring them back. When it came to virtue and modesty, Norah was as uncompromising to the desires of Babylon as her desert was to the wishes of the men lost in its grip.

Chapter 38

Truth within Its Ordained Sphere

Semites had no half-tones in their register of vision. They were a people of primary colours, or rather black and white, who saw the world always in contour. They were a dogmatic people, despised doubt, our modern crown of thorns. They do not understand our metaphysical difficulties, our introspective questionings. They knew only truth, untruth.

T. E. Lawrence, *Seven Pillars of Wisdom*, 1935

Stephen Markham
April 1938
Home of Ulema Abdulkarem
Cairo, Egypt

Al-Ibrahim had convinced his Islamic mentor, Ulema Abdulkarem, to meet with his curious Mormon friend who was full to his ears with questions. However, the invitation to talk with a real Mormon was not received with the warm enthusiasm Al-Ibrahim had hoped. The ulema only accepted the offer to meet with Stephen on the condition that the discussions be held in the privacy his home and not in his majlis at Al-Azhar University.

Because of his unusual views on Mormonism, the renowned Islamic university had censored Ulema Abdulkarem. Although he continued to hold the distinguished title of ulema (a professor of Islamic scholarship), the grand imam of the school removed him from the university's Supreme Council and instructed Abdulkarem to stop teaching about some extraordinary connection between the Christian Mormons' doctrine and the teachings of Islam.

Within moments of Al-Ibrahim and Stephen's entering the ulema's house, the emir emphasized again to Stephen that the American could not speak to anyone about their meeting. Abdulkarem was like a father to Al-Ibrahim, and the Bedouin emir could not bear the thought of his mentor getting into any more trouble at the university. If the ulema were to lose his title and position, it would be devastating. Al-Azhar University, the ulema told Stephen, was the most distinguished center for Sunni Muslims. Established in AD 969, it was the oldest continuously running school of higher education in the world. It was named after the Holy Prophet's daughter Fatima Az-Zahraa, and it was the only scholastic home Ulema Abdulkarem had ever known.

Stephen guessed that the ulema was no more than fifty-five years old, but his long gray beard and piously methodical movements gave him the exterior presence of an elderly man. By this time, Stephen had been in the Arab world long enough to know that you just don't strike up a theological conversation with a person you have just met. You must first exchange gifts and share refreshment together. For the ulema, Stephen brought a bag of high-quality Medinah dates. On Al-Ibrahim's advice, he purchased the dates from a vendor on the Duba pier. Al-Ibrahim must have remembered that his old mentor had a sweet tooth that yearned for dates from the city of the

Prophet. The ulema seemed pleased with Stephen's gift. In return, he presented Stephen with a handprinted copy of the Qur'an. The token of friendship nearly left Stephen speechless.

With time, Stephen was able to steer their small talk toward a resolute discussion on religion. "What can you tell me about the relationship you believe exists between our two religions? It goes without question that the Mormons believe in the divinity of Jesus Christ, while the Muslims reject his godhood. This impasse seems to be as far as most scholars go when trying to understand each other's beliefs. But from what I have read in the Qur'an, I believe we share many theological tenets."

"As a man, my knowledge is limited, so I can only speculate, my friend," the ulema answered. "True knowledge," he added, "is with Allah alone. Before we start, you must understand that I am only a humble servant who follows God's Holy Qur'an."

"I understand that you are not a sage, but only a humble scholar," Stephen responded.

"Good. Your religion is Christian, so you believe that Allah hath begotten a son named Jesus Christ. Chapter eighteen in the Holy Qur'an is meant as a warning to both Muslims and Christians. But in my opinion, it is a warning specifically to the Mormons that Allah wants you to believe in Islam. It is called Al-Kahf, which means 'the cave' in English. Do you remember what Al-Ibrahim told you about the verses in chapter three, the surah known as Ali Imran?"

"From what I recall, the surah said that not all Christians are the same. Some will believe in the last days and be righteous in Allah's eyes. These special Christians will praise God night and day, make his signs, make righteous efforts, and forbid that which Allah has forbidden. Allah will recognize that their deeds are righteous, and he will accept them. These Christians will be joined into ranks of the righteous."[1]

"Ibrahim is a good teacher," the ulema said as he smiled at his ex-student. "I am sure you will agree with me that the only sect of Christianity that comes close to matching that description is the Latter-day Saints. So let's assume for the purpose of our conversation that the righteous Christians spoken of in the Qur'an are the Mormons. This would imply that Allah promised the Mormons that they would eventually be joined with the Muslims. Have you ever wondered when and how our people will be united together?"

"That never occurred to me," Stephen replied.

"As I said, the cave revelation to our Prophet Mohammed, peace and prayers be upon him, appears to be a specific warning to two groups. First, God warns the believers, who are the Muslims.[2] Next, God warns those who believe that God has a son. In my opinion, this is directed toward the Christian Mormons."[3]

"That's interesting." Stephen interrupted the ulema. "I believe Mormons are the only Christians who believe that Mohammed received enlightment from God,[4] so I guess in some limited measure, we already accept the Qur'an as an inspired work."

The ulema continued, "Now let's move on to verse nine where Allah reveals the parable of the cave.

> Or does thou reflect
> That the Companions of the Cave
> And of the Inscriptions
> Were wonders among Our Signs.

"The cave represents the kingdom of God. As I read on, let's assume the companions of the cave are the Muslims and the Mormons. Both groups believe in the one true God, but because of darkness or ignorance, neither group realizes that they are in the same cave with the other."

The ulema continued reciting the Qur'an:

> Then We drew (a veil)
> Over their ears, for a number
> Of years, in the Cave,
> (So that they heard not):
> (Qur'an 18:11)

"What do you think the veil refers to?" the ulema asked.

"In the Bible we are taught that a veil blinds the minds of men so they cannot see things as they really are,"[5] Stephen answered.

"That is correct," the ulema said. "The darkness of the cave represents the ignorance of the world in which the companions dwell, and a veil has been placed to keep them from hearing each other or accepting each other's revelations."

> Then we rouse them,
> In order to test which
> Of the two parties was best
> At calculating the term
> Of years they had tarried!
> (Qur'an 18:12)

"This verse tells us that Allah will test the two parties to see which group can most accurately determine how long they were in the cave together. In verse nineteen, Allah counsels the two parties not to let other groups know about their special relationship. In my opinion, God knows that if they do, other Christian and Islamic sects will persecute them and force them to return to their old ways of thinking."[6]

Stephen added, "I can't image what my non-Mormon Christian friends would say if I told them that the Muslims were my true brothers. They would probably stone me."

"In the twenty-first verse," the ulema continued, "we are told that the final coming together of the two parties will fulfill a promise of Allah. It also says that the two parties in the cave will 'dispute among themselves as to their affairs.' The promise the verse speaks of will be fulfilled in the very hour of the Judgment, which we know includes the Second Coming of Jesus. It is also interesting that the two parties will still 'dispute as to their affairs.' In other words, even after the two parties leave the cave, they will disagree on what is the right way to worship Allah."

Stephen finally interrupted. "I think I might know what the promise is that Allah will fulfill to the people in the cave. It is to gather the house of Joseph."

"I don't understand what you mean. Could you please explain yourself?" the ulema asked.

"I believe that some of the lost tribes of Joseph have mixed into the seed of the Arab nations, and that the promise the Qur'an is speaking of is that God will gather the remnant of the tribe of Ephraim from among the Muslims. Once he has gathered them, he will take them to America, where they will join with their Ephriamite brothers who are already in America."

"America! Of all places, why America?" the ulema questioned.

"The Mormons believe that Ephraim will be gathered there in the last days, along with the other lost tribes. They will be assembled to a New Jerusalem in what is today the United States[7] and that the house of Joseph shall inherit the American continents.[8] Ephraim was the son of Joseph and the tribe that God blessed to rule in Israel. Indeed, the names Ephraim and Israel are interchangeable in the Bible."

The ulema was a little confused with all the new ideas Stephen was presenting. "Who are the Ephraimites you believe are already in America?"

"General Moroni in the Book of Mormon explained that the term *remnant* refers to the house of Joseph.[9] The Book of Mormon tells us that at least some of the Native Americans are also from the house of Joseph.[10] Furthermore, the book tells us that the people it refers to as Gentiles are those who came to America after Columbus. The Book of Mormon also defines the American Gentiles as being from the house of Joseph."

"That's all very hard to believe." The ulema shrugged. "To begin with, why would you think the Muslims are part of the house of Joseph, this remnant you talk about?"

"It's not what I believe. It is what the Biblical prophet Isaiah prophesied. He wrote that the remnant would be gathered from lands that are today predominantly Muslim."[11]

"That would be consistent with the revelation of the cave, but what does this have to do with the Muslims and the Mormons coming together in the last hour of the Day of Judgment?" the ulema asked.

"It means everything," Stephen replied. By this time his excitement was obvious. "You see, in the last days the Lord will bring the remnant, or house of Joseph, to a knowledge of the Lord.[12] In other words, those Ephramites who are gathered from the Muslim nations shall be convinced of the gospel[13] and will know that Jesus is the Christ, the Savior of the world."

"I certainly do not believe that, even if you say a prophet revealed it. If that is what Joseph Smith taught, then he must have been a false prophet."

"He can't be a false prophet, for his prophecies match perfectly the revelation of the cave in the Qur'an. You said yourself that there would be the coming together of the two groups, one Christian and the other Muslim, and that the gathering will fulfill the promise God made to those he gathers. You even said that when the two parties came together, they would disagree on how to worship God. Isn't that exactly what we are doing right now?" Both men broke into a good long laugh.

Stephen finally continued. "Can you see that the coming together of the two people who were in the cave represents the gathering of the house of Joseph?"

"That's only true if what is written in the Bible is true, and who knows, perhaps you are misinterpreting the words of Isaiah."

"That's possible, but if you'll let me continue reading in the Book of Mormon, I think you will agree that what I am saying makes sense."

And when these things come to pass that thy seed shall begin to know these things [the Book of Mormon coming to the Lamanites or Native Americans in the last days], that they may know that the work of the Father hath already commenced unto the fulfilling of the covenant which he hath made unto the people of the house of Israel. (3 Nephi 21:7)

The Mormon continued, "From what you told me about the revelation of the cave, it all comes together for me. When the Gentiles bring the Book of Mormon to the Native American members of the house of Joseph, the faithful should recognize that the Father, or Allah, has already commenced his work in fulfilling the promise he made to the house of Israel in the Muslim world. Please notice that the work with the house of Israel or Ephraim will be the Father's work, and not the responsibility of Jesus Christ. If the house of Israel were Christians, then we would expect Jesus Christ to be responsible for the work. However, it is the Father's work, so the remnant of Joseph from the Old World must be non-Christians at the time of the gathering."

"Well, that's at least something we can agree upon. Islam teaches that Allah will bring the people together," the ulema said.

"Please, let me continue reading," Stephen said.

And when that day shall come, it shall come to pass that kings shall shut their mouths; for that which had not been told them shall they see; and that which they had not heard shall they consider. (3 Nephi 21:8)

"Who are the kings in the latter-days if they are not the Muslim Arab kings? And what is it that will make them shut their mouths? What is it that they have not been told? I believe it could be that Jesus is the Son of God. And that is why they will have to 'consider' that which they had not been told, even though they consider themselves to be faithful Muslims."

"That is an outrageous doctrine! Muslims, especially our faithful kings, will never accept the doctrine that Allah has a son. Can you imagine the all-powerful God of the universe needing a human child in order to save mankind? The concept is preposterous!"

"Not so fast. Let me read on," Stephen pleaded. "In 3 Nephi 21:9 we read, 'In that day, for my [Jesus Christ's] sake shall the Father work a work.'

"This verse explains that Allah will do the work on behalf of his son. God will teach the people that they must worship the Son, their Redeemer. That is the reason Allah will ask Jesus to gather the people to Sinai, so they can offer an offering that will complete the old covenant. Then he will introduce to them the new covenant, the covenant with the Son."

"You are assuming far too much," the ulema interrupted. "I fear that you don't even believe that your own interpretations of the Book of Mormon are correct."

"Perhaps, but let me read on. It explains more about Allah's work. The verse continues: 'Which shall be a great and a marvelous work among them; and there shall be among them those who will not believe it, although a man shall declare it unto them.'

"I suspect that many good and faithful Muslims who have believed with all their hearts that God has no son will find it hard to believe that Jesus is God's son, even when Christ himself declares it to them in the flesh. Remember how you said that in the revelation of the cave the two parties would dispute between themselves? Apparently, not all of those who are gathered will accept Jesus as the Son of God."

"I, for one, certainly will not. Allah has no need for a son. Your notions regarding this concept are overly simplistic."

Stephen looked the ulema in the eyes and said, "I ask you to please read the Book of Mormon and pray about it. Ask Allah if it is not the word of God. If it is, you will have a better understanding of what will happen at the gathering. Look what it says in verse eleven.

Therefore it shall come to pass that whosoever will not believe in my words, who am Jesus Christ, which the Father shall cause him to bring forth unto the Gentiles, and shall give unto him power that he shall bring them forth unto the Gentiles, (it shall be done even as Moses said) they shall be cut off from among my people who are of the covenant (3 Nephi 21:11).

"Abdulkarem, the Book of Mormon is clearly warning you that when our two people come together, you will be asked to believe that Jesus is the Christ."

"Stephen, your interpretation of the Book of Mormon does not convince me. You are a young man. You need to understand that you, like everyone who is born of a mother, came into this world as a Muslim. In your case, you were born into a family of unbelievers. I only pray you will reconvert to Islam before your die. Otherwise, your knowledge of the Qur'an will condemn you before your maker."

"Don't reject my theories so fast," Stephen replied. "You believe in the Old Testament, don't you?"

"Only so far as it is translated correctly. We both believe it is full of errors and has been corrupted by evil men."

"The Book of Mormon declares, 'It shall be done even as Moses' (3 Nephi 21:11). What do you think that means?"

"I have no idea, but I am sure, young man, you have some wild explanation."

"It is not my explanation. It is what Moses himself wrote, and you believe in Moses, don't you?"

"Of course, but if you are quoting Moses from the Bible, it's probably inaccurate."

Stephen went on. "I believe that the promise being fulfilled in the Qur'an's parable of the cave is the promise God made to the house of Israel (Ephraim) through Moses. Moses prophesied that Israel would be scattered among the nations because they would eventually worship idols made from men's hands.[14] Wasn't that exactly what the Arabs were doing before the messenger Mohammed restored the Holy Qur'an and the law of Moses? Didn't the Muslims destroy all the idols in Mecca when the Prophet returned from Medinah?"

"That is historically correct. But if you read on in your Bible, you'll see that Moses promised that one day the people would return to God,[15] and that's what Mohammed did, peace and prayer be upon him; he stopped the people from worshipping idols."

"You are half right, Ulema, but Moses could not have been referring to Mohammed."

"How could you know that?"

"Because the promise God made to Moses was that the people who returned to the Lord would be gathered.[16] As you know, the gathering will take place in the last days of Judgment, and not during the time of Mohammed. Remember, this is the same promise that Jesus made to the Nephites in the Book of Mormon, that in the last days the Father would keep his promise to Moses."[17]

The ulema interrupted. "At least you're right about Allah gathering the tribe of Joseph in the last days. In its sixth chapter, the Holy Qur'an speaks of the remnant and how they will be wrongdoers. Who but Allah could restore them?[18] The sixth chapter also explains that the remnant must submit themselves to God before they will be gathered."[19]

"That's incredible," Stephen said. "The gathering of the remnant is prophesied in the Bible, the Qur'an, and the Book of Mormon. No one should be unprepared for the gathering. The question remains, though: when will the gathering take place?"

"The Qur'an tell us how long they, the two groups, will be in the cave before they discover each other," the ulema said. He then recited a verse of scripture. " 'So they stayed in their Cave three hundred years, and [some] add nine [more]' (Qur'ran 18:25)."

"Three hundred years!" Stephen exclaimed. "But they will disagree—some say it will be 309 years. So what is it, 300 or 309 years?"

"The answer is both," the ulema continued. "Muslims calculate the years in terms of a lunar calendar, while the Christian nations use a solar calendar. Three hundred solar years equals three hundred and nine lunar years. Isn't it amazing that Mohammed, peace and prayers be upon him, would have known that the two parties in the cave in the last days would be using two different calendars, one for the Muslims and the other for the Christians? Of course, only Allah knows the exact time that his two people will come together."[20]

"Even if we're wrong about this, it's still fascinating," Stephen commented. "But three hundred years from what starting point? The Mormons haven't been around anywhere near that long."

"I have an idea," Ulema Abdulraham declared. "I am a Wahhabi Muslim. The Western world has not yet heard of the man named Sheikh Mohammed bin Abdul Wahhab. He was born in 1703. If it were not for him and his followers entering a covenant with the house of Saud, Abdulaziz would probably not be the king of Saudi Arabia today. Not only did Wahhab's followers help bring to power the house of Saud, they are continuing something even more powerful: they are reawakening the Islamic world. They are bringing energy back to our faith. Wahhab was a legal scholar who recognized that the Muslims in Arabia were incorrectly worshipping idols and praying on graves."

"Just a minute," Stephen interrupted the ulema. "You mean to tell me that the greatest Muslim reformer of our time was born in 1703? The most important Christian reformer for Mormons was also born in 1703. The Christian reformer John Wesley taught that the spiritual powers had been lost to all the Christian churches because they had become heathens. He was the founder of the Methodist church. What makes this reformation parallel even more interesting is that the Mormon Prophet Joseph Smith started his search for the truth by attending the Methodist church,[21] and until the day he became a prophet, he seems to have been influenced more by the teachings of Wesley's church than by any other Christian doctrine."[22]

"I hadn't realized that two great religious reformers, one Muslim and one Christian, had been born in the same year, AD 1703. Allah must have had his reasons," the ulema said. "Wahhab taught that the Arab people had strayed from the teachings of Mohammed and needed to return to the Holy Qur'an. The Wahhabi School of Sunni Islam is very conservative, and when his Saudi allies took power, the first thing they did was declare the Holy Qur'an to be the constitution of Arabia. In other words, they made the law of Moses the legal foundation for governing the country. Wahhab had the people return to the law of Moses that was given on Mount Sinai. Thus, the prerequisite for the gathering, as promised to the people through Moses, was fulfilled."

"John Wesley," Stephen responded, "was certainly called of God. He recognized the need for new prophets and apostles, and set in motion the questions that led Joseph Smith to the sacred grove. When the fathers of the American Revolution and other great Christian men appeared in spirit to one of our early leaders, Wilford Woodruff, they were subsequently ordained by proxy as elders in the priesthood. The only exceptions were four great men. These four men were honored by being ordained to the office of high priest. They were George Washington, Benjamin Franklin, Christopher Columbus, and the reformer John Wesley."

Both men could feel the electricity in the air. They were on to something, and they knew it. "So 1703 was when the two reformation movements entered the cave," the ulema said. "Three hundred solar years later would mean that the two groups start to recognize each other in 2003. That will mark the beginning of the Day of Judgment."

"That would be something worth living for," Stephen replied. "But what would we be looking for in 2003?"

"According to the Qur'an, the Day of Judgment will start with the violent period. The Christians call it the Tribulation. In the revelation of the cave, there seem to be two violent events associated with the coming together of the two people that leave the cave. The first is found in verses twenty-nine and forty-two. They describe a large building that implodes on itself and then falls, with many people dying inside.

> For the wrongdoers, We
> Have prepared a Fire
> Whose (smoke and flames)
> Like the walls and roof
> Of a tent, will hem
> Them in if they implore
> Relief they will be granted
> Water like melted brass

That will scald their faces.
How dreadful the drink!
(Qur'an 18:29)

And he remained twisting
And turning his hands
Over what he had spent
On his property, which had
(Now) tumbled to pieces
To its very foundations
And he could only say,
Woe is me! Would I had
Never ascribed partners
To my Lord and Cherisher!
(Qur'an 18:42)

Stephen took up the discussion. "The burning building that falls seems to take place among the Christians who ascribe a partner with Allah, a son named Jesus."

"The second calamity," the ulema continued, "will take place in what Allah calls 'thy garden.'[23] Since the Qur'an is the Muslims' Holy Book, I believe that 'thy garden' is directed to the Muslim people. The sign will be thunderbolts falling from the sky into the garden. From the sequence of the two calamities that is founded in the Qur'an, the thunderbolts in the garden must take place after the burning building falls. The thunderbolts will be so hot they will turn the sands into glass."[24]

Stephen shook his head. "Sand being heated into glass. To me, it sounds like bombs dropping from planes. But where is the garden among the Muslims?"

"The Christians and Muslims have always taught that the great garden was Iraq. It is the land of the Garden of Eden and the hanging Gardens of Babylon. The ruins of Babylon are only seventy miles from Baghdad."

That evening Stephen and the ulema talked for hours, both gaining a greater appreciation for the depth and beauty of the other's religious beliefs. They came together because they both believed religions have more in common than they have in conflict.

Stephen was fascinated by the possible implications of the Qur'an's parable of the cave: two parties, one Christian and the other Muslim, coming together after three hundred years of separation by a veil. He wondered if there would be an ensuing Islamic Wahhabi revolution that would parallel the spread of the LDS Church throughout the world. *And what,* he wondered, *will start the great tribulation in 2003? Why will a Christian air force drop bombs on Baghdad in 2003? Will it be the U.S. Air Corps? Will the bombing of Iraq be in response to the destruction of a building in the United States?* [25]

"But [even so], if they repent, Establish regular prayers, And practice regular charity–They are your brethren in Faith: [Thus] do We explain the Signs In detail, for those who understand" (Qur'an 9:11).

"I did send down fire and destroy them, that their wickedness and abominations might be hid from before my face, that the blood of the prophets and the saints whom I sent among them might not cry unto me from the ground against them" (3 Nephi 9:11).

Notes

1. Qur'an 3:113–15.
2. Qur'an 18:1–3.
3. Qur'an 18:4, 14–18.
4. The Church of Jesus Christ of Latter-day Saints, "Statement of the First Presidency Regarding God's Love for all Mankind," February 15, 1978.
5. 2 Corinthians 3:14.
6. Qur'an 18:20.
7. Tenth Article of Faith.
8. Ether 13:6–10.
9. Alma 46:24–27.
10. 2 Nephi 3:16.
11. Isaiah 11:11.
12. 3 Nephi 5:23.
13. Doctrine and Covenants 90:10.
14. Deuteronomy 4: 27–28.
15. Deuteronomy 30:2.
16. Deuteronomy 30:3.
17. 3 Nephi 21:11.
18. Qur'an 6:45–46.
19. Qur'an 6:71–72.
20. Qur'an 18:26.
21. Joseph Smith—History 1:5.
22. James E. Talmage, *The Great Apostasy* (Salt Lake City: Deseret Book, 2001), 161–62. Joseph Smith—History 1:8.
23. Qur'an 18:40.
24. Ibid.
25. In the year 2003, as a result of the September Eleventh terrorist attacks, the armed forces of the United States invaded Iraq. The first attacks included heavy bombardments on Baghdad by the United States Air Force.

Chapter 39

Bedouin Love

Our doubts are traitors and make us lose the good we oft might win by fearing to attempt.

William Shakespeare

Stephen Markham
April 1938
Cairo, Egypt

As Ulema Abdulkarem said good-bye and closed his door behind him, Stephen knew that his mission to Egypt was over. With Norah's self-imposed internment in her hotel room, his itinerary for Cairo had been abruptly canceled. There would be no spoiling the woman he loved. After she lectured him on modesty, there was no reason to visit the boutiques along Salliman Al-Basah Street that carried the latest French and American fashions. After the fiasco aboard the Duba ferry, a romantic trip up the Nile to the great antiquities at Luxor was unthinkable. However, most disappointing of all, he would not be purchasing an engagement ring from a diamond broker in the Zamalek District.

Leaving the ulema's apartment house, Stephen and Al-Ibrahim flagged a cab and directed the driver to their hotel, the Imperial in Old Cairo. Stephen forced himself to put on a good face. It had only been four days since he was having breakfast with Al-Ibrahim on the ferry. That was when his dreams of marrying Norah dissolved over a ferryboat's breakfast of greasy fried eggs, hard rolls, and warm powdered milk.

Once assured that the driver knew the most direct route to the hotel, Stephen started the conversation. "Al-Ibrahim, I can't thank you enough for arranging a discussion with the ulema. He is a remarkable man and certainly a visionary by any standard. It's one thing to dedicate your life to your own religion, yet so rare for a person to retain an open mind and ponder the doctrine of another faith. I was impressed by his intellect and integrity."

"Well, Al-Mormon, you didn't disappoint me either," Al-Ibrahim replied. "I told Abdulkarem that you were bright, especially for an infidel. But with all the jabbering you two were doing, I didn't see you agreeing on all that much. In my opinion, the modern world is like one big Cairo traffic jam. Every religious sect tries its best not to bump into the other. They spend all their efforts avoiding each other, rather than working together to prepare men for the next life."

Stephen smiled as he thought, *There's just another example of Bedouin wisdom.*

The desert emir continued. "From my perspective, all the religions of the world concentrate on how their doctrines differ from the others. Why don't they seek first to find common ground?

I think the world's religions are still in that dark cave the Qur'an speaks about."

"You're blessed with understanding, my friend," the young America said. "You live in a clean desert, apart from the materialistic world. You have your desert paradise that is still free from the naked temptations of the West and the scum of humanity's dark underbelly."

"So, Al-Mormon," the emir asked the American, "do you still believe there is a special relationship between our faiths?"

Stephen thought about the question before answering. "Yes, I think so, but I still don't understand what exactly it is. Instead of answering you, I will quote the wise men of Cairo: 'Perhaps it is not. Perhaps it is so. To be exactly correct, I do not know.' "

Hearing Stephen use the Egyptian saying he taught him brought a smile to the emir's face. "Maybe my Bedouin life isolates me and makes me vulnerable and naive, but it also allows me to see things that others may pass over. Right now, Al-Mormon, I see the pain you are in. I am truly sorry that you will be leaving us soon. My heart tells me you will take your vacation and never return to Midian. I know you love my daughter, and she loves you, but with time and distance you will be able to go forward again, find a good Mormon wife, and have many children."

Stephen nodded, but he did not initially respond to the emir's consoling. Finally, he said, "I know you love your wives, but Mormons have a special way of looking at marriage. We believe that marriage is forever. A husband and a wife can become one for all eternity. That was my dream for Norah and I, that someday we could go to a temple and be married for all time and eternity."

"Sounds like you have Bedouin love," Al-Ibrahim said. "If so, you might leave Arabia, but you'll be only partly alive."

"What is Bedouin love?" the lovesick cowboy asked.

"Bedouin have arranged marriages. In many cases, a husband and wife will not have met each other until their wedding night. Westerners might think that we do not love our spouses, but if you really knew my people, you would see that just the opposite is true. Our struggle to survive in the desert requires a Bedouin husband and wife to work together so closely that, with time, they can't live without each other. Their struggle has made them one. They become bonded through their day-in, day-out fight with the harsh desert and a mutual and complete love for their children. Like fine steel, the Bedouin husband and wife are forged into one soul. It is common knowledge among our people that if a Bedouin husband dies, his wife usually dies within a few weeks. The same normally happens when the wife dies first. Life just cannot continue without the other."

"Then without Norah, I will be partly dead for eternity."

"Stephen, what makes you think that Norah won't feel the same emptiness in her heart? We Muslims also believe those who are righteous in this life will enjoy their earthly marriages in paradise."[1]

"I didn't know that. My colleagues back at CALTOC joked that Muslim men can't wait to die so they can collect their reward of a harem stuffed with seventy-two virgins."

"Do you really believe that Muslim men would forsake their wives for a cache of strange girls? Would you trade my daughter for seventy-two virgins?"

"Never," replied the cowboy. "But what about the seventy-two virgins?"

"The seventy-two virgins waiting in heaven," Al-Ibrahim replied. "That is a questionable doctrine at best. People reported that the Prophet Mohammed, peace be upon him, said that Muslim martyrs would be rewarded with seventy-two virgins. Perhaps he did say it. Perhaps he didn't. It appears to me that this doctrine was only a tool used by Muslim generals to motivate their bachelor recruits to launch themselves into the heat of a battle. But like I said, Muslims believe that their earthly marriages will continue after death. Of course, there will be some virgins waiting for the unmarried martyrs because no one will be allowed into paradise that is not married.[2] Still, Muslims are allowed four wives on earth, so it would seem likely that we will have four wives in heaven, one for each corner of the house.[3] However, some say that Prophet Mohammed said that believers will have only two wives in paradise."[4]

"It sounds like the Muslim concept of marriage in the next life is similar to ours," the Mormon commented. "To reach the highest level in the celestial kingdom (Mormonism's top sphere in the afterlife) a Mormon has to be married. I apologize for retelling the story I heard in the CALTOC camp about the seventy-two virgins."

"That's nothing, Stephen, and you don't need to apologize. I know you have been taught to respect all of Allah's children. Believe me; we have heard many worse stories from westerners about how we treat our women. The fable about the seventy-two virgins is often used by infidels to make Muslim men appear to treat women as if our marriages were arranged in meat markets. In fact, we love our wives as much as, if not more than, people of other religions. Our brave warriors do not fight and die for the lust of virgin flesh;

they fight for their families and for their beliefs. What we really believe happens to our martyrs is encapsulated in the account of a young *musahadeen*, or freedom fighter, who was killed in battle. He had just married, and his wife was devastated by the loss of her husband. Prophet Mohammed, peace be upon him, comforted the young bride by telling the woman that her husband was in paradise and was waiting for her to join him. I am sure that if Norah were to die today, she would sit by a river in paradise and wait for the day she could be with you."

"The same would be true for me. If I died today, I would wait for Norah to join me," Stephen said with a sad heart.

"If she did join you in paradise, you would be pleasantly surprised. I am sure you have noticed my daughter's natural beauty, but all women will be incredibly beautiful in heaven. The Prophet said, 'If a woman of the people of paradise were to look at this earth, she would light up everything in between and fill it with her fragrance; the veil on her head is better than this world and all that is in it.'[5] Of course, Mary, the mother of Jesus, was selected by Allah and purified by him. She is the best of all the women in heaven."[6]

"That's a wonderful vision of womanhood," Stephen said, "but the last thing I need right now is a dream of Norah being even more exquisite. To me, she is perfect right now. Please forgive me for hurting your sweet daughter. By flirting with her, I have crossed a line that should not have been crossed. I am so, so sorry I have hurt her. I pray God will forgive me. And now, to top it off, I asked for her to come with us to Cairo. Since we left Arabia she has been miserable. Let's leave tomorrow for home."

"I forgive you, my friend, and I am sure Allah will also. The sooner my daughter is home, the sooner she can begin to heal her heart."

"Then it's decided: tomorrow we head back to Arabia, and in June it's back to Utah for me before I cause any more grief to your family. You know something, the first day I arrived in Arabia, the customs agent warned me that if I harmed one of Arabia's daughters, the kingdom's sands would soak up my blood. To tell you the truth, I feel like I deserve that fate. I have even wondered these last four days if I will leave Arabia alive."

Notes

1. Qur'an 13:23; 36:56; 43:70.
2. Sahih Muslim, Kitab Al-jannah, Bab awwal zumrah tadkhul Al-jannah, 4/21/79, hadith no. 2834.

3. Sahih Burkar i, Kitab bid' Al-khalq, Bab sifat Al-jannah, Fath Al-bari, 6/318. (Hadith says that houses in paradise will appear like pearls, with rooms for the wife in each corner.)

4. Ibid. Also narrated by Muslim, At-Tirmidhi, no. 188, Kitab Al-imam, bab adna ahl Al-jannah mazilatan.

5. Mishkat Al-mas ab ih, 3/85, hadith no. 5615.

6. Al-Ashqar, Umar Salaiman, *The Final Day Paradise and Hell in the Light of the Qur'an and Sunnah*, Nasiruddin Al Khattab, trans. (Riyadh: International Islamic Publishing House: 1999), 235–36.

Chapter 40

Neither Rags nor Riches Can Conceal

I've had a wonderful evening, and this wasn't it.

Groucho Marx

Jake Sorensen

Summer 1989
The House of Ahmed—Al-Khobar, Saudi Arabia
Week Nine of Ten-week Internship

I called a taxi to take me from my small bachelor's apartment in the PAMMCO housing camp to the "Gold Belt" district of the city of Al-Khobar. As we reached the upscale district, the sun was starting to set, and the call to prayer echoed throughout the city of over one hundred thousand people. As I traveled through the oil boomtown, I was feeling, for the first time, the rush a reporter experiences when hunting down a hot lead.

Mac Pastore had called Ahmed bin Al-Hajri the night before and requested that he meet with me. Al-Hajri agreed to discuss with me what he remembered of Stephen Markham so long as the conversation took place at his residence. What really sparked my interest was that during his conversation with Mac, Markham's translator referred to the American as his "old friend."

The taxi started slowing along a twelve-foot wall that was a city block long. In the middle of the wall was a huge smoked-glass-and-iron gate. The baroque gate was brightly lit and would have made the perfect backdrop for Cinderella's carriage. I paid the taxi driver and searched the wall next to the gate for a doorbell. *Man, I thought, how could a Bedouin afford such a place? The taxi driver must have brought me by mistake to the house of a Saudi prince.*

I found the doorbell and pushed the button below a camera lens and a six-inch TV screen. Moments later, an Asian-sounding voice came through a speaker, and a Filipino face appeared on the screen. "Are you Mr. Sorensen?"

"Yes, I have an appointment with Mr. Hajri."

"Very well, I will greet you at the front door."

Immediately, the gate doors swung open, and I walked into an estate the size of a large city block. In a land where fresh water is produced by costly desalination plants, Al-Hajri's estate featured several acres of manicured lawn with ponds and oriental bridges like you'd find in a Japanese garden. The landscaping resembled Augusta's famed golf course, including a major water hazard—an Olympic-size swimming pool. As remarkable as the grounds were, they were nothing compared to the circular driveway that led up to a life-size replica of the U.S. White House. Tacky to the point of being obscene, I still couldn't believe how a language translator, even a one-time PAMMCO VP, could afford a house that resembled the home of the United States presidents.

As I approached the house, a uniformed butler opened the door and motioned for me to enter. The large entry hall lacked furnishings. The marble floor was mostly covered by a giant Persian rug that must have cost thousands. An equally impressive crystal chandelier hung from the ceiling. The Filipino butler opened the door on the right and asked me to go in and make myself comfortable in the men's sitting room. He then informed me that Mr. Ahmed would be there momentarily.

Now I was really confused. The men's sitting room had no chairs. The place where Mr. Al-Hajri meets his male guests was a replica of the inside of a Bedouin tent. Arabic tribal rugs covered the floor and pillows were stacked everywhere. In the middle were several coffee tables with bowls of dates resting on them. The walls were covered with colorful Bedouin textiles. I decided that my best option was to sit on a pillow next to a bowl of dates and wait for Mr. Hajri.

I had just devoured my eighth date when a teenage boy entered the room carrying a teapot, a half dozen miniature teacups, and some expensive looking chocolates. The boy said in English that he was Salah bin Ahmed, son of Ahmed, and that his father would be along soon. He started to pour me some tea when I told him I could not accept it. He looked puzzled, as if not knowing what to do. Not wanting to disobey his father's instructions, the boy went ahead and poured the tea, set it on the coffee table, and hurriedly left the room.

I switched from dates to my favorite sweets, chocolates. A sugar rush quickly hijacked my investigator's true senses. I enjoyed the candies so much that I almost didn't notice the gray-haired lord of the mansion step into his Bedouin domain.

"Salaam aleikumm, Mr. Sorensen," Ahmed greeted me. I stood and shook the elderly man's hand. I gave the requisite Arabic reply before opening up the conversation.

"Your son seemed confused when I refused your tea. I hope I didn't upset him or you."

"Of course not," the man said. "Please sit down. You must be a Mormon, like Stephen Markham."

"Yes, I am, sir."

"Good. You Mormons are fine people. When I lived in Houston, my Mormon neighbors were very friendly. They even taught my second wife how to drive an automobile. And don't give me a bad time about having more than one wife. I know all about Brigham Young and his harem. I am just like your Brother Brigham, but as a Muslim, I am restricted to only four wives. However, I could not marry my quota because my first three wives became too darn expensive," Ahmed joked. "Today's Saudi women are nothing like my mother. They want cars, vacations in Singapore and London, and big diamonds on each hand. This modern lifestyle is just too complicated and expensive. All the same, I would never give up my lovely wives and my fourteen children. You met Salah. He is my baby, the youngest son of my third wife. I married her when I was sixty-one years old, the year I retired from PAMMCO."

"So you started with CALTOC and ended up working for PAMMCO in America?" I questioned Mr. Al-Hajri.

"Only my last twelve years were in Houston at the PAMMCO Services Company. I was our company's U.S. vice president over marketing. My family really enjoyed the States. I have a son who is a doctor in Phoenix. I don't think he will ever return to Saudi Arabia."

"You must have seen some dramatic changes during your lifetime."

"Dramatic? Try incredible! Thanks to Allah, I have lived a magical life. Of course, the best thing that ever happened to me was leaving my father's Bedouin camp and traveling to CALTOC in search of a job. Honestly, my brothers still live in the desert and walk around all day following their goats. Today they might drive around in Nissan pickups, but they're still Bedouin and proud of it. For me, I prefer the comforts and challenges of the modern world. Had I not taken that first job with CALTOC, I would still be living a thousand years in the past."

"How did you go from a translator to a vice president?"

"Thanks to Allah, I was, as you Americans say, in the right place at the right time. When I reached the CALTOC camp in 1936, I would have taken any job. I was even hoping I could get a construction job carrying mud on my head from the shoreline to the building sites. But what they needed more than anything were Arabs who could translate for the Americans. They paid me the equivalent of ten U.S. dollars a week and put me into English classes. The Americans found that I had a gift for learning English, and I completed my English studies in only six months. Right out of school they assigned me to be Mr. Markham's translator. I was so happy because they doubled my salary to twenty dollars a week.

"But everything changed in 1938, when CALTOC discovered oil in Dhahran, just outside Al-Khobar. The big money started rolling in. Because I spoke such good English, I was made an English instructor, and I remained a teacher until after the war. Even bigger changes came with the end of World War II. PAMMCO was formed, and it soon became the largest oil producer in the world. The Saudi government put pressure on the company to promote Saudis into managerial positions. I was made the director of training for the entire company.

"The problem was that none of us Saudis knew a thing about running the affairs of a multinational company. I was doing my best, but still, it was a miserable mess. The next thing I knew, the American vice president called me into his office and said he had nominated me to attend a university in the United States. He gave me the choice of studying either business or engineering. I really didn't want to leave Arabia, but if I wanted to keep my management job, I had to take my family and go off to study in America. It was no easy trick. I didn't even have a kindergarten diploma and here I was a freshman at the University of Michigan."

"Were you able to graduate?" I interrupted.

"Graduate? They don't call me Dr. Ahmed for nothing. It turned out that my kids loved being in the United States, and PAMMCO kept paying for everything, including business-class airline tickets back to Arabia each summer for vacation. In all, we spent eight years in the U.S. I earned a bachelor's degree in marketing from Michigan and a doctorate in business administration from the University of Arizona. We froze our butts off, as you say in America, in Michigan, but we felt right at home in Tucson."

"Of course, all good things must come to an end, and I eventually ran out of PAMMCO scholarship money and had to return to Saudi Arabia. As the only man in the marketing department with a doctorate degree, PAMMCO made me an assistant marketing vice president. Three years later, the king nationalized PAMMCO. With the nationalization, I became the first marketing vice president, while my old American boss became my assistant. Just like that, the son of a goat herder became a vice president of the the world's largest oil producer. After ten years as an executive here in Arabia, I had my dream come true. I was able to get myself transferred to Houston. Of course, by that time my children were all grown, so I took my second wife and our children to the States. I am still a Houston Rockets fan. Enough about my life. Please tell me, why are you interested in Stephen Markham? He has been dead for over fifty years."

"I am writing a story about the early oil pioneers in Arabia.

Markham's file came to my attention. Apparently, he worked all alone up in the Tabuk area."

"Not at first. I was with him up there for his first fourteen months. After that he was on his own. He really didn't need me. Markham had a gift for Arabic and even spoke it with a Bedouin accent. He was speaking Bedu Arabic almost as well as I did, so the company decided to bring me back to Al-Khobar."

"What I am confused about is how he died. The old CALTOC files just state he was shot to death. Do you know if this is true?"

"My father is from that area. He knows all the Bedouin tribes in northwest Arabia. From what my father told me, Markham was killed by the Germans."

"There was no record of his body being transported back to America. Wasn't it the policy of CALTOC to ship home the bodies of those who died in Arabia?"

"Not only was it CALTOC's policy, but the religious folks don't like having infidels buried in Arabia. They think the Arabian Peninsula is some kind of holy land, where only Muslims should live and rot away. Even so, I am sure they buried Stephen somewhere in the land of Midian. Believe me, there was no way they could have transported his body back to Al-Khobar for shipping in 1938. I am almost certain they buried Al-Mormon where they found him."

"Excuse me, what did you just call him?"

"Al-Mormon, that was the nickname I called him by."

"Have you ever heard of a white Bedouin who is called Al-Mormon?"

Once Ahmed Al-Hajri realized that I had heard of the White Bedouin named Al-Mormon, his countenance took on a more reserved appearance and his voice shifted from friendly to official.

"Sorry, young man, but I've never heard of a white Bedouin. This is starting to sound like a police investigation of a unsolved crime. Why do you ask such questions?"

"There are stories of an old American who lives with the Bedouin and is called Al-Mormon, the same name you just called Stephen Markham."

"Just because I called Markham Al-Mormon doesn't mean I know some Bedouin by that name or that I know who killed him," the retired PAMMCO VP said. "There are lots of people named Al-Mormon. It just means 'true believer.' "

"Right, but is it possible that Markham, for some reason we don't understand, faked his death and took up the life of a Bedouin?"

"Not possible, young man. Stephen Markham is dead. My father told me that Markham's body was buried by the beni Ibrahim tribesmen. When we worked up there, Sheikh Al-Ibrahim was the emir of a small area near the mountains. Al-Ibrahim was respected as one of the great Bedouin leaders of his day. He was known for his honesty. If Al-Ibrahim told my father that Stephen Markham was dead, then trust me, Stephen Markham no longer lives. If you heard that there was an American living in the desert with the Bedouin, that is nonsense. No westerner could live in the Arabian desert."

"If he is dead, then there must be a grave somewhere. I have heard that the Bedouin mark their graves. Is that true?"

"First of all, Bedouin would not bury an infidel like they would a Muslim, and second, I must dismiss myself. I have another gentlemen coming to see me. It was nice meeting with you. I can only say one more thing about Stephen Markham. Al-Mormon was a good friend and a very decent man. If all Mormons are like him, then Allah favors you. Good evening."

Chapter 41

Marriage to the Emir of Tabuk

You can only go halfway into the darkest forest, then you are coming out the other side.

Chinese Proverb

Stephen Markham
April 1938
Returning to Arabia

Knowing that they were slowly inching their way closer to home, Norah seemed to handle the return to Arabia without the emotional escapades that characterized their journey to Cairo. Still, the air around them was heavy, and their conversations reserved. Norah's instincts told her that Stephen's coolness toward her meant that he had decided to leave Arabia when his contract ended in June. She would never see her American cowboy again. She remained polite the entire three days it took to return to Arabia, but inside she was devastated. *How could I have acted so stupidly on this trip?* she blamed herself. *Stephen would never want such a hotheaded and embarrassing wife. But what could I have done? I was terrified of the city and disgusted by the vulgarity of the Egyptian women.*

Norah was hurt, but not surprised, by what Stephen said once they were back at Al-Ibrahim's camp. After greeting the family members, Stephen and Norah paid a visit to Camelita. Rather than looking Norah in the eyes and telling her what he had decided, the cowboy broke the news to his little camel.

"Well, partner, you're growing into a fine young camel. I am going to miss you."

He petted the little camel and then turned to see Norah's reaction, but she was already running toward her tent. Ashamed to the core, all Stephen could do was to get in his truck and head back to the survey camp. On the way, he wondered what his own mother would have said to him if she were still alive. Perhaps that was part of his problem. Without a mother during his dating years to teach him how to understand the feelings of a woman, he was lost at times when it came to finding the right words to say to a girl.

All that night, Stephen stayed awake. His heart felt like it would collapse and stop beating at any moment. He could not see life without Norah. There was no reason to go back to Utah, and he was no longer wanted among the only people he called family, the beni Ibrahim.

Two days had passed since they had returned from Cairo, and Norah had not left the tent. Finally, Al-Ibrahim commanded that his daughter come out and see him, but she refused. Norah was in mourning for a man who would never be her husband, an American from a foreign land, a man who had seen what she was like in his world and walked away from her. *Why,* she wondered, *couldn't I be someone he could love?*

On the third day, Al-Ibrahim had waited long enough. He came into the tent and sat beside his beautiful daughter.

"Stephen doesn't want to leave you, my daughter," Al-Ibrahim said in a loving tone. "I forbid him to marry you."

Norah looked at her father. "He said he wanted to marry me?"

"Yes, my precious. Al-Mormon asked me on the ferry to Egypt if he could marry you."

"And what did you say to him?"

"Of course, I had to tell him no. You know as well as I that it is forbidden by Allah that a Muslim woman enjoin herself in marriage to a non-believer. I had no other choice."

"But, Abu, I love Stephen."

"I know, and he loves you, and I love the both of you. You are kind and faithful and would have made Stephen very happy. But I told him I would have to kill you if you married him."

"You would?"

"Of course not, but you have to understand that I am both the emir and the imam of our tribe, and the Holy Qur'an states that a Muslim woman cannot marry a non-believer. Norah, Stephen loves you, and he is just as miserable as you are. And because he loves you, he knows it's best that he leave our land and not return."

"Then I will die and wait for him in paradise."

"No, you will marry the emir of Tabuk and give him many fat children and make me a proud grandfather."

Chapter 42

A Ticket to Tabuk

We must sail sometimes with the wind and sometimes against it—but we must sail, and not drift, nor lie in anchor.

Oliver Wendell Holmes

Jake Sorensen
Summer 1989
Mac Pastore's Office
PAMMCO Headquarters—Dhahran
Week Nine of Ten-week Internship

The next morning I debriefed Mac Pastore on my meeting with Ahmed Al-Hajri. I described Mr. Al-Hajri's home to Mac and started my report.

"I'm sure Markham's translator was holding back information. Not only did he call Markham Al-Mormon, but as soon as I mentioned the White Bedouin, he clammed up as if I had caught him cheating on his wife. He quickly ended the conversation, excused himself, and had his butler show me to the door."

"What else did you learn, Jake?" Mr. Pastore quizzed me.

"Ahmed Al-Hajri is from a Bedouin family who lives near Tabuk. Can you believe it? He grew up taking care of goats and retired a PAMMCO VP. His father knew some sheikh up there who seems to have been responsible for burying Stephen Markham."

"Do you remember the sheik's name?"

"Yes, that was easy. It was Al-Ibrahim, the Arabic pronunciation of Abraham. Apparently he was the emir of the beni Ibrahim tribe. Mr. Hajri said his father told him his friend Al-Ibrahim had reported that Markham had been shot. The last thing I wanted to do was tell an Arab that his father is a liar."

"Right. That would have gotten you thrown out of his house for sure. Did Dr. Al-Hajri give you any details about Markham's gravesite?"

"No, like I said, as soon as I brought up the White Bedouin, the conversation was over and the story closed."

"Maybe, maybe not. We have a plant manager at our Tabuk gas plant who comes from the beni Ibrahim tribe. He's some kind of local minor prince, so he could be a relative of this Al-Ibrahim fellow. He's a nice man, and we're friends. Let me give him a call and tell him I am sending you to Tabuk to complete an article on an American who worked and died in their land fifty years ago. Certainly there must be some old members of his tribe who remember an American oilman surveying in their area. And of course, if they cannot produce a gravesite, then bingo—you have circumstantial evidence that Markham faked his own death."

"That would be great." I was excited about the chance to fly to Tabuk and hunt down the White Bedouin, and if not the man, at least his grave. "But what could possibly have been Markham's motive for faking his death if not to dodge a war that hadn't even started?" I wondered aloud.

"Well, Sorensen, finding a motive will be your second reason for flying to Tabuk. Let me get hold of Jameel Al-Ibrahim and see if he can be your guide."

Chapter 43

The Depth of a Father's Love

The only society in which I've found nobility is that of the bedu.

Wilfred Thesiger, *Arabian Sands*, 1959

Stephen Markham
Late April 1938
Stephen's Surveying Camp

How strange it is that the hours can at times pass too quickly, yet suddenly time's passage can appear to be suspended. It happened to Stephen Markham in the deserts of Midian. Before the trip to Cairo, the days were passing too fast. Even more fleeting were the memories of the Thursday afternoons with Norah. They now seemed less than a blurred instant in the past. As for tomorrow, each day felt like an endless imprisonment in Arabia. All he wanted was to finish his two-year contract and leave the desert as quickly as possible. Without the hope of being with Norah, the land he had become so fond of, like the proverbial salt, had lost its savor. The ascending spring temperatures felt even more uncomfortable than before. He was learning once again that reality is the cruelest breaker of dreams, and this awareness left him with no zest for life. He would manage, he figured, but it would have to be in some other oilman's outpost. Perhaps he would go back to west Texas or Libya or Romania, but for now it really didn't matter where.

Surveying was over for the day, and Stephen was about ready to prepare dinner. After eating and cleaning up, his only plan was to sit by the campfire and hold another feeling-sorry-for-himself session. If he could muster enough guilt, he might open his scriptures and read a little. But over the past few evenings he hadn't even touched his scriptures. *Why should I?* he thought. *I've lived all the commandments as best I could. Yet once again, my dreams are crushed. I thought God promised to bless his obedient children. Perhaps I am so insignificant that he has forgotten Stephen Markham. Just look at me. What have I done that God should care for me? I seem to hurt most the women I love. I can't even find oil on a peninsula that experts say is floating on the stuff.*

"Not again," Stephen said aloud on hearing the approaching huffs of camels. "What does Al-Ibrahim want now? Haven't I messed up Norah's life enough?"

Stephen had guessed right. It was another escort the emir had sent to fetch him. He tried to excuse himself, but this group was on strict orders to invite, and if necessary, demand that Al-Mormon come to his camp. When Stephen said he would come on Thursday, the leader of the escort insisted he come immediately. "My uncle," he said, "told us to bring Al-Mormon tonight, even if it means tying you up and throwing you on top of a camel." Since there were twelve beni Ibrahim warriors and only one American cowboy, Stephen grabbed his hat and mounted the spare camel.

At the emir's tent, Al-Ibrahim greeted his American friend. "Thank you for coming, Al-Mormon. I have an important question for you. Do you believe that sacrifice is required in order to receive Allah's blessings?"

"Yes, it is a cardinal principle of Mormonism. Our Prophet Joseph Smith taught us if a religion does not demand the sacrifice of all things, it doesn't have the power to save a man."

The emir then said something that Stephen knew was both wise and hallowed. "The same is true in a marriage. If you're not willing to give up everything for your spouse, the love will not endure the eternities. Al-Mormon, I ask you, how much are you willing to give up for Norah?"

"What have I to sacrifice? Since our trip Cairo, I have realized that without Norah I have nothing, I want nothing, and I am nothing. If I had something worthy to sacrifice, I would give it all for Norah," Stephen said.

"You still have something to sacrifice: yourself," the emir replied, "and I am afraid that is exactly what needs to be sacrificed to make a true marriage between you and my daughter. Al-Mormon, I ask you again, will you sacrifice everything for Norah?"

Stephen smiled at the thought that there could still be a chance that he could be with Norah. "Yes, I would. I would do everything in my power to make Norah happy."

"That's not what I asked you. Let me be more specific. Would you give up your religion so Norah's children could be raised as servants of Allah, the most high God? Will you allow my grandchildren to be Muslims?"

The smile left Stephen's face. He knew the answer to that question. He just needed time to explain to himself and the emir what the answer meant in the context of marrying Norah. He couldn't find the exact words he was looking for, so he gave the first answer that came to him. "No, if my commitment to Jesus Christ means leaving my dreams in the dust, then let it be so. I will not sacrifice my religion for anything." Stephen looked his friend in the eyes and said, "You already knew what I would say. Why did you ask me such a cruel question?"

"I am sorry, Al-Mormon. I am a troubled father. My daughter is as innocent as the spring flowers that bloom after the rain. The joy she has for life radiates from her eyes. Allah controls all things, and for some reason he has brought you to our land. Your life has crossed the life of my daughter, and the consequences are now out of my control. I must decide how to deal with this difficult matter. As you know, Stephen, your world is foreign to Norah. If she leaves the desert, she will be miserable. As her father, I will never allow anyone to take her from her homeland."

"After what I saw in Cairo, I understand."

"Stephen, Mohammed taught that religion should never be compulsory. I would never force you to abandon your faith or keep you from teaching it to your family. But are you willing to sacrifice your way of life, your job as an oilman, even your own identity to marry my daughter? Are you willing to become a true Bedouin and let the name Stephen Markham blow away in the wind?"

"Yes," Stephen said without hesitation, "but why have you suddenly changed your mind?"

"Norah is very sick. She hasn't eaten since I told her I forbid you to marry her. She has lost weight and lies helplessly on the floor of the tent. I sent for a doctor from Al-Bada', but the medicines he gave her didn't work. I had the chief imam from Tabuk come all this way to cure her. He read the Holy Qur'an and spit and yelled and screamed over her body. He swore to me that he extracted an evil genie from her body. Still, she just lies on the floor and mumbles words about you. I told you about the powerful bonding of Bedouin love. My daughter is a Bedouin woman, and she only knows one way to love.

"As you know, Stephen, we believe that our tribal poems and stories contain powerful messages sent down to us by our forefathers. There is a famous story among the Bedouin. I know the story by heart, for I have told it to Norah and my other children many times.

"Once there was a young girl, full of a young woman's liveliness and dreams of one day being married. Her father was the sheikh of a large tribe and often had guests come to his tent to receive his council, seek his authorization, and trade livestock. The sheikh loved his daughter and was set on her marrying a rich prince from his own tribe.

"One day a group of men came to trade with the sheikh. Without anyone seeing her, the girl peeked into the tent and saw the strangers talking to her father. In the group was a handsome young man. Instantly, she fell deeply in love with the boy. From that day on, each night and day she dreamed of marrying him. Yet, being a good Muslim girl, she could not talk with the boy directly, nor could she tell her father she had spied on him and his male guest that fateful evening.

"From that time forth, she watched as visitors came to see her father. She hoped that one day the young man would return. That day finally came. Quickly she ran to the path that led to her father's tent and pretended to gather wood. It was the one thing she could do that would allow the young man to see her beauty. As the young man passed her way, he saw her but did not seem to take notice.

"The girl felt rejected. She refused to eat and soon became very sick. She became so weak that she could not walk and had to stay in bed. Thinking that his daughter had been possessed by an evil spirit, the sheikh brought the imam to cure her. The imam read from the Qur'an, placed his finger upon the back of her ear and pressed hard. He shouted for the evil spirit to leave her. He spit on her to entice the evil genie to leave. Then he cursed at the top of his voice to show that the evil spirit had fled the girl through his own body. It was all for show, for the girl continued to weaken.

"The tribe's medicine woman gave the girl herbs of all kinds, but they didn't work. A doctor was called in, but all he did was place hot nails on the back of her neck to cure her thinking. The lifeless girl would not respond, even to the bite of the hot nails on her skin. She weakened even more.

"Realizing that the girl would soon die, an old Bedouin lady came to her tent to comfort her during her last days. She sat by the poor girl's bed and recited to her Bedouin poems, one after another. As she did, she noticed that the girl responded ever so slightly to the poems about love. The old woman recognized that the young girl's sickness was not of the body but of the heart.

"The old woman told the sheikh to take the girl from the tent and seat her on the side of a mountain. He should then hide and listen to what his daughter would say. The father did as he was advised and took his sick daughter to the side of a mountain where there was a blanket of soft sand. He gently set her on the sand and told her he would leave her alone for a while.

"The girl protested. 'Don't leave me alone,' she cried.

" 'I will come back,' the father promised, 'but you have been in the tent too long. You need sunlight to get well.'

" 'Please, don't leave me,' she cried. However, the father insisted that she sit in the sun alone and promised her once again that he would return. The father left to the cries of his helpless daughter. Once away from her sight, he returned and hid behind a large rock.

"Thinking she was alone, the frighten girl cried out for her father to return. She called to her mother and yelled out the names of her brothers and sisters, but on the mountain, none of them could hear her pleas. Finally, she settled down and started reciting a Bedouin love poem.

"Hearing his daughter's passionate reciting of the poem, the father knew what caused her sickness. She was in love. He returned to his daughter and asked her who it was that she was in love with. She told him about the time she saw the young man and how she knew that he would be the one she would marry.

"The father said that he couldn't remember when the boy had visited the tent, so the daughter told him everything she could recall. She remembered everything in great detail, including the physical features of the lad, his manner of speech, and his fashion in dress. She remembered what they talked about and the direction their camels came from.

"That day the worried father swore to his daughter that even if the boy came from the lowest and poorest of all tribes, he would search for him until he found him. He then promised to pursue the young man until he married her. The daughter's health returned, and the father kept his promise.

"I used to enjoy telling Norah this story at bedtime. She loved it. It was like magic, but now the magic has turned on the magician. She has brought the story back to roost in the life in my own family. I fear that Norah is near death, and I will do all I can to save my beloved princess. You see, Stephen, despite tribe or religion, a father who truly loves his daughter will never break her heart. He will never let her spirit or body die. I have no choice but to allow you to marry Norah. But if you love her, like I love her, then you must never let her joy fade. As you promised me, you must never leave this desert land. Arabia must forever be your home. Do you love her so much that you will sacrifice your old life for a life with the beni Ibrahim?"

"Yes, I do, but I thought it was forbidden for a Muslim woman to marry a Christian, and you know, my dear friend, as a husband I must teach my wife what I believe is true. As a father, I must raise my children as Mormon Christians."

"Yes, it is forbidden for Norah to marry you, but the way I see it, it is also forbidden for me to break my daughter's heart. Besides, the Bedouin have a principle. In family issues, tribe comes before religion. I am the sheikh of this tribe and also its imam. If I say you can marry my daughter, that is all that matters. But remember, Stephen, if you marry Norah, you will become a member of my tribe, even my son, and the beni Ibrahim tribe follows the teaching of the great and last prophet, Mohammed, peace be upon him. So you can teach your children your beliefs, but as the sheikh of the beni Ibrahim tribe, I have declared that I, their grandfather, must teach them about Islam. When your children are in my tent, they will pray beside their grandfather to Allah. When they are in your tent, they can pray the Mormon way. When they are adults they can decide for themselves which prophet they will follow. Are you sure you want to join the beni Ibrahim, Al-Mormon? Are you willing to leave the name Stephen Markham to the ghosts?"

Stephen took a deep breath. "I will give you my final decision by sunset tomorrow."

Chapter 44

The Cowboy and the Anti-Christ

It [Arabia] was a desert peopled only with echoes—a place of
death for what little there is to die in it—a wilderness where,
to use my companion's phase, there is nothing but He, La siwa
hu–ie, where there is none but Allah.

Sir Richard Burton, explorer

Stephen Markham
May 1938
Mount Sinai

Rather than returning to the surveying camp, Stephen stayed the night with the beni Ibrahim. He visited briefly with Norah, but he said nothing to her about his conversation with her father. When offered something to eat, he excused himself. He needed to fast, pray, and deliberate on the consequences of the overwhelming decision he faced.

In the morning, Stephen asked Al-Ibrahim if he could borrow one of his camels.

"You are going to Mount Sinai, aren't you?" Al-Ibrahim questioned his friend.

"That's the idea. I need to commune with God, and that's where Moses found him. Can you think of a better place to pray for an answer?" Stephen replied.

"No, there's no better place to go than up a mountain. But be sure you come down the mountain a new man, a beni Ibrahim man. And Stephen, be careful, my friend. Remember what happened to your two German friends."

"I am not afraid of an evil spirit. What did you call him?"

"Al-Dajja. And he might be there. Beware, he is the anti-Christ. He is more than an evil genie. His powers can kill a man in an instant."

"Well, I am not afraid of him. Evil spirits are found all over the world. You and your men seem to have no trouble with him, why should I?"

"He's more than just a dark genie. He is ruthless. When we go near Mount Sinai we constantly repeat in our mind the last chapter of the Qur'an. It gives us protection from evil spirits. You must learn it before you go to the mountain and you must recite it while you are there. Wait and I will write it down for you."

Stephen still had plenty of anger inside him and two large fists at his sides. He figured that if he ran into this Al-Dajja fellow, he had everything he needed to avenge the death of his friends. Stephen believed in evil spirits, but man was the only animal who would kill in the fashion Al-Dajja slaughtered Klaus and Gerhard. Stephen felt he had enough righteous cause to handle any man who got in his way. *Come on out, Al-Dajja,* Stephen thought. *You killed the two kind scholars, but you haven't met me!*

"Here, Stephen," Al-Ibrahim pleaded as he handed him a small piece of paper. "Take this surah from the Holy Qur'an and keep reciting it. Let me say it for you so you have the proper pronunciation.

I seek refuge with the Lord and Cherisher of Mankind.
The King of Mankind, The God of Mankind—
From the mischief of the Whisperer (of Evil)—who withdraws
Who whispers into the hearts of Mankind—
Among the Jinns (Genies) and among Men.
(Qur'an 114:1–6)

"Please, my son," Al-Ibrahim insisted, "start reciting these verses as you come close to the mountain of God."

Stephen had no intention of reciting what he considered a superstitious prayer. Still, he was touched by Al-Ibrahim's calling him son. "Will do," he replied. "And as I promised, I'll be back by sunset with my answer. Please take care of Norah. I will be as fast as I can, but in the meantime, I don't want her getting any weaker. I just need to be alone and pray about my decision."

"I appreciate the attention and care you are taking in deciding whether or not to marry Norah. Neither of us wants her hurt again. May Allah be with you. Inshalah. I'll see you before sunset."

As an experienced cowboy and geologist, Stephen had no problem finding his way back to Mount Sinai. To his trained eye, each mountain had its own story. He remembered the topography of the terrain and read the earth's storybook all the way back to the sacred mountain.

Within two hours, Stephen found himself riding up to the base of the holy mountain. He got off his camel and shackled the animal's feet. Everything seemed peaceful. He removed the piece of paper that contained the verses Al-Ibrahim wanted him to recite. He looked it over. "Whispers and genies," he chuckled and then threw the paper on the ground.

But Stephen had his own superstitions. Before starting his climb, he removed his boots and climbed carefully to a level stone shelf where he could look to the valley below one way and to Elijah's cave in the opposite direction. The climb took longer than he had first anticipated. On the way up, he almost stepped on a scorpion. It was midday in late May. The seasonal scorpions awake mean and hungry from their winter hibernation. All the same, he didn't question the wisdom of his decision to remove his boots. He needed his Heavenly Father's help in making a complex decision of the heart that held eternal consequences. There was no way he could come to a conclusion without divine guidance.

When he finally reached the shelf, Stephen knelt to pray and meditate. He first thought of what his earthly parents would think. Even though they were dead, he knew they watched over him. He was sure that they would not approve of him marrying someone of another religion, especially a Muslim girl who had no real understanding of his commitment to the Savior.

However, his thoughts soon focused on his heavenly parents' will. Stephen had been through the temple and had made sacred promises to God. Throughout his youth, his life's mission had been to build up the kingdom of his Heavenly Father, and now he was seriously contemplating never returning to Utah. If he married Norah, he would probably never sit in another sacrament meeting or go to one of the Lord's temples. Where had he gone wrong? He'd gone from returning from a mission to seriously considering never returning home. Was he breaking every covenant he had ever made? By marrying a Muslim, was he turning his back on the Savior? And what realistic chance would he have of raising his children in the gospel? Even if he could one day convince Norah of Christ's Atonement, could she help him raise his children with a testimony of the Savior? Even if she did, there would still be their powerful and impressive grandfather. As emir of the tribe, Al-Ibrahim would teach their children to be faithful Muslims. How in the world had he moved so far away from his childhood dreams?

Suddenly, a strong gust of wind swiped up from the valley below, causing Stephen to brace himself. It took both hands to keep him from being blown off the rock he was kneeling on. As the gust passed, he first heard and then saw several loose rocks crashing down the mountainside in his direction. He sprang to his feet and jumped to a higher rock to avoid being struck by the tumbling debris.

What kind of wind was that? Stephen asked himself. He knew it was not from a natural source. Perhaps it was a sign from God that he was displeased with Stephen's desire to marry a Muslim. The Mormon boy got back on his knees and asked Heavenly Father if he should marry Norah. Nothing came to his mind, only confusion and a cold, dark void. Certainly, he must be offending God by even considering marrying a non-Christian and giving up all the blessings his Father in Heaven had provided him: a Mormon upbringing; a chance to serve mission; a good education; a solid career; and the chance to return to Utah in two months, where he could look for a Mormon wife. But despite the enormous cost, he still felt that his eternal companion should be a beautiful Bedouin girl named Norah.

His thoughts then turned to Norah. He meditated on the happiness and pleasure he believed he would enjoy by marrying her. How could he ever find another woman who understood the essence of life so clearly? To her, obeying God was good, and disobedience was unthinkable. She believed that happiness came from God, family, the simple desert life, and marriage to a faithful husband. Norah's love was an uncomplicated art form and her religion an unpretentious pattern for her life.

As he thought, he felt a small tremor. It was no illusion. The entire mountain seemed to have moved. This time he looked up to see a torrent of rocks descending upon him. Again, he ran to higher ground, and he just about made it before a grapefruit-size rock smashed against his right calf. It hurt like the devil, but putting his weight on his leg, he knew it wasn't broken.

What's next? he thought. Was God so disappointed in him that he was trying to end Stephen's life? Certainly, God was sending him a message, and he was not pleased. Still, Stephen needed a clear yes-or-no answer about Norah. If the answer was no, then he needed God's wisdom on how to save her life. He would need confirmation that he could live without her for the rest of his life. He tried praying again. This time he sought a different answer. "Dear Father, please confirm to me in my heart that I should not marry Norah, but instead that I should return to Utah." There was no answer, only a coolness that was growing in intensity.

Still concentrating in prayer, waiting for even the slightest indication of an answer from God, Stephen heard a voice that he immediately recognized. "So you think you can get an answer from Father?"

It was Al-Dajja, and Stephen knew that his troubles had just begun. He opened his eyes, and there he stood, dressed in black as before. He was just as handsome and had the same charismatic smile as the day they met in the midst of the sandstorm.

"You stupid goathead," the cocky Al-Dajja said. "Even I don't have the nerve to ask Father for permission to marry a non-Christian. Do you seriously think Father is going to waste his time on such a dumb question? Didn't he include a brain in that body he gave you?"

"You are not the clever genie you believe yourself to be," Stephen replied. "In your hunger to destroy human bodies, you killed the two men who could have placed the entire German army at your command. They had the means to bring Hitler and his army right here to Midian. The dictator and his armies would have been at your disposal, right here on this mountain. But your lust to destroy the bodies of two men has cost you your chance to rule Arabia and take control of her future oil wealth. You have no idea what you have lost and what your donkey brain has cost your evil empire. Ephraim will rise again in America and Arabia, and now you can't stop it."

"How did you ever serve a mission, you deaf, dumb, and blind fool? Hitler will eventually serve me. Perhaps I have lost my chance to use the Germans to rule Arabia, but I will see to it that my Nazi friends kill millions of people and spill the blood of your American brothers. The death and destruction of man is my glory, and today it is my delight to kill you."

"I do not fear you. I am here to call upon my father, so adios, partner."

But Al-Dajja didn't move. "Asking Father for permission to marry? In love are you? Ha ha ha!" His evil laugh rang out over the valley. "Brother Markham, you are a Mormon simpleton, and your mind is so easy to read. You Saints are so predictable. Look, you fool, if you want to marry that desert harlot, go ahead; you have my permission."

"That's enough," Stephen stood up to face Al-Dajja. "That's the second time you have offended a virtuous daughter of our Father." Stephen sprang at the devil with both fists tightened to strike. But he didn't get halfway to the beast before a blast of wind lifted him and slammed his body with great force against a sharp boulder. Stephen collapsed below the rock. His body shook uncontrollably, as if he had been struck by a train.

"How would you like your liver? Fried like Gerhard's or scrambled like Klaus's? You see, Mormon boy, I don't appreciate donkeys like you pissing on my altar. Did you like that wind? Try this one." And with that, the evil spirit let out a foul breath from his internal wickedness. When the vile gases reached Stephen, he could not breathe. Al-Dajja's breath had the concentrated essence of a billion sins.

"Now, wouldn't you say that's a meaner way to die than being smashed against a rock? And don't try to pull that Jesus Christ stuff on me. It won't save you this time. When we met in the Nafud desert, you were still worthy and had honored the prophets that Father sent to your people. But now you are a disgrace. You are powerless. You are nothing."

Stephen tried to speak, but in intense pain, he vomited instead.

"Brother Markham, I once respected you as a worthy foe, but now you are as unworthy as Osama, my servant that you disposed of for me. It was I who tempted him to confess what he did for me to his brother. By having you kill him for me, I have already planted the seeds of anger that will destroy the enemy—the beni Ibrahim tribe. Clever, aren't I? Destroying you is no challenge for me. The emir's daughter, the desire of your pathetic heart, requires you to give up your sacred covenants. Why? So you can marry a simple desert girl who could care less about your prophets? Don't blame the Lord for forsaking you. You gave up on him."

Stephen began to turn blue before he felt a gentle breeze coming from a different direction. The fresh air cleared away the stench, and Stephen started to regain his wits and strength. His mistake was believing the devil's words. Stephen was born of the noble birthright of Ephraim, and he was now asking to give it all away for the simple girl he loved. He had turned his back on the Lord. How could he expect the Lord to come to his aid?

"So you're getting your strength back," Al-Dajja said. He stepped over to Stephen and kicked him in the head. The force of the blow flipped the American over on his back and he tasted blood filling his month. "That one was for Osama, the time you rammed your boots into my servant. Are you surprised I have a body? Believe me, bodies are easy to trade for. Fools like you give up their physical birthrights for cheap thrills and the tender throbbing of the heart."

Stephen felt like he had been kicked by a mule. He tried to think, but he couldn't put his thoughts together. Finally, he realized he was dying, so he simply stopped thinking, closed his eyes, and waited for the final blow.

Enjoying belittling a believer, Al-Dajja continued his verbal attack on the motionless Mormon. However, Stephen was no longer able to hear him or experience any of his other senses. Instead, softer thoughts had taken control of Stephen's mind. He remembered his mother telling him that even though we try our best, we are all imperfect, but Jesus Christ loves us and will never forsake us. He remembered his father telling him that the devil's most effective tool is destroying our self-esteem, making us believe that we are not worthy of the Lord's blessings.

Al-Dajja kept assaulting the motionless body. "Enough of my time has been wasted on camel crap. I think I'll quarter your body and place it on the golden calf altar. Right where you pissed."

"No," Stephen's feeble voice said. Still laying on his back and unable to lift his head, Stephen barely raised his hand and said in near silence, "No, I have not broken my covenants. My master is the Lord, Jesus Christ. Norah is a righteous daughter of God."

Stephen closed his eyes and waited for the final blow. He felt only incredible pain and the hot sun scorching down on his body. He was too weak to get up, and pain rang out from every part of his body. However, he began to sense a strange calmness. He could do nothing but lie there and take in the pleasant peace that came over him. His mind began to release its memories, and images of his childhood flashed back before him.

For what seemed like hours, his entire life seemed to pass before him, but eventually he felt a sweet spirit coming over him, and his pain faded away.

A glorious feeling filled his heart, and he heard a still small voice whisper, "I love you, my son. I brought you to Arabia for my own purposes. It is my will that you die in this land. Norah will be yours in paradise." Tears filled his eyes as the sky slowly turned black.

Chapter 45

What Stays within the Family

I sense that they [the Bedouin] have lost the freedom that they had—the freedom of the desert. The Bedu were always above everyone else: they were more civilized and more noble, and they despised the villagers, the cultivators, and the townsmen.

Wilfred Thesiger, *Arabian Sands*, 1959

Jake Sorensen
Summer 1989
To the Land of Midian
Week Ten of Ten-week Internship

Mac Pastore had been a great supporter all summer. My father's friend had made my internship with PAMMCO a genuine learning experience. From that first dinner at the Commissary Inn with Willy and Hank to our hunt for the White Bedouin, his help had been something special. My flight to the city of Tabuk this morning was just another example of his thoughtfulness. Mac arranged for me to catch a free lift on the PAMMCO jet to Tabuk. Even more important, he gave Jameel Al-Ibrahim a day off and asked him to meet me at the airport and take me to the gravesite of Stephen Markham.

As Jameel and I drove out of the city of Tabuk, we first took the divided highway north toward the Jordanian border. After about a half hour, we turned off the main highway onto another modern road that led to the Gulf of Aqaba. Both highways were new and as good as any road found in Utah. Jameel was proud of his new Toyota Land Cruiser, but mentioned that the few members of the beni Ibrahim tribe who still lived on their traditional lands preferred Nissan pickups.

Jameel explained that members of the beni Ibrahim family held many key positions at the PAMMCO gas plant in Tabuk. Another cousin had earned an MBA from Columbia University in New York and was the president of a local bank. When I told him I had thought his family was a Bedouin tribe, he answered in the affirmative, but I sensed he was a little embarrassed that he was from nomad stock. He said that he didn't go very often to the beni Ibrahim lands, perhaps only once or twice a year to have a picnic with his family and to visit the cousins who insisted on holding to the Bedouin ways. Most tribal events now took place in the city of Tabuk, where the majority of the beni Ibrahim tribe lived and where they had built their own family wedding and social hall.

As we drove, I asked Jameel if he had heard of a tribal emir named Al-Ibrahim.

"Of course," he replied. "All Bedouin families keep a genealogy and a history of their ancestors. Al-Ibrahim was our last great prince. However, he was a man who lived in the past. He died over thirty years ago. My father told me that Al-Ibrahim had tried to discourage him and the other tribesmen from leaving their desert camps. Despite his pleas, after oil was discovered, most of the tribesmen relocated to the city where the high-paying jobs were.

"However, there was something else," Jameel continued. "Something happened that broke up our tribe. Al-Ibrahim executed one of his own nephews. The man he had beheaded was named Osama. The nephew had been the captain of the beni Ibrahim militia. As the story goes, the emir executed Osama for betraying the tribe to the evil one. Whatever happened, several of Al-Ibrahim's brothers were angry with him for executing Osama. Over time, one thing led to another, and the upset brothers eventually broke away and moved their families to Tabuk. The tribe really hasn't been the same since. You might say the so-called evil one eventually won."

"Who is this evil one?" I asked.

"That was part of the problem. Al-Ibrahim believed that some dark ghost lived in the mountains. No wonder his brothers were mad at him. You see, Al-Ibrahim supposed himself to be a spiritual man, but he was also an unrealistic dreamer. Why would anyone want to stay in the desert and tend goats when he could live in the city and have all the conveniences of the modern world? The younger generation thinks Al-Ibrahim was an old-fashioned religious fanatic. Still, our parents respected him and say that he died of a broken heart after the tribe broke apart and most of the families rejected the old ways."

"I guess he must have loved the Bedouin way of life," I commented.

"Yes, he did, and it was also his belief that the beni Ibrahim tribes had some special responsibility. He thought we were supposed to stay in the desert to guard some holy mountain. It sounds like the guy was a little nutty, but that's the way all the old folks were back then. They believed in genies, ghosts, and sacred mountains. When I try to tell my children about our old tribal stories and poems, they just roll their eyes and keep playing their Nintendo games. I guess it's the same way in the States. As you know, you can't turn back the clock."

It didn't take long to discover that Jameel liked to talk, so it made me all the more curious when he gave a brief answer to my next question. "Have you ever heard of a man named Al-Mormon?"

"No, never have. But you might want to ask Sheikh Saad. He is Al-Ibrahim's son and our current emir."

"What do you remember about Stephen Markham?"

"Nothing, of course. He died before I was born. My father told me that German spies killed him. You'll need to ask Saad about him. I think he might have met him when he was a teenager."

About an hour and a half from Tabuk, we turned off the highway and headed down a dirt trail that led into the mountains. The landscape was beautiful, especially the tall granite mountains to the west. After traveling what seemed to be about five miles, we arrived at a small Bedouin camp. I counted only four tents, three Nissan trucks, and several dozen goats, but not a single camel. The temperature that day was over 115 degrees. From inside our air-conditioned Land Cruiser, I could see at least one reason Jameel's people had given up the harsh desert life and migrated to the city.

A tall, handsome Bedouin greeted us. He was Saad bin Al-Ibrahim, the son of Al-Ibrahim. He offered me tea, and when I declined, he just looked at me and asked, "So you are a Mormon? Have your people finally come to take home the body of your brother?"

Obviously, he knew that Markham had been a Mormon, and he was trying to find a connection between my arrival at his tent that day and Markham having been a Latter-day Saint. "No, I'm just writing a magazine story about the early pioneers in the oil industry. Can you tell me what you know about his death?"

"All I remember is something about our warriors finding his body near the sacred mountain. Apparently that's where the elders buried him. I really don't remember much about it, just that they thought German spies killed him, took his radio, and burned his clothes."

"They burned his clothes?" I asked. "Why?"

"I don't really know. I just remember something about his clothes having been burned."

"Can you take me to his gravesite?"

"Of course."

As we drove to Markham's grave, I decided to bring up the name of Al-Mormon and see what kind of reaction I got.

"Do you know if Stephen Markham ever went by the name Al-Mormon?"

Like a well-rehearsed line, the emir quickly replied, "Sorry, I have never heard of him being called Al-Mormon."

The grave revealed to me about as much as Sheikh Saad had— very little. Stones had been placed on the grave. An acacia tree stood over the plot. Saad told me that when he was a boy he remembered seeing a cross made from branches of an acacia tree standing over the grave.

We returned to the sheik's tent, where I was served date cake and goat's milk. I tried to get the emir to open up, but he remained closed-lipped about Markham and Al-Mormon. I could tell these people knew more about Stephen Markham, but they weren't about to tell me about it. I decided to head back to the airport. Sheikh Saad walked with me back to Jameel's Land Cruiser. Just before I got into the vehicle, a young Bedouin girl, perhaps six years old, ran over to Sheikh Saad and wrapped her arms around his legs. In the security of the emir, she looked at me over her shoulder and said something in Arabic. I was startled; her eyes were a light blue color. I asked Jameel what she had said. He replied, "She said, 'Why does that man look like Grandpa?' "

Chapter 46

The Day of Transformation

Here are people that sift the pure fine gold of Arabia Felix . . . the Arabs that ever shift their dwellings.

Miguel de Cervantes, *Don Quixote*

Stephen Markham
Late April 1938
Midian

Using his long razor, Stephen started removing his beard, He nearly decapitated himself when he heard the distant pounding of Arab war drums. Getting a clean shave, putting on his favorite shirt and only tie, and slapping on his Stetson were the only things the cowboy thought he needed to do to finish getting ready for his wedding. He knew the beni Ibrahim tribesmen were coming to get him, but he hadn't expected the rhythmic pounding of a dozen bass drums. The energizing beat of the drums meant either a battle was ready to break out or a Bedouin marriage was about to be celebrated with the traditional wedding feast.

A quarter of an hour had elapsed from the time he first heard the far-off drums to the arrival of beni Ibrahim warriors. Stephen had expected an escort, but he wasn't expecting it to be led by the emir himself. Like the first day he met his good friend, Stephen saw that the party carried their flags and Al-Ibrahim was positioned in the middle of the troop. Beside Al-Ibrahim was a camel with no rider. Colorful ropes hung from the camel's ears and reins. Its red velvet saddle looked like a seat in a Union Pacific dining car. Draped over the camel's neck was a gold-colored sash. This time, the cowboy would be going to the beni Ibrahim camp in style.

It was about four o'clock when the beni Ibrahim arrived at the survey camp. Stephen greeted each warrior with kisses on each cheek and a warm hug. He thought he had the greeting sequence down pat and already had a pot of mint tea brewed for the men. He was wrong. To his surprise, Al-Ibrahim said they had no time for the standard formalities, for he had his own special ceremony to conduct.

The emir started by presenting the Utahn with a gift from the members of the tribe. He handed Stephen a cloth-covered package tied together with string. Stephen opened the gift to find a top-quality white robe, a pair of new leather sandals, an ornately netted prayer cap, a red and white gutra headdress, and a *shagal* (the black head ropes that hold the Saudi-style headdress in place). There was one last item in the bundle, a thin black overcoat or dress shield. The shield's golden trim indicated to all that this man was either the groom or a respected elder of the family.

"Thank you so much," Stephen said to Al-Ibrahim. Then he turned to thank the other men in the party.

"Go put them on, Al-Mormon," the emir cheerfully instructed. "No decent Arab can go to his wedding dressed like a dead oilman."

Stephen did as he was instructed, and a few minutes later he exited his tent looking like an Arab who had been caught in a windstorm. The prayer cap was positioned too far back on his head, making the headdress appear as if it would fall off at any moment. "Come here, my son," Al-Ibrahim commanded. "If you want to make your abu proud, you need to look like a man."

With the kindness of a natural father, the emir helped Stephen adjust his clothes. "Now that's better. Pack up those western clothes you were wearing and bring them here."

Stephen returned a moment later with the clothes he had just removed. He figured the emir thought it would be a good idea to bring a second set of clothes along for the honeymoon. Not so.

"Here, give them to me. Remember, Al-Mormon, you said you would become a Bedouin and ride with the beni Ibrahim. You won't need these anymore. Al-Ibrahim dropped Stephen's clothes in a pile on the sand, took a tin of gasoline from Stephen's stores, and poured it on his western clothes. He then announced loud enough so that all the warriors could hear, "Here, Al-Mormon, is a match! Destroy your past. Today you are born anew. From this moment on, you are to be known only as Al-Mormon. If any man asks you about Stephen Markham, I order you to say that he is dead. Say his body rests in the gravel where we buried the Germans. The famous phoenix returns to Arabia to die a fiery death, and from its own ashes the bird rises again as a strong young raptor. Like the phoenix, today Al-Mormon starts a new life. He is now my son and your brother! From this day on, he rides with the great beni Ibrahim!" Hearing the emir's impassioned declaration, the warriors let out a war cry to honor their new brother.

Stephen lit the match and started his pile of clothes on fire. He had no regrets. It was what he had promised, to give up everything in exchange for Norah, including the identity of Stephen Markham. As the flames grew, Al-Mormon was surprised by one last request of his new father-in-law.

"That's a good start, Al-Mormon," the emir said, "but you're still holding on to symbols of your old life. Where is that silly hat you wear and those pointed boots that make you look like a Persian magician?"

"No, you must be joking . . . not my Stetson and cowboy boots!"

"Don't argue, son. You are now a Bedouin, and when a beni Ibrahim tribesman makes a promise, his word is his bond."

With head bowed, Al-Mormon returned for the last time to his CALTOC tent. He carried back to the fire his treasured hat, boots, and every other piece of western clothing he had owned. As he dropped them into the fire, he realized for the first time that he had broken free from his past. He could never go back, only forward into the timeless world of the nomad.

With his clothes ablaze, the ritual was completed. To endure life in the desert, the cowboy knew he must have no second thoughts. He promised he would give up his life for Norah. He found his wallet and passport and threw them on the fire. He added another good measure of gasoline to the mix.

Next, Stephen grabbed the rifle and a bag that contained the only items he would carry with him from his old life into world of the Bedouin. The bag contained his scriptures, the English translation of the Qur'an, and the faded picture of his parents. The men mounted their camels and rode toward the beni Ibrahim camp where the women and servants were preparing the wedding feast. The grand event would be the public recognition of the marriage contract that Stephen and Norah had signed the day before. Thereafter, they would be allowed to live as Bedouin husband and wife.

"I see that the bruise on your face is almost gone," Al-Ibrahim noted. "It's a miracle. When we found you on Mount Sinai, we thought you were dead."

"I might have been if you had not come to help me. I could hear wolves howling around me."

"I had to find you. You said you wanted to marry my daughter, and then you ran off to the sacred mountain to figure out if you had made the right choice. I don't understand you Mormons. Anyway, I had to find you. I had already promised my daughter you would marry her, so you were going to marry her whether you were dead or alive."

"Do you believe that's possible?"

"What are you talking about?"

"Getting married when you're dead. Mormons can arrange that."

"You Mormons really are peculiar. Anyway, I can't figure out how you've been attacked twice by Al-Dajja and are still alive. You must be an odd being."

"Like I told you before, I am not afraid of that old ghost. But he has the worst case of bad breath I've ever encountered."

"Son, when will you listen to our elders? Stop angering Al-Dajja. Just leave him alone."

"I wish I could, but I'm afraid I'm going to be a pain in his side for a long time. As I said before, I still owe him some payback for

Gerhard and Klaus, and now for the bruise on my face. The next time we meet, I'm going to kick his butt."

"Well, don't try to kick Al-Dajja's butt until you've given me at least one grandson. By the way, where are you planning to take Norah on your honeymoon? I recommend anywhere but Cairo."

Stephen laughed at his new father-in-law's joke. "I thought of a cruise on the Duba ferry, but finally I decided on a better idea. Besides, I promised you that I would never take Norah from the desert. I know a very beautiful place were we can be alone. There is a great canyon with a small river running through it. There are wild flowers and berries and dates in the canyon. The canyon opens onto a white beach and a palm-lined cove. We can swim together in the moonlight and have fires beneath the stars."

"I know the place," Al-Ibrahim interrupted. "I will bring my wives and children, and we'll meet you there."

Stephen didn't know if his father-in-law was joking or not. Perhaps it was the Bedouin custom for the entire family to go on the honeymoon together.

Al-Ibrahim finally let out a broad smile. "Sorry, I was only joking. You and Norah will enjoy the valley. The canyon belongs to the emir of Al-Bada'. He is a friend of mine. He will be at the wedding festival tonight. I will ask him to place a guard at the entrance to the canyon so no one will disturb you.

"Thank you," Stephen said with a smile. "It is a special place for me. I believe the prophet Nephi and his wife spent their honeymoon there."

"I don't know Mr. and Mrs. Nephi, but I'm sure you and Norah will play Adam and Eve. The valley is like a beautiful garden. Its real name is Wadi Tayyib Al-Ism."

"No, its real name is the Valley of Lemuel," Stephen replied. "Look, we've only been family less than one day and we're already arguing."

Both men laughed again. "Al-Mormon, I see it's going to be a joy having you as my son. Besides, you're wrong. The original name of the valley is Elim. It is where Moses camped by the twelve wells."

"You could say it is where the children of Israel honeymooned after leaving Pharaoh." The men laughed again.

To announce the arrival of the groom's wedding party, the men started beating their drums as the riders neared Al-Ibrahim's camp. Their flags blew in the breeze and on their final approach to the camp the women started screeching their eerie war cry. The scene made Al-Mormon feel like he was the central character of a fantastic fairy tale, one from which he was awakened by the firing of rifles.

There were at least two hundred men assembled in the camp, and all of them were shooting their rifles in the air. "Is there trouble in the camp?" Stephen asked Al-Ibrahim.

"Oh, I forgot to tell you, my son," Al-Ibrahim answered. "Like your western love, Bedouin love involves the passions of love and war. Welcome to married life, my son. If your new wife declares war on you, don't come running to me with your problems. Norah is your wife now. Besides, I warned you that I had no power over my daughter because I have always spoiled her. She is now yours to deal with and yours to spoil. My final advice on your wedding night: spoil her, but do so with great passion. And that's why we shoot our rifles into the air, to welcome the groom to the wedding feast and to wish him a marriage full of passion."

The wedding feast venue consisted of two large tents, one for the men and one for the women. As the events of the evening unfolded, Al-Mormon realized that he was in the wrong tent. As the groom, he was stuck on the men's side of the party. In the men's tent, tea and dates were served and everyone sat around discussing the weather. What made it seem all the more boring was that the ladies seemed to be having the time of their lives. From the ladies' tent came plenty of laugher mixed with feminine war cries. Midway through the evening, the music of drums, flutes, and tambourines broke out on the ladies' side of the camp. When Al-Mormon heard the clanging of small bells, he was sure the women were dancing the night away. However, he had no envy that night, he only hoped that Norah was experiencing a fullness of joy on her wedding night.

The groom's party wasn't a total loss. In fact, it turned out to be quite profitable for the new Bedouin. Al-Mormon started the day's festivities by burning the only clothes he owned. Before the night was over, he owned a tent and all the means he needed to prosper in the desert. As each guest approached the groom and his new father-in-law, he announced to all the men the gift he was giving to the new couple. By the time the last gift was presented, Al-Mormon owned, not counting Camelita, over two hundred camels.

But of all the gifts, none matched that given by a grateful Al-Ibrahim. The emir announced that he was giving Al-Mormon and Norah two tents and a prized Persian prayer rug to remind his son-in-law to prostrate on his knees when he prayed. Next, he asked for all the men's attention. He wanted to show them the dowry his son-in-law had given him. Without exception, they were amazed when Al-Ibrahim asked one of his servants to fire up the CALTOC generator. He then unveiled the radio Stephen had given him and proudly turned up the volume. It was tuned to a channel playing belly-dancing music from a

Palestinian radio station. The nomads could hardly believe their ears; music was coming out of a box! It didn't take long for them to warm up to the latest technology, and within minutes they had all drawn their swords and were dancing in a circle. Swinging their swords over and over again toward the sky, the men chanted along with the music.

"At last," Al-Mormon thought. "This might not be the dance floor at Saltair, but finally the men are doing up the Ritz Bedu-style." Al-Mormon hoped that Norah and the other women could hear that the men could have fun too. The merrymaking lasted about an hour, until the men were summoned to an open area where the traditional goat, rich rice, vegetable dishes, fruits, and sweets were served to the guests. The dinner break gave Al-Ibrahim an opportunity to discuss his business plans for his new son-in-law. That was fine with Al-Mormon. Just minutes away from the start of his honeymoon, he was too nervous to eat.

"What are you going to do with all your camels?" Al-Ibrahim asked the groom.

"I have no idea," Al-Mormon replied. "I guess I start my new job in the morning."

"It's no mystery why all the families gave you camels. I asked them to. They usually give goats, but I demanded camels. Our camel herds are the finest in all Arabia. I want you to establish a camel trade with the tribes in southern Arabia. The tribes near the Empty Quarter will pay thousands of riyals for a fast racing camel. Now we sell our camels to tribes in Tabuk. In turn, they trade the camels for goods in Riyadh. Eventually, our camels are sold in southern Arabia for several times the amount we received for them. Al-Mormon, you can help our people by taking our camels each winter to the south. Norah is strong; she and your children can make the journey with you each winter."

"Sounds like the same job I had back in high school. Instead of going on a cattle drive, you want me to drive camels to the south. Can I get a new cowboy hat?"

"No, my son," the emir said with a hardy laugh. "You are now full-blooded Bedu, not a cowboy."

In the middle of the briefing Al-Mormon was receiving from his new father-in-law, the camp erupted into chaos. Not only had the radio been turned to full volume, but some of the men picked up the drums and started a war beat. Others pulled out their revolvers and started shooting in the air.

"It's time! It's time!" one of Al-Ibrahim's sons shouted. "The women are ready for Al-Mormon."

"What's this all about?" Al-Mormon pleaded for an answer from

Al-Ibrahim.

"Sorry, son. I can't tell you. You'll soon find out. Good luck. You'll need it."

With that brief explanation, the emir stood up and led Al-Mormon to the ladies' tent. Ibrahim opened the tent door but remained outside. "May Allah be with you," Al-Ibrahim said with a smile. He motioned Stephen into the tent.

As he entered the women's domain, they suddenly veiled their faces and let out the loudest war cry yet. The women were sitting on rugs, except for the beautiful Norah who was seated in a large throne-like chair. She was dressed in a white wedding gown with a white headscarf but no veil. She was lovely. Stephen thought she looked like an angel of light. Using the natural herb *hayna*, Norah's sisters had painted elaborate designs on her hands. Next to her was another chair. Norah smiled at her husband and waved for him to sit next to her.

Once the groom was seated, the fun began. The odds were definitely against Al-Mormon. The women could see the groom, but they were veiled from his eyes. Besides, he was the only man in the tent.

"Look how skinny he is," an old woman spoke up. "You'll need to feed that skinny boy if you want to call him a man." All the ladies laughed.

"He is so tall. His legs will drag when he rides Camelita," another said. "Norah, you will need to buy that strange man a giant camel."

"What have you married? The poor thing must be sick. He is as white as a ghost. You will need to roast him in the sun each day." And on and on the ribbing went, until it was time to turn the table.

"He has big muscles, and see how intelligent he looks. Does he have a brother?"

"I like his blue eyes," said another. "You must promise me, Norah, that your first son will marry my next granddaughter."

The praises didn't last as long as the roasting had, but that was fine with the wedding couple. The time had finally come for them to be led to the honeymoon tent. It was a special tent the Bedouin pitch for the couple's wedding night. A lavish bed had been placed in the center of the tent and mirrors had been hung on all the walls. Rose water and exotic perfumes scented the room.

Finally, Al-Mormon was alone with his wife in the honeymoon tent. His heart was racing with desire. It was only then that he learned of another Bedouin tradition. By long and honored convention, a Bedouin bride is supposed to act reluctant and shy for at least the first three days of marriage. In Norah's case, feeling Al-Mormon's love for her burning inside her bosom, her Bedouin bridal shyness disappeared in less than three minutes.

Chapter 47

My Brother in the Desert

They are all gone, these great ones. . . . Can the sorry little crowd of us today be in their tradition, even? I fear not.

T. E. Lawrence, *Seven Pillars of Wisdom*, 1935

Jake Sorensen
Summer 1989
Leaving Saudi Arabia
En Route to the United States

"Please fasten your seat belt in preparation for our descent into the Salt Lake City International Airport. We will be landing shortly."

In a few minutes I'll be back in Utah, and a week later I'll be walking the slightly-hallowed halls of BYU. What a summer it has been. How can you explain what it's like to live in Saudi Arabia? In so many ways, Arab culture is immeasurably different from how we live and think in America.

During the three months I worked for the PAMMCO magazine, I never lost my fascination with Arabia and its people. What vivid memories I brought back with me from that mysterious land of camels, falcons, crusty expatriate Jacks, and the nouveau Arab billionaires.

"Cabin crew, please be seated for landing."

Before the plane touched Utah soil, I had already decided that if PAMMCO invites me back next summer, I'll return to the enchanted sandbox.

Without a doubt, of all the bizarre experiences I had this summer, the hard-to-believe story I heard at the Commissary Inn topped the cake. The Empty Quarter massacre, a white Bedouin, the anti-Christ, and a nomadic oilman named Al-Mormon were all part of a story that still needs to be told. But who would believe such a story based on the meager information I was able to glean? Would my hero, Jack Anderson, submit a story for publication based on the information I had? Not for a minute! I had to return and find the smoking gun. I had to get back to Arabia!

So what did I learn this summer about the White Bedouin? I know that in 1938 Stephen Markham was still alive in Tabuk. I also know that he was a Mormon. I know that today there is an old Bedouin chief in Tabuk who a PAMMCO dentist believes is an American draft dodger. I saw with my own eyes a little blue-eyed Bedouin girl who thinks I look like her grandfather.

But there are still so many important questions I don't have definitive the answers to. Is Stephen Markham dead or alive? Did he fake his death in 1938? If so, what was his motive for abandoning his life in Utah? Why would he have just faded away into the culture of the nomad?

Of all the questions that kept haunting me, the most compelling was this: If Steven Markham is still wandering in the deserts of Arabia, what religious secrets did he take with him when he vanished?

As I walked toward the baggage claim area, I recalled with surprising clarity a scripture I read while on the plane.

Thus saith the Lord God; Behold, I will take the children of Israel from among the heathen, whither they be gone, and will gather them on every side, and bring them into their own land: And I will make them one nation in the land upon the mountains of Israel. (Ezekiel 37:21–22)

About the Author

Many consider George Potter to be today's leading Book of Mormon explorer. He has been credited with discovering the best candidates for the Book of Mormon sites of the valley of Lemuel (Wadi Tayyib al-Ism), Shazer, Nahom, Nephi's Harbor, and Lehi's Trail. His articles have been published by the Neal A. Maxwell Institute in the Journal of Book of Mormon Studies. George and his exploring companion wrote the milestone book *Lehi in the Wilderness: 81 New, Documented Evidences that the Book of Mormon Is a True History.*

George has lived in Saudi Arabia for sixteen years, where he has made twelve documentary films on the Book of Mormon and Biblical archaeology, dealing with such themes as Lehi's trail, the Jaredite trail, and the trail to the real Mount Sinai. He has shared his research with the Ensign, the Foundation for Apologetic Information Research (FAIR), the LDS Chaplains Conference, LDS institutes of religion, the BYU Management Society, and numerous stake firesides. He is the co-founder of the Nephi Project, an independent research organization. For more information on his research, visit www.nephiproject.com.

Brother Potter, a CPA, works in Saudi Arabia as a consultant. He has taught at universities in the United States, Canada, Switzerland, and Saudi Arabia. He served an LDS mission in Peru and Bolivia. He is married to Susan Jenson Potter, and they are the parents of ten children.